This monograph offers a thorough examination of good faith in international arbitration, bridging theory and practice. Dr. Martsekis analyzes the substantive, procedural, and interpretive functions of the principle while highlighting the potential for a transnational standard – a valuable resource for practitioners and scholars.

Gary Born, *International Commercial Arbitration (2020)*

This original, important and outstanding book offers an illuminating analysis of the concept of good faith in international commercial arbitration, its application across different legal systems and legal contexts. Martsekis convincingly demonstrates that good faith is neither silver bullet nor empty shell, but a nuanced principle that plays a critical role in the law.

John Fellas, *Arbitrator, Fellas Arbitration, Adjunct Professor of Law, NYU, Honorary Professor of Law, Durham Law School*

An excellent work which explores the operation of good faith in international commercial arbitration (ICA). Dr. Martsekis employs civil and common law perspectives to demonstrate how good faith infuses all stages of ICA. The book analyses good faith's role in balancing between party autonomy and arbitrator discretion. It considers how good faith underpins the gap-filling and contract interpretation functions which tribunals routinely carry out. This is important when abuse of rights and due process issues are increasingly raised in ICA. For academics and practitioners, this monograph provides valuable insights into the integrity of ICA as a means of dispute resolution.

Anselmo Reyes, *Arbitrator, Professor of Law, University of Hong Kong, International Judge of the Singapore International Commercial Court*

Good Faith in International Commercial Arbitration

This book demystifies the effectiveness of good faith in international commercial arbitration law.

In the growing universe of international commercial arbitration, it is more pressing than ever to discuss the role of good faith and challenge residual conservative skepticism regarding its usefulness. The book employs principles, standards and concepts which are normatively ingrained in good faith. These include the principle of pacta sunt servanda, the estoppel doctrine, the transnational standard of cooperation and fair dealing among merchants. It also discusses the pertinence of good faith to corrective justice, proportionality, prohibition of discrimination and unconscionability, international public policy and due process, among other concepts. This granular approach demonstrates how good faith is integrated into the practice of international commercial arbitration. The book sheds light on the technical functions of the principle in parties' substantive protection, contractual interpretation and arbitral procedure, with an ultimate view to reinforcing the soundness and persuasive value of arbitral decision-making. Throughout, the book establishes a uniform and enforceable conceptualization of good faith in transnational disputes.

The book will be of interest to practitioners and researchers in the fields of commercial law, arbitration, transnational disputes and international law.

Georgios Martsekis is Associate at Plesner's International Arbitration Practice Group in Copenhagen, Denmark, where he focuses on complex and high-value investment and commercial arbitration cases. He holds a PhD (Summa cum Laude) from the National and Kapodistrian University of Athens. He is also an attorney-at-law licensed to practice before the Court of Appeals in Greece. George possesses one LLM from Queen Mary University of London (Merit) and another LLM from Georgetown University Law Center (Distinction & Dean's List). He has served for several years as a foreign associate and consultant at national and international law firms in New York, Washington D.C., London and Athens in the field of international arbitration, public international law as well as corporate and commercial law.

Routledge Research in International Commercial Law

Available titles in this series include:

International Commercial Arbitration and the Arbitrator's Contract
Emilia Onyema

Jurisdiction and Arbitration Agreements in International Commercial Law
Zheng Sophia Tang

Progressive Commercialization of Airline Governance Culture
Jan Walulik

Economic and Environmental Regulation of International Aviation
From Inter-National to Global Governance
Steven Truxal

Combining Mediation and Arbitration in International Commercial Dispute Resolution
Dilyara Nigmatullina

Non-State Rules in International Commercial Law
Contracts, Legal Authority and Application
Johanna Hoekstra

Commercial Law in the South Pacific
Mohammed L Ahmadu and Bridget Fa'amatuainu

Digital Finance Law
Common and Civil Law
Robert Walters

Good Faith in International Commercial Arbitration
Georgios Martsekis

Good Faith in International Commercial Arbitration

Georgios Martsekis

Routledge
Taylor & Francis Group
LONDON AND NEW YORK

First published 2025
by Routledge
4 Park Square, Milton Park, Abingdon, Oxon OX14 4RN

and by Routledge
605 Third Avenue, New York, NY 10158

Routledge is an imprint of the Taylor & Francis Group, an informa business

British Library Cataloguing-in-Publication Data
A catalogue record for this book is available from the British Library

ISBN: 978-1-032-85672-8 (hbk)
ISBN: 978-1-032-86454-9 (pbk)
ISBN: 978-1-003-52759-6 (ebk)

DOI: 10.4324/9781003527596

Typeset in Times New Roman
by Apex CoVantage, LLC

Contents

Foreword

Good faith is a fundamental general principle of law with many faces and functions. It is prevalent across almost all legal systems as it expresses fairness and thus has potentially – despite variations among national laws – a translational character. To some authors, it belongs to the so-called *lex mercatoria*. The concept of good faith is classical in the context of civil national law yet also inevitably germane to international arbitration. Dr Martsekis has taken on the intellectual challenge of exploring a highly critical topic and offers us this precious monograph that has not only theoretical interest but practical value as well. Dr Martsekis has adopted a functional analysis of good faith, a clearly symbiotic approach toward the fundamental aims of private international law. He distinguishes interpretive and procedural good faith and its many manifestations from substantive good faith, which mostly depends on the applicable law to the merits of the dispute.

In his chapter on the anatomy of substantive good faith, the author analyzes the different idiosyncratic expressions of good faith with respect to notionally neighboring principles. As argued in subsequent chapters, the two main sub-categories of substantive good faith – normative and corrective – which pertain to the application of national law to the merits, determine and delimit parties' contractual rights and reflect a mechanism of balancing and fairness. That same idea of fairness is served by the principle of good faith in the procedural arena, as Dr Martsekis exemplifies in his last chapter through the increasing demand for procedural predictability, integrity and efficiency. Of particular interest is the chapter dedicated to the application of interpretive good faith that showcases the talent of the author in conducting an original analysis. It explains that beyond the interpretative function, good faith becomes a corrective and somehow a creative tool in balancing parties' rights and upholding justice. The author masterfully explains the precise boundaries of that function, especially in terms of balancing the need to respect parties' will on the one hand and fairness on the other. Finally, the chapter on transnational good faith explores the evergreen but contemporary theme of *lex mercatoria*, particularly in the realm of metaverse disputes as part of a broader *lex metaverse*. It is effectively supported that an "elevated" good faith could act as a metanational uniform device accelerating the harmonization of laws.

This monograph not only constitutes a comprehensive study of international civil and commercial arbitration but also contains findings of comparative law importance. It certainly enriches the literature of international arbitration by offering an intellectually stimulating contribution. Dr Martsekis has succeeded in combining analytical rigor with intellectual originality and has thus embellished the art of arbitration with a vigorous, distinctive and user-friendly guide, both for practitioners and scholars.

Charalambos P. Pamboukis
Professor at University of Athens

Preface

In the universe of international commercial arbitration, it is more pressing than ever to demystify the essence of the principle of good faith and challenge any misunderstanding about its application. This monograph sheds light on the three core functions of the principle, namely substantive, interpretive and procedural functions. It dispels the skepticism toward the application of good faith by illustrating the potency of good faith in the exercise of the parties' rights and obligations and explaining how it regulates the impact of changed circumstances upon the contractual equilibrium. To that effect, it illuminates the power of the arbitrator to supplement or correct the parties' intentions. The author also analyzes whether good faith can constitute a cause of action itself and what the consequences of a breach of a duty of good faith would be, both at a substantive and procedural level. Delving into a comparative analysis of good faith between national court litigation and arbitration, this monograph offers several concretizations of the interpretive principle of good faith. Further, it explains the practicality of the principle in the determination of the proper law applicable to the merits of the dispute. Finally, it elaborates on the formulation of a standard of procedural fairness by identifying the consequences of the breach of good faith in the procedure, portraying the limits of the parties' conduct thereof, as well as the limits of the arbitrator's procedural discretion. Importantly, the author attempts to showcase the contextual value of good faith and elevate it to a transnational standard that is uniformly understood and enforced in cross-border disputes.

The purpose of the monograph is not to prompt the arbitral community to adopt a liberal interpretation of good faith, which frustrates the careful negotiations of parties' agreements, thereby negating contractual predictability, but to enhance parties' accountability, the arbitral system's legitimacy and the persuasiveness of arbitrators' reasoning. The aim of this monograph is to explore a common ground across diverging legal cultures and enhance their dialectic symbiosis. An in-depth analysis of the underpinnings and the connecting threads between various legal systems helps the reader understand the vital role of a uniform standard of good faith in cross-border transactions and the resolution of disputes. A real culture of arbitrating such disputes is therefore nurtured, especially in the era of AI-assisted arbitration and metaverse disputes. In the wake of pandemics, market disruptions and all kinds of irregular conduct, its originality lies in the effort to bolster the legitimacy of arbitration by discovering the tools that uphold the fair and efficient resolution of disputes.

I owe a special debt of gratitude to Prof. Haris Pamboukis for his invaluable guidance and comments, as well as his unwavering support. His kindness and generosity offered a sense of uplift and motivation throughout this journey. My gratitude also extends to Columbia Law School, where I spent a significant amount of time conducting research and giving shape and form to my ideas. In particular, I would like to thank Mr. Robert H. Smit for his insights on the procedural aspects of good faith. Also, thanks to Prof. Alejandro Garro for his enthusiasm about my decision to write on such seminal topics and for inspiring me to focus on the technicalities of my proposal rather than merely navigating the unknown in an academic fashion. I am deeply indebted to Prof. Pierre Mayer and Prof. Mistelis for critiquing my results and sharpening my methods of analysis. It would be an omission not to acknowledge Prof. Karampatzos (from University of Athens) for his thought-provoking perspectives on the civil law aspects of good faith, which benefited the development of this book. Further, I am grateful to Prof. Constantine Calavros and Asst. Prof. Dimitris Stamatiadis (from Democritus University of Thrace) and Prof. Dimitris Tsikrikas, Assoc. Prof. Chrysa Tsouka and Asst. Prof. Anastasios Gourgourinis (from University of Athens) for their authoritative comments. I would also like to offer my special thanks to Mr. John Fellas for our productive conversations about the various functions of good faith and Prof. John Facciola (from my alma mater, Georgetown University Law Center), who has always been available to assist me with puzzling questions on American contract law. Words cannot express my gratitude to Assoc. Prof. Mary Mitsi (from Queen Mary University of London), whose continuous guidance and support have been instrumental in shaping the direction of this monograph. Above all, this monograph is dedicated to my family, who stood by me all these years of sleepless nights and always encouraged me to follow my dreams, particularly, to my father, Loukas, and my mother, Eirini, who taught me the value of ethos, kindness and discipline. Their uncompromising integrity has been, and will be, a source of great inspiration.

Georgios Martsekis
Copenhagen, November 2024

Abbreviations

AI	Artificial Intelligence
Arb.	Arbitration
Areios Pagos	Supreme Court of Greece
BAC	Beijing Arbitration Commission
BGB	Bürgerliches Gesetzbuch (*German Civil Code*)
Bull.	Bulletin
BW	Burgerlijk Wetboek (*Dutch Civil Code*)
C.P.C.	Code de procédure civile (*French Code of Civil Procedure*)
CAA	Chinese Arbitration Association
Cal. App.	California Court of Appeal
CAM	Camera Arbitrale di Milano (*Milan Chamber of Arbitration*)
CCIR	Curtea de Arbitraj Comercial Internaţional (*Romania*)
CEITAC	China Economic and Trade Arbitration Commission
cf	*confer* (*compare*)
Ch.	Chancery
CIAM-CIAR	Centro Internacional de Arbitraje de Madrid-Centro Iberoamericano de Arbitraje (*Madrid – Iberoamerican Arbitration Center*)
CISG	United Nations Convention on Contracts for the International Sale of Goods
Civ	Civil Division
cmt.	comment
Comm.	Commercial
CPR	Conflict Prevention & Resolution
CRCICA	Cairo Regional Centre for International Commercial Arbitration
CUP	Cambridge University Press
Del.	Delaware
e.g.	*exemplum gratia* (*for example*)
ECHR	European Convention on Human Rights
Ed./Eds.	Editor/Editors
et seq	*et sequens* (*what follows*)

EWCA	England and Wales Court of Appeal
EWHC	England and Wales High Court
GCC	Astikos Kodikas (*Greek Civil Code*)
HKIAC	Hong Kong International Arbitration Centre
i.e.	*id est* (*that is*)
IACAC	Inter-American Commercial Arbitration Commission
IBA	International Bar Association
ICC	International Chamber of Commerce
ICCPR	International Covenant on Civil and Political Rights
ICDR	International Centre for Dispute Resolution
ICJ	The International Court of Justice
ICSID	International Centre for Settlement of Investment Disputes
Id.	*Ibidem* (*in the same place*)
INCOTERMS	International Commercial Terms
K.B.	King's Bench
LCIA	London Court of International Arbitration
NAFTA	North American Free Trade Agreement
NAI	Netherlands Arbitration Institute
NYC	The 1958 Convention on the Recognition and Enforcement of Foreign Arbitral Awards
OUP	Oxford University Press
para./paras.	Paragraph/paragraphs
PECL	Principles of European Contract Law
PIL	Private International Law
QB	Queen's Bench
Restatement	The Restatement (Second) of the Law of Contracts
Rv	Wetboek van Burgerlijke Rechtsvordering (*Dutch Code of Civil Procedure*)
S.D.N.Y.	Southern District of New York
SCC	Stockholm Chamber of Commerce
SIAC	Singapore International Arbitration Centre
U.C.C.	Uniform Commercial Code
UDHR	Universal Declaration of Human Rights
UNCITRAL	The United Nations Commission on International Trade Law
UNCITRAL Model Law	UNCITRAL Model Law on International Commercial Arbitration
UNIDROIT	The International Institute for the Unification of Private Law
UNIDROIT Principles	UNIDROIT Principles of International Commercial Contracts
VCLT	The Vienna Convention on the Law of Treaties (1969)
Y.B.	Yearbook
ZGB	Schweizerisches Zivilgesetzbuch (*Swiss Civil Code*)

1 Introduction

1.1 Understanding the Value of Good Faith

International commercial arbitration, as the primary dispute resolution method of cross-border disputes, is deeply associated with contract law. That is surely true for the substantive protection of the parties, including the determination of whether a breach of contract occurred, a termination of contract is reasonable and whether certain remedies such as rescission, specific performance and damages are available. International commercial arbitration is also inextricably related to the regulation of parties' conduct in the proceedings. In particular, whether an objection to jurisdiction was brought in bad faith, whether the right to be heard has been complied with or guerilla tactics employed by a party need to be sanctioned. The source of the power to regulate such procedural conduct is the arbitration agreement. The core principle that underpins such contractual or procedural arrangements, and without which every sort of contract would be devoid of its binding nature and enforceability, is good faith. Good faith not only prevents exploitation but is a requirement for the very existence of a contract.[1] Even if not expressly provided in the contract, it is firmly recognized

> that in every contract there is an implied covenant that neither party shall do anything which will have the effect of . . . injuring the right of the other party to receive the fruits of the contract, which means that in every contract there exists an implied covenant of good faith.[2]
>
> (citation omitted)

It even constitutes a mandatory rule, the waiver of which is, and should be, precluded.[3] The omnipresence of good faith is a reality in international business transactions, notwithstanding the diffused criticism of its meaning and scope. Likewise, in the procedural context, the very principles of equality of arms and fair trial governing the

1 Daniel Markovits, *Good Faith as Contract's Core Value, in* Philosophical Foundations of Contract Law 293 (Gregory Klass et al. eds., 2014).
2 Kirke La Shelle Co. v. Paul Armstrong Co., 263 N.Y. 79, 87 (1933).
3 Markovits, *supra* note 1, at 284.

DOI: 10.4324/9781003527596-1

conduct of the parties in the proceedings are reflected in the arbitration agreement, and more specifically, the inmost contractual duty to arbitrate in good faith.[4]

1.2 Purpose of the Monograph

The purpose of this monograph is to comprehend the principle of good faith in international commercial arbitration. In particular, the focus is to examine and effectively establish in international commercial arbitration the three functions of good faith. First, the substantive function will be explored, which prescribes good faith as a normative rule imposing different standards of conduct, the breach of which may result in damages. The substantive function may also give rise to a special rule of good faith, namely the corrective rule, the latter giving leeway to the arbitrator to do justice when the original intention of the parties proves inadequate to give a satisfactory solution to the dispute. Second, the interpretive function of good faith will be scrutinized, pursuant to which good faith acts as a principle in the interpretation of the contract and the arbitration agreement. By virtue of the disparate approaches within the ecosystem of civil and common laws in relation to the interpretation of the contract, the author will attempt to reconcile the tension between textualist and contextualist interpretation by resorting to good faith. Additional emphasis will be put on how good faith can be utilized to determine the limits to the selection of the applicable substantive law. The analysis of the procedural function of good faith comprises the last objective. Contrary to the substantive function, the procedural rule of good faith regulates the conduct of the parties in the proceedings. Four principles dictate what a procedural duty of good faith consists of. These are procedural certainty, equality, integrity and efficiency. Overall, the ultimate purpose is to contribute to the practice of international commercial arbitration by exploring all possible applications of the principle. Importantly, it provides an authoritative account of the functions of good faith and aims to assist scholars, arbitrators and practitioners in navigating the mechanics of the principle while pushing the frontiers of arbitral jurisprudence forward at the same time. The exhaustive doctrinal analysis does not aim to provide a rigid and monolithic exegesis of the principle. Quite the contrary, pragmatism and flexibility comprise the crux of the present monograph.

1.3 Reasons Behind the Critical Analysis of Good Faith

1.3.1 Gap in Literature

Admittedly, good faith as a concept is not newfangled. Lando has characterized good faith as the 'king' principle of the BGB.[5] Going back in time, Immanuel Kant's

4 See Felix Dasser & Danielle Gauthey, *La bonne foi dans l'arbitrage*, 33(2) ASA BULL. 239, 265 n.135 (Kluwer Law International 2015).

5 OLE LANDO, *Is Good Faith an Over-Arching General Clause in the Principles of European Contract Law?*, *in* LIBER AMICORUM GUIDO ALPA: PRIVATE LAW BEYOND THE NATIONAL SYSTEMS 601, 604 (Mads Andenas et al. eds., 2007).

categorical imperative proclaiming that "your behavior shall be governed by such principles as if you were a legislator in a society of reasonable beings obeying common laws"[6] is associated with the principle of good faith. The edifice of international arbitration is interwoven with the trust of all actors that the legal relations have arisen in good faith, and it is on that assumption that a professional solution must be sought.[7] Unfortunately, the omnipresence of good faith does not eliminate doubts about its understanding and systematic application. Effectively, there is a gap in both theory and arbitral case law. For example, the newest Greek Law 5016/2023 on International Commercial Arbitration is by far clearer – and much more aligned with UNCITRAL Model Law – than its predecessor Law 2735/1999 as to the interpretive function of good faith and the establishment of the parties' procedural duty of good faith. However, one may still wonder what the role of the "principle of good faith" exactly is "in the interpretation of the present law"[8] or what the perimeter of a good faith conduct is insofar as it stipulates that "the one awarded interim relief is obliged to reasonable compensation, if . . . she obtained the issuance or maintenance of it with acts or omissions in violation of the duty to conduct the proceedings in good faith."[9] One may naturally wonder what precisely those acts or omissions are. The urge to bravely demystify the principle is more topical than ever.

1.3.2 Failure to Understand the Concept Uniformly

The failure to comprehend the principle uniformly across the universe of different legal traditions is not only frustrating, but it also constitutes a reality that cannot be overlooked. Different legal systems ascribe a different content to the principle of good faith. However, what this monograph aspires to show is that these differences are significantly less than originally thought. The principal reason is that what is considered to be a prohibited conduct, either in the form of a delaying or contradictory conduct, a failure to cooperate or failure to raise in a timely fashion any irregularity in the procedure, constitutes the same intolerable conduct everywhere.[10] The anti-fragmentation trend will be approached both from a comparative perspective of diverse national laws where, for example, a homogeneous reading of the requirements and consequences of *force majeure* upon the contract is justified under the prism of good faith, as well as from a transnational law perspective integrating a unifying approach of what an acceptable or intolerable conduct must be.

6 PETAR SARCEVIC & PAUL VOLKEN, THE INTERNATIONAL SALE OF GOODS REVISITED 178 (Kluwer Law International 2001).
7 Bernardo M. Cremades, *Good Faith in International Arbitration*, 27 AM. U. INT'L L. REV. 761, 788 (2012).
8 Law 5016/2023 on International Commercial Arbitration – Regulations on the function of the Hellenic Court of Audit and Other Emergency Provisions [Διεθνής Εμπορική Διαιτησία – Ρυθμίσεις για τη λειτουργία του Ελεγκτικού Συνεδρίου και λοιπές επείγουσες διατάξεις] OFFICIAL GAZETTE OF THE HELLENIC REPUBLIC 2023, A:21, art. 5(1) (Greece).
9 Law 5016/2023, *supra* note 8, at art. 25(6).
10 Dasser & Gauthey, *supra* note 4, at 259.

It must, however, be borne in mind that the purpose thereof is not to simplify or replace specific national legal rules with a general principle of good faith. Nor is it to propose a universal solution[11] stemming from good faith. As a matter of fact, it does not even suggest that good faith should be frozen in amber. The purpose is rather to advance the argument that, in certain cases, good faith points to the common understanding of different cultures about what unacceptable conduct is. Good faith may also be appropriate to address a set of issues without overregulating the arbitral system,[12] but that admission requires an inquiry into whether we need more rules in the system of international arbitration or the dogma that minimalism is effective[13] should be preferred.

1.3.3 Science Deprived of Conscience

"Science without conscience is but the ruin of the soul."[14] On this basis, good faith is seen as the soul of arbitration, without which the entire system would fall apart.[15] Is good faith merely a moral principle or a social policy norm? Is it just aspirational, as a product of suasion and empty rhetoric, or a rule having legal teeth instead? The latter suggests that the existence of good faith as a rule reflects sound reasons for compulsion, the non-enforcement of which entails legal consequences for all actors involved in arbitration, including arbitrators, too. Both the substantive and procedural conduct of the parties frequently raise questions of good faith, the latter being inevitably resorted to by arbitrators with a view to regulating the parties' conduct as needed. The rupture between a race-to-the-bottom approach (deregulation) resulting from less reliance on good faith and the race-to-the-top approach (more regulation) is increasingly relevant as the moral premise of good faith is deeply endangered by the progressive, yet uncontrolled, rise of AI in the administration of justice.[16]

1.3.4 Inadequacy and Rigidity of the Law

A prominent barrister has recently argued that complete compliance with the law may not be desirable because the applicable law may not be very good or strict

11 Dasser & Gauthey, *supra* note 4, at 273.
12 Dasser & Gauthey, *supra* note 4.
13 Dasser & Gauthey, *supra* note 4, at 270.
14 François Rabelais, Pantagruel (1532).
15 Dasser & Gauthey, *supra* note 4, at 271.
16 Meriam Al-Rashid & Ulyana Bardyn, The Role of Artificial Intelligence in International Arbitration, GAR, Jul. 25, 2019, *available at* https://globalarbitrationreview.com/review/the-arbitration-review-of-the-americas/2020/article/the-role-of-artificial-intelligence-in-international-arbitration (last visited Mar. 5, 2023) ("[I]t is not clear how the robo-arbitrator will be able to apply intangible concepts, such as, for example, good faith, reasonableness, materiality or best efforts. Such concepts are frequently incorporated into legal norms and the application of a given norm may turn on these concepts. A robo-arbitrator that has difficulty analysing and applying such concepts will be unable to correctly decide the application of the relevant legal norm").

enforcement of the law in a particular case may be rather harmful than beneficial.[17] Although there are clear instances of what lawful or unlawful conduct is, the ultimate purpose may be more than just total and complete compliance with the rule of law.[18] The attempt of this monograph would be to show that recourse to good faith oils the wheels of the system by providing the legal justification of one solution over the other, especially when new unforeseen contingencies, *i.e.*, the outbreak of the COVID-19 pandemic, impact upon the natural course of things. The law is not perfect. As such, any inadequacy of the law or the contractual arrangement of the parties, irrespective of how technical or sophisticated it may appear, cannot always fulfill the mission of the law as a practical science destined to give practical solutions. There comes the principle of good faith potentially capable of yielding the proper response to the problem.

1.4 Obstacles and Reservations

One of the main obstacles in the process of demystifying the principle is the vagueness and indeterminacy of it, which will be addressed at greater length hereinafter. Another hurdle seems to be the misconception that good faith lies in the eyes of the beholder. Good faith is a highly relative concept, the application of which depends on the applicable law, the parties' reliance on it, the cultural background, training and discretion of the arbitrators. It would be an omission not to refer to the reluctance shown by practitioners and tribunals to ascribe to it meaningful content and who repetitively contend that good faith fails to replace mechanical rules. Even if such rules are not adequate, there is no compelling reason why recourse to good faith should be justified. As a result, arbitral theory and practice have failed to systemize the applications of good faith. Overcoming these reservations is not straightforward. The author acknowledges that good faith is not, and should not be, a panacea. What is purposive instead is to distill certain standards fulfilling the mission of the principle by sketching *de lege artis,* the outer boundaries of good faith, including the premise that party autonomy shall always be upheld.

1.5 The Main and Peripheral Questions

The preliminary appraisal of substantive good faith hinges upon the question what the constituents of good faith are. It further hinges on whether it is a creature of suasion or has any enforcement capacity, whether it can give rise to autonomous obligations for the parties or instead functions as an ancillary mechanism confined by the explicit contractual undertakings. The next array of questions pertains to the circumstances under which the normative and corrective rules of good faith are

17 National and Kapodistrian University of Athens NKUA, Honoring Alan Vaughan Lowe, KC, Emeritus Chichele Professor of International Law, University of Oxford [ΕΚΠΑ NKUA, Αναγόρευση Alan Vaughan Lowe, KC, Emeritus Chichele Professor of International Law, Παν. Οξφόρδης, YouTube, Nov. 29, 2022], *available at* www.youtube.com/watch?v=I5GSv_Fb0Ao.

18 National and Kapodistrian University of Athens NKUA, *supra* note 17.

admissible in arbitral practice. It will be analyzed, therefore, whether the diverse platform of civil and common laws in arbitration confirms the existence of a duty of good faith in the phase of pre-contractual negotiations, as well as at the stage of the actual performance of obligations.

Most importantly, the author will attempt to explore the positive and negative standards of good faith during performance. The scope of good faith will also be examined, specifically whether its application entails the importation of extra-contractual standards. The special issue of whether good faith can act as a 'sword' is then to be examined. This idea suggests that an autonomous breach of good faith may constitute a cause of action. On the other side lies the restrictive function of good faith, also referred to as the 'shield' function. The question is whether good faith can be employed to limit the *pacta sunt servanda* principle both in light of a public policy defense and in a *force majeure* situation.

Does good faith play any role in the termination of the contract? What is the relationship between good faith and mitigation of damages? Can punitive damages be employed as a remedial response to a breach of contractual good faith? Could the principle of good faith function as a rule, indulging the arbitrator to interfere with a contract to the extent that they are able to correct it or even adjust it? On what basis should they be allowed to do so? Are there any limitations? Finally, is there a need to justify a transnational standard of good faith in international commercial arbitration, and if so, what are its contours? Can the argument that such a standard may function independently of domestic legal systems be sustained? The compendium of all the previously mentioned questions are the most seminal – though cloudy – issues that the arbitral jurisprudence has systematically failed to explain thus far.

The next set of questions concerns the interpretive function of good faith. The first question is whether there is any scope for good faith in the subjective and objective interpretation of parties' contractual rights and obligations. The second question analyzes the specific concretizations of the interpretive principle of good faith. The third revolves around the exceptional effects of a good faith interpretation. Pertinently, the aim is to discover on what basis a good faith interpretation justifies supplementation and correction of the contract and where the line should be drawn. The last inquiry is whether the emerging need for more uniformity in international commerce calls for the systemization of a transnational good faith interpretation that would be less confined by domestic law idiosyncrasies. Ultimately, a novel question of certain practical value is whether good faith can be used by arbitrators as a methodological tool in order to ensure the appropriateness of the law governing the merits.

The last catalog of questions is focused on the procedure. They pertain to whether a procedural duty of good faith is justified for both the parties and arbitrators. The content of such a duty will be clarified by resorting to certain uncompromising procedural safeguards. The monograph will then grapple with whether a uniform procedural standard of good faith is justifiable in practice, whether it imposes more obligations than those required by existing arbitral rules and what the consequences of its violation are. The ultimate challenge would be to define the arbitrator's procedural duty of good faith and explain under what circumstances their procedural discretion must be restrained thereto.

1.6 Scope of Examination

For purposes of accuracy and clarity, the examination of good faith is strictly focused on the practice of international commercial arbitration. Good faith is not some pre-existing or pre-determined norm. It borrows its contours from the specific branch of law that is called on to serve. Thus, its conception and application vary among public international law, private international law and international commercial arbitration.[19] Surely, there are certain similarities. For example, good faith is presumed, whereas bad faith must be proven,[20] which seems to be a particularly high threshold.[21] However, any effort to conflate good faith in commercial arbitration with good faith as applied in public international law or investment treaty arbitration would disregard a primordial distinction among these areas of practice. Under a national law applicable to the commercial dispute, good faith potentially remediates the effects of an unequal bargaining power upon the contract, whereas

19 An emblematic crystallization of the principle of good faith in public international law is reflected in the VCLT, which in Article 26 pertinently provides: "Every treaty in force is binding upon the parties to it and must be performed by them in good faith." Article 31(1) further stipulates that, "[a] treaty shall be interpreted in good faith in accordance with the ordinary meaning to be given to the terms of the treaty in their context and in the light of its object and purpose," as well as in the ICJ practice. The Court in the *Nuclear Tests (Australia v. France) case* emphasized that, "the very rule of *pacta sunt servanda* in the law of treaties is based on good faith." Nuclear Tests (Australia v. France) (Judgment) [1974] ICJ Reports, para. 46. On the other hand, the cosmopolitanism of international commercial arbitration suggests the escapism of good faith from the patronage of lexforism, as envisioned in private international law, in terms of delocalization, detachment of *jus* from *forum*, maximum convergence achieved among parties, procedural freedom as a result of deviation from national law peculiarities, as well as procedural economy, speed and simplification. George A. Bermann, International Arbitration and Private International Law, paras. 43–47 (The Hague Academy of International Law 2017). Unlike in private international law, in international arbitration, *lex mercatoria* may also be the 'law' applicable to the dispute, by virtue of explicit references to "rules of law" applicable to the substance of the dispute, such as in Article 28 of UNCITRAL Model Law.

20 Without a presumption of good faith, it is advanced that one party may get the benefit of making unmeritorious contentions, whereas the other would have to prove the regular course of things. Frederic G. Sourgens, *By Equal Contest of Arms: Jurisdictional Proof in Investor-State Arbitrations*, 38 N.C. J. Int'l L. & Com. Reg. 875, 950 (2012); In that vein, *Kolb* explains that the good faith "presumption we are dealing with favours the stability of international transactions and is based on the socially useful consideration that regularity is the rule and fraud the exception." Robert Kolb, Good Faith in International Law 20 (Hart Publishing, 2017); *accord* De Rendon et al. v. Ventura et al. (ICC Case No. 19728/ASM), Final Award, Apr. 26, 2017 (Arbitrator Intelligence Materials, Kluwer Law International), para. 402 (discussing the presumption of good faith under the applicable Colombian law).

21 Simon Weber & Julie Martinez, *Good Faith in International Arbitration: Comparative Approaches in ICC Awards*, 2 ICC Disp. Res. Bull. 112, 115 (2020), *available at* www.trans-lex.org/109210 (discussing the high threshold of proving bad faith in ICC Cases Nos. 12198 and 11651).

in public international law, there is no legal asymmetry between states.[22] On the other hand, in investor-state treaty-based arbitration, good faith forms the bedrock of standalone standards, such as the fair and equitable treatment (FET), the latter being absent in contract-based commercial arbitration, where national or transnational law (*lex mercatoria*) is usually applicable. Not to mention that the standard to prove a breach of good faith in investment arbitration is quite high considering the heavy presumption that a state as a respondent acts in good faith under international law. On the contrary, in commercial arbitration, the cause of action is typically the violation of a contractual proviso, not the standards of international law or state responsibility. However, in light of the fluidity of cross-border disputes, no rigid distinction should be admissible. Brower has coined the term 'investomercial' arbitration, reasonably suggesting that the dichotomy between private-public and private-private arbitration is false.[23]

To be precise, the analysis will only focus on contract-based arbitration germane to commercial arbitration, notwithstanding the relative insufficiency of the term 'commercial' to justify a clear divide between commercial and investment arbitration. Even if states or state-owned entities act as parties to arbitration, such states or state entities act in a commercial capacity (*fisc*), usually in the case of state contracts. Hence, good faith will be approached from a contractual perspective. That is because, as Mann elegantly observed, an express contractual exemption from a change in legislation has no effect on international law since that exemption is not able to exclude the state's exercise of police powers.[24] The content of good faith in commercial arbitration is determined by domestic or even transnational law, not by public international law. Nevertheless, certain useful parallels will be drawn in order to defend the criticality of good faith for the system of international commercial arbitration as a relatively autonomous area of law.

It must be stressed further that the concept will not be approached from the perspective of a general idea of equity ('*ex aequo et bono*' or 'amiable composition'). The reason is that equity is independent of the application of municipal law or transnational law, including the *lex mercatoria*. Indeed, equity is parallel to good faith but different in that it describes an entire system of law and reflects the practices of the English judiciary purported to be the 'keeper of the King's conscience.'

In addition, the scope of the present analysis is confined in the application of good faith by arbitral tribunals. It is not the aim to explore in detail how different national courts approach the concept of good faith. Nonetheless, it is critical to analyze the consequences of the breach of the procedural good faith at the stage of annulment of the award in the place of arbitration or the enforcement of it in the country where enforcement is sought, as further illustrated in Chapter 8. Finally, it

22 Steven Reinhold, *Good Faith in International Law*, 2 UCLJLJ 40–63 (2013), Bonn Research Paper on Public International Law No. 2/2013.

23 See Charles N. Brower, *State Parties in Contract-based Arbitration: Origins, Problems and Prospects of Private-Public Arbitration*, 1(2) ITA IN REVIEW 103 (2019).

24 F.A. Mann, *State Contracts and State Responsibility*, 54(3) AJIL 572, 587–88 (1960).

is not part of the objective to provide a detailed account of the manifold applications of good faith in contract law, first because this analysis is not an exhaustive compilation of all or the most representative legal systems, and second, because that exercise would undermine the role of the arbitrator to stand "above the law, since he is the one who renders it applicable,"[25] including his own perception of the 'foreign' law they are required to apply on every occasion, which is markedly different from a state judge's viewpoint.

1.7 Methodology

The method of analysis is constituted of first identifying the principle in the express provisions of national codes, arbitration rules and international conventions. Treatises, journal articles, dissertations, surveys and online materials weed the tapestry of the analytical and descriptive method of analysis. Arbitral case law is further utilized to show the connection between theory and practice. Reference to state court decisions will also be available, however, to a limited extent, to justify a constructive dialogue between state courts and arbitral tribunals. The topic will be approached from a comparative perspective, both from a civil and common law perspective, as well as from a truly international perspective. In that vein, the comparative perspective aims to reveal the connecting threads between various legal systems. The technique of comparison will also be employed insofar as the demonstration of both the supporting and opposing arguments proves to be critical. The empirical analysis of good faith will be prioritized by giving precedence to inductive reasoning. That would mainly be achieved by resorting to case law to infer a general conclusion. Where necessary, deductive reasoning will also be applied to support a conclusion that only theoretical reflections have thus far underpinned. The author does not offer rigid solutions but flexible ones. The reason is the high level of vagueness of good faith and the fact that it is not frozen in time. Much will change over time, and new arbitral decisions will be rendered, but what this analysis aspires to offer is shelter amidst the storm. It aims to restore the stability and integrity of the system by examining good faith as a safety valve that regulates the conduct of the parties and better informs arbitrators' decision-making.

1.8 Structure

The structure of this monograph is grounded on the various functions of good faith. Part I focuses on the substantive function of good faith. Chapter 2 introduces the concept and components of good faith by drawing upon civil and common law traditions as well as international commercial instruments. Chapter 3 explains the

25 Pierre Mayer, *Reflections on the International Arbitrator's Duty to Apply the Law*, *in* 16 Arbitration Insights: Twenty Years of the Annual Lecture of the School of International Arbitration, Sponsored by Freshfields Bruckhaus Deringer, para. 15.27 (Julian David Mathew Lew & Loukas A. Mistelis eds., 2007).

specific normative standards of good faith as a substantive rule when national law governs the merits of the dispute. Chapter 4 explores the arbitrator's capability to intervene and correct the contract by virtue of good faith under special circumstances and criteria. Chapter 5 examines the rationale for, and scope of, a transnational standard of good faith in parties' substantive protection as well as its added value in the era of metaverse disputes.

Part II focuses on the interpretive function of good faith. Chapter 6 grapples with the essence, contours and limits of good faith interpretation both with respect to the parties' contract and the arbitration agreement. Chapter 7 addresses a novel issue. That is how the interpretive principle of good faith can be utilized by an arbitral tribunal to guide the determination of the applicable law, including the potential to supplement or correct it.

Part III analyzes the procedural function of good faith. Chapter 8 focuses on the parties' procedural duty of good faith as well as on deciphering the arbitrators' duty of good faith in the procedure and the ensuing limits thereof.

Part I

Substantive Function of Good Faith

2 Anatomy of Substantive Good Faith

2.1 The Indeterminacy of Good Faith

Good faith or *bona fide* is so old a concept as much as law itself. In the same way that natural sciences are founded on core tenets without which their existence is meaningless, the same assumption that the system is governed by principles and rules is true for law too. Just like geometry, which dictates that "if equals be subtracted from equals, the remainders are equal,"[1] it is equally logical to assume that the system of law is anchored in canons, which sometimes exist in a dialectical symbiosis with each other by lending their content to others.

The aim of this chapter is to answer what good faith is constituted of and why good faith is so important for the genesis, operation and evolution of international commercial arbitration. First, the indeterminacy of good faith must be explained. Discussing the indeterminacy of good faith is not tautological to say that good faith does not exist. Had it been true, good faith would have just been an empty shell in all domestic legal systems as well as in international instruments. Nor does it entail the other extreme reflected in Justice Stewart's famous phrase, "I know it when I see it,"[2] as this would suggest an "equation of seeing and knowing"[3] and undermine the search for the critical understanding of it.

Reference to good faith can be found in almost every arbitral award. However, the omnipresence of good faith is interwoven with its indeterminacy in the sense that it is not clearly understood; the involved parties do not always know how to use it or even predict what this concept means to arbitrators or how it would be employed by the tribunal.[4] The oxymoron is that, although it is supposed to act as a safety valve for the system of international commercial arbitration, there is a generic assumption about its existence and not a precise, coherent and effective definition.[5]

1 W.D. Ross, Aristotle 70 (Mariliza Mitsou trans., 3rd ed., National Bank of Greece Cultural Foundation 2001) (referring to a known Euclid's axiom).

2 Paul Gewirtz, *Essays on "I Know It When I See It"*, 105 Yale L. J. 1023, 1023 (1996).

3 Gewirtz, *supra* note 2, at 1024.

4 Bernardo M. Cremades, *Good Faith in International Arbitration*, 27 Am. U. Int'l L. Rev. 761 (2012).

5 Duarte Gorjão Henriques, *The Role of Good Faith in Arbitration: Are Arbitrators and Arbitral Institutions Bound to Act in Good Faith?* 33 ASA Bull. 514, 516 (2015).

DOI: 10.4324/9781003527596-3

The question that one may naturally pose is the following: Is it because of its inherent polymorphic character that good faith cannot be specified? That might be true considering the various values that fair persons share and which good faith is arguably comprised of, such as honesty, loyalty, diligence, cooperation, integrity, transparency and confidence, the latter protecting the legitimate expectations of the parties.[6] These concepts can be employed by the contracting parties in the performance of their obligations by not taking advantage of the other party in a manner that offends fairness, not using trickery and half-truths or, finally, not hiding certain information or misrepresenting that important information is available or not.

It is also critical to note that in international commercial arbitration, which involves parties from different cultural backgrounds, political and geographical mentalities, as well as dissimilar expectations and probably bargaining positions, the same words do not necessarily connote the same views. From Asian to European and American legal systems, the content of good faith changes apparatus depending on the *sui generis* societal circumstances and standards of right and wrong that each state law is obliged to protect. This indeterminacy is also enhanced if one considers each party's special role in the arbitral process. The LCIA Rules provide that each of the parties and the tribunal shall always act in accordance with good faith.[7] What is the standard of good faith applied to the parties and arbitrators? Is it the same or different? Further, good faith is not only subject to a conflict of opposite views about its very essence but essentially acts as a chameleon pursuant to what time and historical contingencies command thereof. However, this conflict is supposed to be complementary and not contradictory, as philosopher Heracleitus first articulated about the harmony of things being opposite,[8] suggesting that behind the differences, there is an underlying common denominator. The objective of the present research is to reveal a common denominator among cultures and bolster the argument that there exists an evolving convergence rather than a divergence.

2.2 The Rivalry of Civil and Common Law

Admittedly, there has been a recurring rivalry between common and civil law traditions in terms of the understanding of good faith in commercial dealings. A comparative examination of good faith against the backdrop of civil and common law tradition sheds light on the underlying nuances and clearly suggests that the devil is in the details.

6 Henriques, *supra* note 5.

7 LCIA Arbitration Rule (2014), art. 32.2 ("[T]he Registrar, the Arbitral Tribunal, any tribunal secretary and each of the parties *shall act at all times in good faith*, respecting the spirit of the Arbitration Agreement, and shall make every reasonable effort to ensure that any award is legally recognised and enforceable at the arbitral seat") (emphasis added).

8 Heracleitus, *Ancilla to the Pre-Socratic Philosophers* 8 (Kathleen Freeman trans., Harvard University Press 1983).

2.2.1 Civil Law Tradition

The *New French Civil Code* stipulates that "contracts must be negotiated, formed and performed in good faith."[9] Article 8 of the Enabling Law of 16 February 2015 clarifies that the reform, among other reasons, is targeted at affirming the general principles of law, including good faith (*bonne foi*).[10] As Terré emphasized, such principles "allow [the Legislature] to broadcast in the clarity and transparency, the essence of contract law and spirit that animates it,"[11] thus revealing its importance within the French civil system. The gravitas attached to good faith is so great that Article 1104 further provides that this provision is a matter of public policy. This is not merely incidental since the principle of good faith is associated with the lawful cause underlying the obligations of the parties, which constitutes the fourth requirement of the validity of the contract, thus suggesting that promises are binding as a matter of fidelity and honesty.[12] Although there is no explicit definition of good faith, what has invariably been perceived as good faith in the French legal system lies in the concepts of loyalty, cooperation and coherence.[13]

The *BGB*, which originally entered into force in 1900, provides in Section 242 that the obligor has an obligation to perform pursuant to the requirements of good faith and take into account customary practice.[14] In addition, Section 157 provides that contracts shall be interpreted according to the principle of good faith.[15] The result is a system of specific duties, prohibitions, sub-rules and doctrines, all of which form part of *Treu und Glauben*,[16] where *Treu* means faithfulness, honesty and loyalty (by paying regard to other party's interests) and *Glaube* means belief in terms of faith or reasonable reliance.[17] Indeed, the importance of good faith in the German civil system is reflected in the fact that most German legal scholars regard good faith as a rule that supplements or even corrects the law.[18] The effort of such concretization has made the content of good faith more comprehensible and the decisions based on Section 242 more predictable and rational.[19] It is worth

9 CODE CIVIL [C. CIV.] art. 1104 (Fr.)

10 Mustapha Mekki, *The General Principles of Contract Law in the "Ordonnance" on the Reform of Contract Law*, 76 LA. L. REV. 1193–94 (2016).

11 Mekki, *supra* note 10, at 1197.

12 Nadia E. Nedzel, *A Comparative Study of Good Faith, Fair Dealing, and Precontractual Liability*, 12 TUL. EUR. & CIV. L. F. 97, 110 (1997); see also Code civil [C. civ.] [Civil Code] art. 1108 (Fr.) (current art. 1128).

13 Solene Rowan, *The New French Law of Contract*, 66(4) INT'L & COMP. L.Q. 805–31 (2017).

14 BGB § 242.

15 BGB §157.

16 MARTIJN W. HESSELINK, *The Concept of Good Faith*, *in* TOWARDS A EUROPEAN CIVIL CODE 471–98 (A. S. Hartkamp et al. eds., Kluwer Law International 2004), *available at* https://ssrn.com/abstract=1098856 (last revised Apr. 8, 2011).

17 REINHARD ZIMMERMANN & SIMON WHITTAKER, GOOD FAITH IN EUROPEAN CONTRACT LAW 30–31 (CUP 2000).

18 MARTIJN W. HESSELINK, THE NEW EUROPEAN PRIVATE LAW: ESSAYS ON THE FUTURE OF PRIVATE LAW IN EUROPE 213 (Kluwer Law International 2002).

19 HESSELINK, *supra* note 18, at 199.

mentioning, though, that in German law, the role of good faith does not form the basis of a course of action; however, it serves as a binding commitment underlying the legal relationships formed between the parties and a limitation to their conduct.[20] Thus, it may not be asserted that it imports an autonomous obligation, yet its significance lies in that it specifies and supplements the contractual obligations of the parties[21] and effectively constitutes the soul of every contract.

Dutch law adopts the methodology of *Fallgrupen* that objectifies the principle of good faith by categorizing court decisions depending on the different applications of good faith, thus classifying the different functions of good faith and developing an "inner system of good faith."[22] The content of good faith is shaped by reference to general principles, judicial views and the societal and private interests involved,[23] while an objective test of good faith is adopted. As Article 3:11 of the BW stipulates, the parties have not acted in good faith if they knew or, under the very special circumstances of the case, reasonably ought to have known the facts or rights based on which they act.[24] In fact, "good faith in this sense not only requires that the party concerned *did not know* the relevant state of affairs, but also that he *should not have known* it; this implies that he may be under a duty to investigate"[25] (emphasis added).

In *Swiss law*, the approach that the party has to exercise its rights and perform its obligations in good faith and that a manifest abuse of rights is not protected by law is contained in the Civil Code.[26] It is effectively established that good faith is presumed when the law makes a legal effect conditional upon the good faith of a person.[27] The principle of good faith, albeit objectified in terms of interpretation of contracts in the sense that it is more connected to how a third reasonable person would understand the contract, the subjective theory of good faith, which attaches importance to the intent of the contracting parties, is still decisive in Swiss law.[28] The fuzziness of the concept of good faith is well-known to Swiss scholars and practitioners, yet it is accepted that it does not kill the black letter of the contract,

20 Kevin Bork & Manfred Wandt, *"Utmost" Good Faith in German Contract Law*, ZVersWiss 109, 243–45 (2020).

21 A similar approach is reflected in the Dutch literature where good faith supplements rights or obligations not expressly envisioned in the contract or a statute, yet those may arise under the contract. Arthur S. Hartkamp, *Judicial Discretion Under the New Civil Code of the Netherlands*, 40 Am. J. Comp. L. 551, 555 (1992).

22 Ewood H. Hondius & H. J. Van Kooten, The Principles of European Contract Law and Dutch Law: A Commentary 49 (Kluwer Law International 2002).

23 BW art. 3:12 ("In determining what reasonableness and fairness require, generally accepted principles of law, current juridical views in the Netherlands and the societal and private interests involved in the case must be taken into account").

24 BW art. 3:11.

25 Hartkamp, *supra* note 21, at 554 n.6.

26 ZGB art. 2(1) and (2).

27 ZGB art. 3.

28 Ahmet Cemil Yildirim, Interpretation of Contracts in Comparative and Uniform Law 69, 79 (Kluwer Law International 2019).

nor does it render the contract barren.[29] As the Swiss Supreme Court and legal commentary have confirmed, its significance is to give the contractual terms the meaning that a reasonable third person in similar circumstances would ascribe to when it is not possible to ascertain the common intentions of the parties based on the available factual evidence.[30]

A more detailed, yet similar, approach is found in *Spanish law*. Spanish law does not introduce a definition of good faith. However, it is inferred *a contrario* that the content of good faith is made of the flip side of abuse of rights or the antisocial exercise of it.[31] As the same law implies, the scope of good faith is determined with reference to the normal limits of exercising such a right, the manifest excess of which gives rise to liability. Moreover, the Spanish Civil Code, as much as its Chilean counterpart, set forth that the contract must be performed according to the requirements of good faith, implying, therefore, that the parties are not only bound by what is agreed upon but also by what emerges as a consequence of the contract and its nature.[32]

The Italian law is equally vocal on good faith. The parties must behave in good faith at the negotiation stage, and contract formation and the contract must be interpreted in good faith; the debtor and creditor must behave according to the rules of correctness and performance cannot be refused if that refusal would be contrary to good faith, having regard to the circumstances of the case.[33] In the Italian civil system, good faith is not regarded as a pre-determined kind of behavior, the content of which can be established from the outset but an open-ended term that has to be specified by judges and which is dependent on the circumstances of the case.[34]

Greek law incorporates the principle mainly in Articles 197, 200, 281, 288 and 388 of the Greek Civil Code. The contract must be interpreted in accordance with good faith and fair dealing and the exercise of the right is prohibited if it manifestly exceeds the limits imposed by good faith, good morals or the social or economic purpose of the right.[35] In addition, the debtor has the obligation to perform its obligation as good faith requires, taking into account fair dealing. Given that these rules aim to protect against bad faith and immorality, they are effectively

29 Elliott Geisinger, *President's Message: The Wizard of Oz (or "Good Faith and Swiss Law")*, 35 ASA BULL. 803, 803 (2017).

30 Geisinger, *supra* note 29, at 804.

31 See CÓDIGO CIVIL [CIVIL CODE] art. 7(2) (Spain); Cremades suggests that "the prohibition of the abuse of a right or antisocial exercise thereof is a clear *normative consequence* of good faith as a general principle of law." (emphasis added). Cremades, *supra* note 4, at 769.

32 CRISTIANO DE SOUSA ZANETTI, *Filling the Gaps: A Civil Law Tradition*, *in* 18 LEGITIMACY: MYTHS, REALITIES, CHALLENGES 1006, 1015 (Albert Van Jan den Berg ed., ICCA Congress Series, 2015).

33 Codice Civile [C.C.] art. 1337, 1366, 1175 and 1460 (It.).

34 Tommaso Febbrajo, *Good Faith and Pre-Contractual Liability in Italy: Recent Developments in the Interpretation of Article 1337 of the Italian Civil Code*, 2 THE ITALIAN LAW JOURNAL 291, 293 (2016).

35 The prohibition against the abusive exercise of a right is primarily founded on art. 25, para. 3 of the Greek Constitution reading "[t]he abusive exercise of a right is not permitted."

considered rules of public order.[36] Similar to the continental civil legal systems, good faith in Greek law is ascertained on objective criteria. From a Greek law perspective, good faith is cemented on the prevailing view of honesty and integrity in business transactions and social symbiosis, meaning that a beneficiary should not harm the other party in disproportion to the benefits realized from the exercise of its right and in any case it must prefer a less harmful exercise of its right.[37] Good faith is also ascertained based on the *venire contra factum proprium* doctrine, especially when the long inaction of exercising a right creates the belief that the right will not be exercised. Its significance is widely affirmed in case law. Indicatively, the Supreme Court (*Areios Pagos*) has emphasized that good faith applies in every contract, regardless of whether this contractual relationship arises from a particular kind of transaction or the law itself.[38]

The *Nordic legal system* is very close to the continental legal tradition with respect to the understanding of good faith. Good faith refers to the general understanding of loyal and decent behavior and, more specifically, to the rules of good business practices.[39] As Lilleholt illustrates, if a potential buyer reveals that they are going to buy a new house close to a railway station by virtue of the construction of a new line, the seller must inform the buyer before entering the contract if they know that such construction plans came to an end, whereas the seller is not obliged to inform the buyer if they are doubtful about whether such line is going to be constructed.[40]

The preceding comparative analysis showcases that civilian legal orders across the globe perceive – to a great extent – the concept of good faith alike. In particular, the parties are not only bound by what is expressly agreed upon in the contract but also by what emerges from good faith. If the seller has delivered more goods than the quantity agreed, the buyer is not permitted to decline performance but instead she shall invite the seller to take the rest of it back.[41] The same applies to the termination of the contract, particularly in long-term contractual endeavors where termination may be allowed, yet that alone does not give the leeway to the counterparty to do as they want.[42] Prior notice might be necessary, in line with good faith.[43]

Good faith is also used to re-allocate the risks between the parties when a change of circumstances causes hardship to one of the contracting parties and which was not originally foreseeable. Indeed, the Portuguese Civil Code stipulates that the

36 See Apostolos S. Georgiades, General Principles of Civil Law 205 (ANT. N. SAKKOULAS 2007).
37 Georgiades, *supra* note 36, at 209.
38 Areios Pagos, Case No. 2154/2007.
39 Kåre Lilleholt, *Application of General Principles in Private Law in the Nordic Countries*, 20 Juridica International 15 (2013).
40 Lilleholt, *supra* note 39.
41 Zanetti, *supra* note 32, at 1016.
42 Zanetti, *supra* note 32.
43 Zanetti, *supra* note 32.

contract may be adapted in this case as required by good faith, provided that the balance of risks agreed upon by the parties is not trumped.[44] True, in civil law traditions, good faith helps integrate the contract by filling gaps pursuant to what is perceived to be necessary in a bid to protect the value of mutual trust between the parties.[45] However, good faith has been cautiously used by civil courts to that effect because a wide construction of good faith might import undesirable exogenous parameters into the contract.

2.2.2 Common Law Tradition

The common legal system treats good faith differently. Although the father of English commercial law, Lord Mansfield, believed that good faith was a superior principle governing all contracts and negotiations,[46] modern English law adopts a literal interpretation of contracts. It is indicative that Lord Steyn underlined that there was no need for English law to insert a general duty of good faith so long as the courts respected the reasonable expectations of the parties.[47] The rationale of that effect is that the concept of good faith in English jurisprudence is regarded as quite vague a notion running against the parties' goal to pursue their own interests. The Court of Appeal opined in 2013 that "there is no general doctrine of 'good faith' in English contract law."[48] When the English courts had to deal with issues of fairness, they came up with piecemeal solutions[49] in the sense that particular facts merit a particularized analysis of fairness. In the English law jurisprudence, the notion of good faith is not established. What civil law treats as a general principle, English law associates it with notions of equity, undue influence, misrepresentation, mistake, duress and promissory estoppel. Recently though, there has been a shift in this adamant attitude.[50] In *Yam Seng PTE Ltd v. International Trade Corporation Ltd*, the High Court found that the distribution agreement contained an implied term in the performance of the contract obligating the parties to act honestly in the sense that

44 ZANETTI, *supra* note 32, at 1018; see CÓDIGO CIVIL [Civil Code] *art. 437(1) (Port.) ("Should the circumstances on which the parties decided to enter an agreement have suffered an abnormal change, the affected party is entitled to terminate the agreement or to have it amended based on equity principles, provided that the performance of the obligations undertaken by such party seriously breaches the principles of good faith and is not covered by the risks set forth in the agreement*"). I would like to thank Mrs. Ana Carolina Freire Gentil for her contribution to this translation.

45 ZANETTI, *supra* note 32, at 1019.

46 See Carter v. Boehm [1766] 3 Burr 1905, 1910 ("The governing principle is applicable to all contracts and dealings").

47 Lord Steyn, *Contract Law: Fulfilling the Reasonable Expectations of Honest Men*, 113 LAW Q. REV. 433, 439 (1997).

48 Mid Essex Hospital Services NHS Trust v. Compass Group UK and Ireland Ltd (t/a Medirest) [2013] EWCA Civ 200, [105].

49 Interfoto Picture Library Ltd v. Stiletto Visual Programmes Ltd (CA) [1989] QB 433, 439.

50 Klaus Peter Berger & Thomas Arntz, *Good Faith as a 'General Organising Principle' of the Common Law*, 32 ARB. INT. 171 (William W. Park ed., OUP 2016).

one party should not knowingly provide false information that the other is likely to rely upon. As Justice Leggatt put it, there are

> other standards of commercial dealing which are so generally accepted that the contracting parties would reasonably be understood to take them as read without explicitly stating them in their contractual document. A key aspect of good faith, as I see it, is the observance of such standards.[51]

These standards include the fidelity to the bargain, non-arbitrary or irrational exercise of a right, and a high degree of cooperation with respect to 'relational' contracts, which, by nature, involve mutual trust and expectations of loyalty "implicit in the parties' understanding."[52] Further, consent must not be withdrawn in an unreasonable manner and any onerous or unusual term that a party intends to rely on has to be brought to the notice of the other.[53] The test for ascertaining good faith is an objective one. In this vein, the decision highlighted that what matters is not the perception of the parties but whether a reasonable and honest person in these particular circumstances would consider the conduct as commercially inappropriate,[54] which is also endorsed by later English court rulings.[55] A further remarkable development in trumping hostility against good faith is the requirement for the parties to conduct negotiations in a genuine, honest and fair manner with the ultimate view of resolving their dispute,[56] as well as the finding of the English judiciary that good faith is a *general organizing principle* in common law which informs more specific rules.[57] In the same vein, the Supreme Court of Canada in *Bhasin v. Hrynew* held that a *minimum standard* of honest contractual performance is imposed on parties in the sense that they should not lie or mislead each other: This duty of good faith is not *per se* an implied term of the contract, nor does it depend on the intentions of the parties,[58] but it is to be determined objectively by what a reasonable commercial person should have understood.

In contrast to English law, the *American legal system* has codified the principle. The U.C.C. sets forth that every contract imposes an obligation of good faith in its performance and enforcement.[59] U.C.C. Section 1–201 observes that good faith "means honesty in fact and the observance of reasonable commercial standards of

51 *Yam Seng Pte Limited v. International Trade Corporation* [2013] EWHC 111 (QB) [138] [hereinafter *Yam Seng*].

52 *Yam Seng, supra* note 51, at [142].

53 *Yam Seng, supra* note 51, at [145].

54 *Yam Seng, supra* note 51, at [144].

55 See, *e.g.*, Bristol Groundschool Ltd v. Intelligent Capture and others [2014] EWHC 2145 (Ch) [196].

56 Emirates Trading Agency LLC v. Prime Mineral Exports Private Ltd [2014] EWHC 2104 (Comm) [53], [64] [hereinafter *Emirates Trading*].

57 MSC Mediterranean Shipping S.A. v. Cottonex Anstalt [2015] EWHC 283 (Comm) [97] [hereinafter *MSC Mediterranean*].

58 Bhasin v. Hrynew, 2014 SCC 71, [2014] 3 S.C.R. 494, paras. 73–75 (Can.).

59 U.C.C. § 1–304.

fair dealing."[60] The Restatement similarly imposes on parties a duty of good faith and fair dealing in the performance of their contractual obligations.[61] While the official comments do not explicitly provide for an abstract definition, it is stated that good faith "excludes a variety of types of conduct characterized as involving 'bad faith' because they violate community standards of decency, fairness or reasonableness."[62] Characteristic examples of bad faith conduct include "evasion of the spirit of the bargain, lack of diligence and slacking off, willful rendering of imperfect performance, abuse of a power to specify terms . . . interference with or failure to cooperate in the other party's performance."[63] Other forms of bad faith include dishonest conduct by devising claims for an ostensible disagreement, interpreting the contract against one's own understanding, falsification of facts, intended failure to mitigate damages or rejection of performance with no reasons provided.[64] Further, what constitutes bad faith is the parties' effort to take advantage of opportunities which were already foregone upon contracting.[65]

Although there are three main schools of thought in the US jurisprudence as to the meaning of good faith, namely the theory that good faith is "simply a rechristening of fundamental principles of contract law,"[66] Burton's analysis that good faith is a limit to the discretion of the parties to "recapture opportunities foregone on contracting"[67] and Summer's view that good faith can be understood as excluding different forms of bad faith,[68] these variations are not, in reality, incompatible with each other. Under the American law perspective, good faith implies reasonableness, too. When the contract leaves the specification of the particulars of the performance to one party, this specification has to be made in good faith and within the limits of commercial reasonableness.[69] As Markovits highlights, when the parties fall short of making arrangements in relation to some eventuality *ex ante*, they have to employ good faith to make arrangements *ex post*.[70] For example, the termination of a contract shall definitely be governed by good faith in case the parties

60 U.C.C. § 1–201 (20); Burton draws a distinction between "honesty in fact" and "reasonable commercial standards", the former corresponding to a subjective standard, whereas the latter to an objective one. See Steven J. Burton, *Good Faith in Articles 1 and 2 of the U.C.C.: The Practice View*, 35 WM. & MARY L. REV. 1533, 1539 (1994).

61 Restatement § 205.

62 Restatement § 205 cmt. [a].

63 Restatement § 205 cmt. [d].

64 Restatement § 205 (e).

65 Steven J. Burton, *Breach of Contract and the Common Law Duty to Perform in Good Faith*, 94 HARV. L. REV. 369, 387 (1980).

66 Allan Farnsworth, *Duties of Good Faith and Fair Dealing under the UNIDROIT Principles, Relevant International Conventions and National Laws*, TUL. J. INT. COMP. L., 47, 59 (1995) (citing Tymeshare v. Covell, 727 F.2d 1145, 1152, D.C. Cir. 1984).

67 Farnsworth, *supra* note 66, at 60 (quoting Burton, *supra* note 65).

68 Farnsworth, *supra* note 66, at 59 (citing Robert S. Summers, *"Good Faith" in General Contract Law and the Sales Provisions of the Uniform Commercial Code*, 54 VA. L. REV. 195, 196 (1968)).

69 U.C.C. § 2–311 (1).

70 DANIEL MARKOVITS, *Good Faith as Contract's Core Value, in* PHILOSOPHICAL FOUNDATIONS OF CONTRACT LAW 273 (Gregory Klass et al. eds., 2014).

have not agreed on the applicable rules. A party that is about to terminate may not do so unless a "reasonable notification" is provided to the other, which means "reasonable time to seek a substitute agreement."[71] In the same vein, good faith in the performance of the contract is used by courts to effectuate parties' intentions and serve their reasonable expectations.[72] Alas, the principle of good faith should not be exclusively identified with the standard of reasonableness as the former means honesty and fairness, whereas the latter has "diligence in its essence and is more exacting than the usual contractual duty of good faith."[73] In support of this, the Kansas Supreme Court observed that the standard of best or reasonable efforts goes farther and beyond the implied duty of good faith.[74] In addition, good faith should be distinguished from any sort of loyalty to the counterparty. As US courts have observed, good faith does not reflect loyalty to the counterparty but faithfulness to the content and purpose of the contract of the parties.[75] It would be a stretch to equate good faith with loyalty. This resonates with English law in that pursuing self-interests for whatever purpose is appropriate.[76] Although the duty of good faith cannot constitute an independent cause of action as the U.C.C. sets forth, a failure to perform a specific duty or obligation in good faith can indeed constitute a breach of contract.[77] As Judge Posner noticed, "the contractual duty of good faith is thus not some newfangled bit of welfare-state paternalism or . . . the sediment of an altruistic strain in contract law"[78] (citation omitted) that could readily be enforced regardless of parties' specific duties.

Having sketched a stark comparison between common and civil law tradition, it can be deduced that civil law practitioners employ the amorphous principle of good faith to manifest other principles or rules, whereas common law practitioners might not easily imply a duty of good faith since to them predictability is far more important than serving than fairness – broadly speaking.[79] Even if courts do imply such a duty, at least from an English law perspective, they might do so in the context of relational contracts and under extreme circumstances.[80] In that vein, common law still persists that the specific notions of equity, misrepresentation and estoppel do not need to be substituted by a general concept of good faith. Finally, even if there is an express duty of good faith under English law, the courts will hesitate to

71 Markovits, *supra* note 70; see U.C.C. § 2–309 cmts. [5] and [8].

72 Steven J. Burton, *Good Faith Performance of a Contract Within Article 2 of the Uniform Commercial Code*, 67 iowa L. Rev. 1, 3 (1981).

73 E. Allan Farnsworth, 2 Farnsworth on Contracts 383–84 (2nd ed., Aspen Law & Business 1998).

74 T.S.I. Holdings Inc. v. Jenkins, 260 Kan. 703, 719–20, 924 P. 2nd 1239 (1996).

75 Markovits, *supra* note 70, at 277 (citing ASB Allegiance Real Estate Fund v. Scion Breckenridge Managing Member, L.L.C., 50 A.3d 434, 440–41, Del. Ch. 2012).

76 Markovits, *supra* note 70.

77 U.C.C. § 1–304 cmt. [1].

78 Market Street Associates Limited Partnership v. Frey, 941 F.2d. 588, 595 (7th Cir. 1991).

79 Roy Goode, The Concept of "Good Faith" in English Law 7 (Centro di Studi e Ricerche di Diritto Comparator e Straniero 1992).

80 Candey Ltd v. Bosheh & Anor [2022] EWCA Civ 1103, [31].

automatically import a wider meaning unless the parties have explicitly authorized the court to do so.[81] However, it must be accepted that piecemeal solutions would not help instill consistency in decision-making.[82] In light of recent case law, small steps have been taken both at a domestic and international level to reflect a progressive convergence of both worlds despite their congenital dissimilarities.

2.3 The International Landscape

In the international legal order, there has been an effort to merge the benefits of the historical, cultural, philosophical and purely legalistic idiosyncrasies regarding the meaning of good faith in a dialectical symbiosis. First-hand experience of this osmotic effect is detected in the UNIDROIT Principles.[83] It is observed that their purpose is associated with the promotion of contractual good faith, which is elevated to an *international standard* regulating a variety of practical matters in cross-border transactions. Article 1.7 requires that "each party must act in accordance with good faith and fair dealing in international trade" and further that "the parties may not exclude or limit this duty." As the comment emphasizes, and despite the absence of special provisions on the direct or indirect application of good faith, the parties' conduct throughout the lifetime of the contract, including the negotiation phase, must comply with good faith and fair dealing.[84] In addition, general applications of good faith include abuse of rights[85] and inconsistent behavior.[86]

More specific applications of good faith permeate a variety of provisions of the UNIDROIT Principles to ensure fairness in cross-border commercial relations, the latter being forged in a rapidly changing environment.[87] Among others is Article 2.1.15, establishing the liability resulting from bad faith negotiations where bad faith means entering into, or continuing, negotiations when the intention is not to reach a final agreement.[88] Although it is argued that good faith, as formulated in the

81 Re Compound Photonics Group Ltd [2022] EWCA Civ 1371, [196]; see also David Lewis KC & Fiona Petersen, Good Faith in English Law – As Elusive as Ever? Twenty Essex, Bulletin Nov. 2022, *available at* www.twentyessex.com/good-faith-in-english-law-as-elusive-as-ever/ (last visited Apr. 9, 2023).

82 See Daniele Bertolini, *Toward a Framework to Define the Outer Boundaries of Good Faith in Contractual Performance*, 58 Alberta L. Rev. 573 (2021).

83 See also PECL, art. 1:102, 1:201.

84 UNIDROIT Principles, art. 1.7 cmt. [1].

85 UNIDROIT Principles, art. 1.7 cmt. [2].

86 UNIDROIT Principles, art. 1.8.

87 UNIDROIT Principles, art. 4.8 stipulates that in supplying an omitted term to the contract regard has to be had to good faith and fair dealing; art. 5.1.2 provides that implied obligations stem from good faith and fair dealing; art. 5.1.3 provides for the duty to cooperate as an application of the principle of good faith; art. 5.3.3(1) provides for the duty to cooperate when that is reasonably expected; finally, art. 7.1.6 reads that a clause excluding liability or permitting performance other than what is expected may not be invoked if that is grossly unfair and against the purpose of the contract.

88 UNIDROIT Principles, art. 2.1.15 ("(2) [A] party who negotiates or breaks off negotiations in bad faith is liable for the losses caused to the other party. (3) It is bad faith, in particular, for a party to enter into or continue negotiations when intending not to reach an agreement with the other party").

UNIDROIT Principles, is applied very differently across a number of jurisdictions and this fragmentation allegedly constitutes one of the main conceptual reasons why the UNIDROIT Principles are simply a restatement of transnational contract law that cannot be applied directly to actual cases,[89] there is ample evidence to the contrary.

The exact purpose of the promulgation of this set of 211 rules is to provide a neutral compromise among national traditions, which are ill-suited for what international trade is made for.[90] For example, there is a considerable divergence between civil and common law on whether a duty to negotiate in good faith is enforceable. Civil law has doctrinally formulated the duty to negotiate in good faith on the basis of *culpa in contrahendo*, whereas the common law counterpart has markedly displayed an aversion to this concept. What the UNIDROIT Principles achieved is to bridge the gap by recognizing the duty of good faith in negotiations, especially when the negotiating party's intent is exactly this: not to reach an agreement with its counterparty. This is amply supported by recent common law judgments and the solid argument that otherwise, "the expectations of parties who reasonably rely on reciprocal good faith in negotiating contracts"[91] would be frustrated.

On the other hand, the CISG is less vocal, given that it reserves for good faith only an interpretive function and that it is within the convention's boundaries. Indeed, it is provided therein that "[i]n the interpretation of this Convention, regard is to be had to its international character and to the need to promote uniformity in its application and the observance of good faith in international trade."[92] Albeit the result of a hard-fought debate on whether the CISG imports a general duty of good faith or not,[93] the middle ground was adopted, which recognizes good faith *merely* as an interpretive principle,[94] and even more restrictively "[i]n the interpretation of this Convention,"[95] thus excluding it as an interpretive principle in the performance of parties' contractual obligations. It may be inferred, therefore, that the evolution of a duty of good faith to a full-fledged doctrine in international commerce is rather slow.

2.4 The Polysemy of Good Faith

The concept of good faith in arbitration is not philosophical. It is practical. What should be sought after is a logical methodology to discover the components of

89 Ralf Michaels, *The UNIDROIT Principles as Global Background Law*, 19 Unif. L. Rev. 643, 668 (2014).

90 Klaus Peter Berger, *UNIDROIT Principles of International Commercial Contracts, an Article-by-Article Commentary*, 34(3) Arb. Int'l. 469, 469 (2018).

91 See generally Leon E. Trakman & Kunal Sharma, *The Binding Force of Agreements to Negotiate in Good Faith*, 73 The Cambridge Law Journal 598, 627 (2014); see also *United Group Rail Services Ltd v Rail Corporation New South Wales* [2009] NSWCA 177, ¶ 71 (Austl.); see also *Emirates Trading, supra* note 56, at [42]–[46].

92 CISG, art. 7(1).

93 Boris Praštalo, Uniformity in the Application of the CISG: Analysis of the Problem and Recommendations for the Future 15–16 (Kluwer Law International 2020).

94 See ICC Case No. 8611/HV/JK, Jan. 23, 1997, *available at* www.unilex.info/cisg/case/229.

95 CISG, art. 7(1).

good faith and the dynamics between them and good faith. Leading minds in international arbitration have observed that good faith provides the foundation of more specific rules that, in turn, become principles.[96] The explanation of such a phenomenon is grounded in the fact that good faith is the *whole* and the specific rules or principles generated out of it are the *parts*. Such principles are *pacta sunt servanda*, estoppel, reasonableness and abuse of rights. However, what has not been elucidated thus far is that good faith is not just the sum of its components. The whole is prior to the sum of its parts.[97] It is also greater than the parts added up. Indeed, as one cannot possibly talk about some part of a whole if this whole does not pre-exist, similarly, each of the principles or parts of good faith cannot be construed without any reference to good faith. In other words, good faith can survive the lack of one of the following principles, but none of them has some worth or practical value should good faith be absent.

2.4.1 Expression of or Limitation to Pacta Sunt Servanda

The Latin *pacta sunt servanda* means agreements must be kept[98] (*sanctity of contracts*). This was eloquently conveyed in an ICC award, whereby the arbitrators noted that this principle means that a contract governing the legal relationships between the contracting parties has to be performed in conformity to its terms and other stipulations, which *inter partes* have the quality of the rule of law.[99] It is indeed a principle that has to be applied more rigorously in international contracts, for it would be disruptive and contemptuous from a policy perspective for the parties to an international contract to escape the contractual stipulations, assuming the language of the contract is unambiguous.[100] In the well-known case of *Malicorp Ltd. v. The Government of the Arab Republic of Egypt and others*, the tribunal observed that there was ample evidence that the Republic of Egypt had sought to shape a secure regime for the attraction of foreign investments in the country. As a result, any effort on the part of Egypt seeking to challenge jurisdiction, on the basis that the government official who entered into the arbitration agreement did not have the authority to bind the Republic to arbitration, would produce a result against the principle of *pacta sunt servanda* as a manifestation of good faith.[101]

The connection to good faith is so great that the commentary to the Trans-Lex Principles provides that *pacta sunt servanda* is an expression of good faith in terms of keeping the faith in the contractual undertakings, without which international

96 Emmanuel Gaillard & John Savage, Fouchard Gaillard Goldman on International Commercial Arbitration 820 (Kluwer Law International 1999).

97 See Aristotle, Politics 6 (Benjamin Jowett trans., Batoche Books 1999).

98 Black's Law Dictionary 3508 (Bryan A. Garner ed., 8th ed., Thomson West 2004).

99 ICC Case No. 18489, 42 Y.B. Comm. Arb. 172, 193 (A. J. Van den Berg ed., 2017).

100 ICC Case No. 12456, Collection of ICC Arbitral Awards 2008–2011, at 811, *available at* www.trans-lex.org/212456.

101 Malicorp Ltd. (UK) v. The Government of the Arab Republic of Egypt and others, Final Award, CRCICA Case No. 382/2004, Mar. 7, 2006, at 17 and 18.

contract law would be ridiculed.[102] Nonetheless, good faith acts as a limit to the principle of the sanctity of contracts, too. The arbitral tribunal in *ICC Case No. 4761* reasoned that, much as national systems and the *lex mercatoria*, Libyan law employing the doctrine of *imprévision* dictates that the principle of *pacta sunt servanda* is limited by the principle of good faith.[103]

2.4.2 Estoppel or Abuse of Rights

Another principle of paramount practical importance that forms part of good faith is *estoppel* or *venire contra factum proprium (non valet)*. There are many types of estoppel in common law, including promissory estoppel,[104] equitable estoppel,[105] acquiescence,[106] and issue estoppel (or collateral estoppel).[107] On the other hand, estoppel *per se* does not exist in the civil law tradition. Instead, what resembles the fundamentals of estoppel from a civil law perspective is embodied in *culpa in contrahendo* translated into 'fault in conclusion of a contract,' and which is cemented in that a party's ending of negotiations without a valid reason following inducement to the other party of reliance on the contract is not permitted.[108] As a Louisiana court opined, *culpa in contrahendo* is the "civilian equivalent of the common law concept of promissory estoppel."[109]

From the perspective of international arbitration, the thrust of estoppel echoes a more generic understanding of both worlds. In that spirit, the arbitral tribunal in the ICC case of *Sales Representative (Iraq) v. Manufacturer (France)* neatly portrayed

102 Trans-Lex Principle No. IV. 1.2., cmt. [1], *available at* www.trans-lex.org/919000. Comment 2 further adds that it is good faith that helps integrate these two principles into one in the performance of contract such that it coins the term "*pacta sunt servanda bona fide.*"

103 ICC Case No. 4761, Clunet 1987, at 1017, *available at* www.trans-lex.org/204761.

104 The doctrine pursuant to which a party is not supposed to make the other party rely on an unequivocal promise and then make a U-turn by taking it back. See Marquardt v. Perry, 200 P. 3d 1126 (Colo. App. 2008).

105 Equitable estoppel is slightly different in that it connotes *inducement* to the other party and is more associated with ideas of fairness. See L.A. Sheridan, *Equitable Estoppel Today*, 15 The Modern Law Review 325, 334 (1952).

106 The distinguishing feature of acquiescence is related to a *silent* acceptance "by the plaintiff of the *status quo,* the defendant acting in reliance upon that acceptance and doing such consequential acts as to make it inequitable that he should be asked to undo it all in order to satisfy the plaintiff's claim" (emphasis in the original). Sheridan, *supra* note 105 (quoting McCausland v. Young [1948] 1 N. Ir. 72, at 100–12 (Ch.)).

107 The Supreme Court of the United States affirmed a long time ago that "collateral estoppel, like the related doctrine of res judicata, has the dual purpose of protecting litigants from the burden of relitigating an identical issue with the same party or his privy and of promoting judicial economy by preventing needless litigation" (citation omitted). Parklane Hosiery Co., Inc. v. Shore, 439 U.S. 322, 327 (1979).

108 Günther Kühne, *Promissory Estoppel and Culpa in Contrahendo*, 10 Tel Aviv U. Stud. L. 279, 287 (1990).

109 David V. Snyder, *Comparative Law in Action: Promissory Estoppel, the Civil Law, and the Mixed Jurisdiction*, 15 Ariz. J. Int'l & Comp. 696, 704 (1998) (quoting Snyder v. Champion Realty Corp., 631 F.2d 1253, 1255, 5th Cir. 1980).

the principle as barring a party from contradicting itself.[110] As the same award affirmed, given that Swiss law does not recognize estoppel, the analog of estoppel in Swiss law is an abuse of rights of Article 2(2) of the Swiss Civil Code.[111] In Chapter 3, whether estoppel or abuse of rights are totally distinct concretizations of good faith will be explored. It suffices to note here that both notions refer to the same contemptible unfairness of a conduct. As the United States Court of Appeal held: "[E]stoppel precludes a party from asserting rights he otherwise would have had against another when his own conduct renders assertion of those rights contrary to equity" (internal quotation marks omitted; citation omitted).[112]

2.4.3 Expression of Parties' Reasonable Expectations

Arbitrators should not honor any kind of expectations except for the reasonable expectations of the parties. These expectations are not any different from 'fair and legitimate expectations' or 'justified expectations.' Therefore, they might be used interchangeably. The element of reasonableness is profoundly entrenched in good faith. Article 8 of the CISG sets the scene for the quest for the meaning of reasonableness by providing that if the statements or conduct of one party cannot be interpreted according to their intent that the other party knew or could have been aware of, such interpretation can be made in accordance with the understanding of a reasonable person of the same kind in same circumstances.[113] The test is an objective one.

Despite a lack of accurate definition of reasonable, a Greek analog of the term is '*εύλογος,*' the etymology of which describes a virtue accorded to a person demonstrating rational reasoning.[114] Rationality as the flip side of reasonableness is confirmed in an ICC award where the tribunal ascertained that parties to a contract pursue reasonable aims in the sense that they should "be viewed as behaving *rationally* and striving for the conclusion of contracts with which they can achieve their common purpose"[115] (emphasis added). It went on that "[t]he aim of contract interpretation is not to read possible inconsistencies into the language but rather to ascertain the real and rational will of the parties to be found behind the words

110 ICC Case No. 16684 of 2012, 41 Y.B. Comm. Arb. 52, 80 (A. J. Van den Berg ed., 2016).

111 ICC Case No. 16684 of 2012, *supra* note 110, at 79.

112 International Paper Co. v. Schwabedissen Maschinen & Anlagen GMBH, 206 F.3d 411, 417–18 (4th Cir. 2000).

113 CISG, art. 8(1)–(2).

114 Etymology in ancient Greek: *εύλογος* < ευ + λόγος (< *λέγω*), which indicates one having a good reasoning – the rational or prudent person.

115 ICC Case No. 13585, Partial Award on Jurisdiction, Aug. 31, 2005 [Enforcement of the award was sought and challenged in Germany. The German Supreme Court rendered a decision confirming that the Arbitral Tribunal had properly construed the arbitration agreement. See BGH III ZR 214/05 of Jan. 12, 2006, ASA Bull. 1/2013, at 194. See also Simone Stebler, *The Problem of Conflicting Arbitration and Forum Selection Clauses*, ASA Bull. (Jan. 2013), at 27] 31(1) ASA Bull. 57, 61 (Kluwer Law International 2013).

used in the contract."[116] Even if such rationality does "not arise from the immediate expressions of assent of the parties, [it is] still properly regarded as part of the parties' contract because their reasonable expectations always include the context of which the normative structure is an essential part."[117] In *Gephar LLC v. Danstar Ferment AG* the arbitral tribunal reasoned, by discussing what good faith actually means in the context of a contract governed by Swiss law, that "an obligation to behave in good faith"[118] requires that "the parties observe a reasonable commercial standard of fair dealing, be faithful to the agreed purpose of the agreement, and act consistently with the legitimate expectations of the other party."[119]

Were it not for the test of a rational person in the same circumstances and of the same kind, which reflects the commercial sense of people in the same business community as the parties, good faith would be superfluous and would merely be exhausted to an exercise of seeking the esoteric will of the parties. Jettisoning the idea of an esoteric will does not imply whatsoever that certain subjective standards of good faith do not exist, such as honesty in fact. A concrete example of such reasonable expectations may be utilized to determine whether one arbitration clause in a contract serves as an 'umbrella' for other separate contracts concluded between the said parties[120] or whether a state party can invoke its local law as it pleases to circumvent its obligation to arbitrate the dispute.

2.4.4 Fairness

Even the proponents of the natural law theory of respecting the parties' will did not envisage the supremacy of party autonomy as necessarily being independent of its consequences, the latter being an indication of what fairness actually requires.[121] Even under the prism of fairness, good faith is still vague. Three observations help demystify the relationship between the two notions. First, the interplay of good faith and fairness should not only be understood in terms of *restricting* the parties' will but also in terms of establishing confidence among the parties and inspiring predictability within the system of international arbitration. It is the vindication of the reliance principle that a "contracting party may be bound by its actions, even if it did not intend this,"[122] as well as the "justified confidence"[123] of the other

116 Stebler, *supra* note 115.

117 Jay M. Feinman, *Good Faith and Reasonable Expectations*, 67 Arkansas Law Review 525, 567 (2014).

118 ICC Case No. 9890/EMT, Aug. 5, 2015, para. 364 (Arbitrator Intelligence Materials, Kluwer Law International).

119 ICC Case No. 9890/EMT, *supra* note 118.

120 Marc Blessing, Introduction to Arbitration – Swiss and International Perspectives, para. 515 (Helbing & Lichtenhahn 1999).

121 Nagla Nassar, Sanctity of Contracts Revisited, Dordrecht, Boston, London 1995, at 7, *available at* www.trans-lex.org/105700/_/nassar-nagla-sanctity-of-contracts-revisited-dordrecht-boston-london-1995/.

122 ICC Case No. 16920, ICC Disp. Res. Bull. No. 2, 136, para. 148, 2016.

123 ICC Case No. 16920, *supra* note 122.

party. The tribunal in *ICC Case No. 16920* explained that it would be unfair for sophisticated market-leading contracting parties to get protection against contractual clauses that they agreed to in the first place.[124] Second, fairness constitutes the heart of good faith. Contractual clauses that are so oppressive and one-sided or take advantage of the lack of experience, imprudence or hardship of one party grossly violate good faith (and the underlying principle of proportionality).[125] Under this prism, the notion of fairness must be generally understood as the most sacred aspect of public policy, by virtue of which it is determined whether the particular terms of the contract or the arbitration agreement are enforceable or not.[126]

2.5 Doctrinal Debate Over the Role of Good Faith

Except for the multiple contours of good faith crystallized in the previously discussed concepts, its coherent application in international arbitration depends on resolving a few quandaries: whether good faith is subjective or objective; an autonomous contractual obligation or ancillary mechanism; an expression of suasion or compulsion; and eventually creature of morality or social policy.

2.5.1 Subjective v. Objective Good Faith

The civil legal systems usually provide for both subjective[127] and objective good faith.[128] The distinction lies in that subjective good faith refers to the inner confidence of the party that their acts are legitimate, whereas the objective good faith has a more tangible foundation. It refers to the social crystallization of good faith. Thus, it can be ascertained by reference to trade practices or fair dealing and can even be used to mitigate the unfairness produced as a result of the law or contract. It becomes apparent that the objective good faith has certain enforcement value in terms of certain consequences imposed by virtue of its violation. As explained in Chapter 3, the subjective good faith might be easily conflated with the inner or esoteric honesty of a person who escapes the imposition of sanctions; thus, it

124 ICC Case No. 16920, *supra* note 122, para. 152.

125 Nassar, *supra* note 121, at 195 n.6; see also GCC 1:179 ("Invalid as violating fair dealing is mainly the agreement by which the freedom of a party is excessively restricted or the agreement by which someone takes advantage of the need, the naivety or inexperience of the other party and in that way succeeds in entering into an agreement or gain for themselves or some other person, in return for some performance, benefits which under the circumstances are obviously disproportionate to their own performance").

126 Vlad Movshovich et al., Cool Ideas 1186 CC v. Hubbard and Another [2014] ZACC 16, Constitutional Court of South Africa, CCT 99/13, June 5, 2014 (A contribution by the ITA Board of Reporters, Kluwer Law International).

127 See, *e.g.*, GCC 3:1036 ("With the disposal of a movable asset according to article 1034, they who acquire become the owners even if the ownership of the asset does not belong to the person disposing it, except if during the transfer of the possession the acquiring person is in bad faith").

128 See, *e.g.*, GCC 2:288 ("The debtor has the obligation to perform their obligation in accordance with good faith, having regard to fair dealing").

should better fall under an *inter*-subjective standard of good faith, which must be pegged to the *mutual* trust between contracting parties and the *mutual* effort toward upholding the purpose of the contract. Only then can it function as a source of a measurable standard of conduct.

2.5.2 Rule Imposing Autonomous Obligations v. Principle Informing Existing Rules

Whether good faith operates as an autonomous obligation or ancillary mechanism has produced conflicting schools of thought. From a practical point of view, an award under the auspices of the Italian Arbitration Association, which was based on a claim seeking termination of a distributorship agreement and damages, confirmed the "autonomous obligation of good faith arising in the performance of the contract, to afford proper co-operation and assistance to the suing claimant."[129] Even if, the tribunal reasoned, a contractual duty of cooperation was provided to be borne by the distributor to the licensor for the protection of the trademark, this does not mean that a similar duty of cooperation should not be borne by the defendant licensee pursuant to the duty of good faith, as enshrined in the governing Italian law, which is "beyond the specific provisions of the agreement and not capable of exclusion by the will of the parties."[130] Similarly, the arbitrators of another case held that the defendants breached under the applicable Italian law their "autonomous obligation of good faith in the negotiation process" because they did not maintain transparency in their dealing and delayed their decision not to extend the duration of the agreement.[131]

However, it is rather rare that a duty of good faith will constitute an independent source of breach of contract. True, in the majority of civil and common laws, and as expounded previously, good faith cannot form an independent legal basis upon which one can act, nor does it produce a direct legal effect.[132] Normally, the arbitrators mandated to resolve international disputes will perceive the superior principle of good faith as an ancillary and supportive mechanism, allowing them to measure the conduct of the co-contractors and shape more uniform and coherent rules of behavior.[133] Such firm belief is also embedded in public international law, where good faith functions as a general principle guiding the process of

129 Exclusive Distributor v. Principal, Final Award, AIA Case No. 76/98, Nov. 24, 1999, 25 Y.B. Comm. Arb., para. 56 (Albert Jan Van den Berg ed., ICCA & Kluwer Law International 2000).

130 Exclusive Distributor v. Principal, Final Award, AIA Case No. 76/98, *supra* note 129, at 370 (discussing Article 1375 of the Italian Civil Code).

131 CAM Case No. 8803, Feb. 24, 2006 (Stefano Azzali, A contribution by the ITA Board of Reporters, Kluwer Law International).

132 U.C.C. § 1–304 cmt. [1]; *accord* BGB § 242.

133 Filali Osman, Les Principes Généraux de la Lex Mercatoria, Paris 1992, at 19 et seq., *available at* www.trans-lex.org/106300.

decision-making.[134] The ICJ indeed ruled that good faith is "not in itself a source of obligation where none would otherwise exist."[135]

Despite the previous accurate observations, it would be meaningless to maintain that good faith does not enjoy an enforcement status. Reinhold argued that "good faith serves a mediatory role between a rule and a principle."[136] Thus, a main objective of the present monograph is to prove that good faith has the capacity to act as a rule, too, the breach of which has certain consequences for the parties and the award itself. To the extent it informs existing rules or helps arbitrators justify their solution, good faith acts as a general principle. To the extent it imposes certain standards of conduct, the breach of which results in certain consequences, or corrects the contract by importing specific rules the latter deriving from trade usages, good faith acts as a rule. Good faith also acts as a rule to the extent it functions as a public policy limit to the parties' rights and obligations or in case it expresses an idea of fairness within the metes and bounds of the governing law that the parties themselves have selected.

2.5.3 Suasion v. Compulsion

The argument that the principle of good faith is a product of mere suasion among the parties or the product of rhetorical elaborations topping off a lawyer's arguments[137] is all the more defective and impractical. The general phenomenon of the underenforcement of good faith[138] contradicts the very purpose of the philosophy around the genesis of the contract. Good faith is so vital for the existence of the contract that it is rightly argued that it provides the matrix of the shared perspective of the parties and facilitates the "joint project fixed by the contractual intentions."[139] Under this spectrum, it is an inter-subjective principle in that one party's commitment to the contract is dependent on the faith that the other party will honor in good faith its own contractual obligations. Indeed, it would be a Pyrrhic victory for the arbitration system itself if, for example, a distributor of goods could give up on its good faith commitment to the supplier to accept the merchandise, based on orders already made, by invoking the *force majeure* defense, especially when the latter is used as a pretext of unprofitability, or when the *force majeure* event is readily foreseeable. Such conduct should be condemned in the form of damages or specific

134 Emily Sipiorski, Good Faith in International Investment Arbitration, para. 1.27 (OUP 2019); *accord* Ronald Dworkin, Taking Rights Seriously 25 (Harvard University Press 1978).

135 Border and Transborder Armed Actions (Nicaragua v. Honduras) (Jurisdiction and Admissibility) [1988] ICJ Reports 69, para. 94.

136 Steven Reinhold, *Good Faith in International Law*, 2 UCLJLJ 40–63 (2013), Bonn Research Paper on Public International Law No. 2/2013, *available at* https://ssrn.com/abstract=2269746.

137 Ragnar Harbst, A Counsel's Guide to Examining and Preparing Witnesses in International Arbitration 59 (Kluwer Law International 2015).

138 See generally Paul MacMahon, *Good Faith and Fair Dealing as an Underenforced Legal Norm*, 99 Minn. Law Rev. 2051 (2015).

139 Markovits, *supra* note 70, at 293.

performance in the sense that it disturbs the essence of good faith to compel parties to enforce their original contractual faith to each other. In other words, as important as party autonomy is to international commercial arbitration, as also envisioned in the UNCITRAL Model Law,[140] so is the enforcement of good faith in safeguarding the parties' binding commitments resulting from such autonomy.

An *ad hoc* tribunal explained that the dominant shareholder's legal independence of the company is disregarded when good faith in business affairs requires so or reliance on such independence would constitute an abuse of rights or gross violation of the party's legitimate interests.[141] It would be hypocritical to maintain that good faith is reduced to just an exercise of suasion. That is particularly true in arbitration. Even the proponents of the underenforcement of good faith advance that "[m]ore than courts, which tend to be staffed by generalist judges and juries who lack expertise, arbitrators are often in a better position to identify unreasonable contractual behavior"[142] (citation omitted).

2.5.4 Morality v. Social Policy

It is reasonable to argue that good faith does not function as a moral rule in arbitral practice. The morality argument collapses if one considers first, whose morality is fulfilled when resorting to good faith and second, the assumption that the parties to an international contract merely pursue, and should be allowed to pursue, their self-interests.[143] More workable seems to be the proposition that good faith reflects a social policy norm, or the ubiquitous *boni mores* of the society, as a concept distinct from individual morality, even justifying in the field of international arbitration the discreet introduction of a corrective form of equity.[144] That is certainly justified given that "there are all sorts of moral (or public interest) constraints on the kind of agreements that the parties can enforce."[145]

140 Sunday A. Fagbemi, *The Doctrine of Party Autonomy in International Commercial Arbitration: Myth or Reality?* 6 AFE BABALOLA UNIVERSITY J. OF SUST. DEV. LAW & POLICY 223, 224 (2015); see UNCITRAL Model Law, art. 19(1) (2006) ("Subject to the provisions of this Law, the parties are free to agree on the procedure to be followed by the arbitral tribunal in conducting the proceedings"); see also English Arbitration Act 1996 § 1(b) ("[T]he parties should be free to agree how their disputes are resolved, subject only to such safeguards as are necessary in the public interest").

141 Alpha SA v. Beta & Co. (Ruritanian State Company), Award, 1991, 10(2) ASA BULL. 202, 224–25 (Kluwer Law International 1992).

142 MacMahon, *supra* note 138, at 2108.

143 Roger Brownsword, '*Good Faith in Contracts' Revisited*, 49(1) CURR. LEG. PROBL. 111, 113 (1996). ("[C]ontractors . . . should pursue their individual self-interest in a way that is consistent with the community's sense of fair dealing") (alteration to the original).

144 Mayer, Pierre, Le Principe de Bonne Foi devant les Arbitres du Commerce International, Festschrift Pierre Lalive, Basel, Frankfurt a. M. 1993, at 546, *available at* www.trans-lex.org/115700.

145 ROGER BROWNSWORD, Positive, Negative, Neutral: The Reception of Good Faith in English Contract Law, in GOOD FAITH IN CONTRACT (Roger Brownsword et al. eds., 1999), at 38, *available at* www.trans-lex.org/131100.

2.6 Conclusion

The previous analysis explains that, despite the indeterminacy of good faith, the full spectrum of the substantive content of good faith manifests through the specific concepts of *pacta sunt servanda*, estoppel or abuse of rights, reasonableness and fairness. Measuring it is still elusive as different legal systems perceive good faith quite differently. As the gap between civil and common law still remains apparent, it becomes increasingly debatable whether on the international plane of cross-border arbitration, the practicality of good faith corresponds to the proposition that more specific and technical rules (or principles) can adequately substitute it. It remains to be seen whether a true convergence or homogeneity is gaining momentum. It suffices to note that good faith does not merely have moral connotations. It is not even an empty shell or a sign of hollow rhetoric. Good faith's enforceability lies in its substantive content, which guides arbitrators in inducing specific standards for the purpose of measuring the appropriateness of parties' conduct or diagnosing its permissiveness. It even constitutes the premise for ascertaining liability and imposing certain consequences, such as damages, arising from the breach of it.

3 Normative Good Faith when National Law is Applicable to the Merits

3.1 Pre-contractual Negotiation

Arbitral case law is not particularly affluent in decisions requiring the parties to negotiate their contract in good faith. The reason is that common and civil law traditions are quite divided on the firm establishment of a duty to negotiate a contract in good faith. A typical example is the *caveat emptor* maxim in the common law system, pursuant to which the seller is not obliged to inform the buyer about characteristics or facts around the merchandise to be sold, even if there is evidence during the negotiation phase that the buyer is deprived of such material knowledge.[1] English law has admittedly distanced itself from recognizing such a duty. The leading judgment of the House of Lords in *Walford v. Miles* is illuminating. *Lord Ackner* reasoned that:

> A duty to negotiate in good faith is as unworkable in practice as it is inherently inconsistent with the position of a negotiating party . . . [w]hile negotiations are in existence either party is entitled to withdraw from these negotiations, at any time and for any reason.[2]

On the other hand, the landscape in civil law countries is quite different. German law requires the seller to notify the buyer about the legal characteristics of a product without the latter being obliged to request such information.[3] Along the same lines, the recent reform of the French Civil Code has firmly established a non-waivable duty of good faith in pre-contractual negotiations. Parties are permitted to cease negotiations, except if such termination is against good faith.[4] Article 1112(1) imposes a duty upon the party that has knowledge of information decisive for the other party's consent to inform it in case the other contracting party

1 Beata Gessel-Kalinowska vel Kalisz, *Representations and Warranties in Cross-Border Mergers and Acquisitions: The Challenges of Cultural Diversity*, 24 Icc Bull. No. 1, 31–32 (2013).

2 Gary B. Born, International Commercial Arbitration §5.08 (3rd ed., Kluwer Law International 2021).

3 Gessel-Kalinowska vel Kalisz, *supra* note 1, at 33.

4 Code civil [C. civ.] [Civil Code] art. 1112 (Fr.).

DOI: 10.4324/9781003527596-4

is legitimately unaware.[5] Under the new revolutionary regime in France, such an enhanced duty of good faith also includes the duty of confidentiality, pursuant to which disclosure of confidential information obtained without permission through negotiations incurs liability and thus forms the basis of a claim for damages.[6]

Greek law also espouses the concept of *culpa in contrahendo*, which is cemented on GCC Article 197. It accordingly stipulates that the parties have a duty to negotiate in line with good faith and fair dealing. Pursuant to Article 198, compensation might be awarded to the aggrieved party in case the other party conducted negotiations in bad faith. Even in American law, it appears that good faith notions have emerged in preliminary negotiations and have been fused to doctrines of estoppel or are linked to an "increased duty to disclose."[7] It is astonishing that as early as 1964, American scholars recognized the importance of good faith in their common law system, the existence of which "is vital to an open system of contract justice and to a restriction of contractual freedom in the interest of its own preservation."[8]

The comparative study of a duty to negotiate an international contract in good faith reveals the strong tension between common and civil law traditions as to the understanding and application of good faith in negotiations. Indeed, it would be rather difficult to reconcile the dissimilarities in international arbitration, where domestic law usually governs the dispute. However, two observations are critical. First, even jurisdictions that traditionally resist the application of good faith tend to acknowledge the importance of its application to some extent. *Goode* has succinctly remarked:

> English law does not have anything equivalent to . . . good faith found in the civil law; *we require good faith in particular situations*. For example, a party who opens *negotiations* leading to a contract has a duty not to deceive the other party by false statements or by any concealment.[9]

Second, its application by common law jurisdictions is gaining momentum with major implications in international arbitration, too. In evaluating agreements to negotiate in good faith, the English courts have traditionally ruled that such agreements are unenforceable since "good faith is too open-ended a concept or criterion to provide a sufficient definition of what such an agreement must as a minimum involve and when it can objectively be determined to be properly concluded."[10] Contrariwise, the Australian Court of Appeal in *United Group Rail Services v. Rail Corporation*

5 Code civil [C. civ.] [Civil Code] art. 1112(1) (Fr.).
6 Code civil [C. civ.] [Civil Code] art. 1112(2) (Fr.).
7 Friedrich Kessler & Edith Fine, *Culpa in Contrahendo, Bargaining in Good Faith, and Freedom of Contract: A Comparative Study*, 77 HARV. LAW REV. 401, 448 (1964).
8 Kessler & Fine, *supra* note 7, at 449.
9 ROY GOODE, THE CONCEPT OF "GOOD FAITH" IN ENGLISH LAW 4–5 (Centro di Studi e Ricerche di Diritto Comparator e Straniero 1992).
10 Wah (Aka Alan Tang) and Another v. Grant Thornton International Ltd and Others [2012] EWHC 3198, [57] (Ch).

New South Wales corrected the false impression that to negotiate in good faith is "vague, illusory or uncertain."[11] The commitment of the parties to a good faith standard in negotiations implies "notions of honesty and genuineness."[12] It went on that "[w]hilst the activity is of a self-interested character, the parties have not left its conduct unconstrained."[13] Instead, a duty to negotiate in good faith is pegged to "the requirement . . . to do all things necessary to enable the other party to have the benefit of the contract"[14] (citations omitted). Third, international arbitration practice is aligned with the previously stated view in that the parties have an obligation not to make any misrepresentations if they are requested to disclose.[15] The understanding is that of a "minimum standard of honesty in fact, where one is not expected to care for others or share his fortunes with them. His only obligation is not to cause his partner's ignorance for the purpose of increasing his profits or securing a contractual advantage."[16]

3.2 Performance of Contractual Obligations

3.2.1 The Content of Good Faith in Contractual Performance

The content of good faith in international arbitration depends on the fabric of the applicable national law and the unique facts of the case. The ICDR award in *Samwhan v. Louis Berger* explained that one party intentionally withheld critical information from the other in the execution of their contract, while the full extent of such superior knowledge was only revealed thereafter.[17] The tribunal found that the standard of good faith and fair dealing was breached by virtue of the violation of a duty of disclosure; thus, it awarded compensatory damages under the laws of New Jersey.[18] Another embodiment of good faith is offered in *ICC Case Nos. 6515 and 6516*, where the tribunal held that any ambiguous conduct that misleads the other party "into doing or not doing something which was not provided for in the contract, or into doing or not doing something it would be excused from

11 United Group Rail Services Limited v. Rail Corporation New South Wales [2009] NSWCA 177, para. 74 (Austl.).

12 United Group Rail Services, *supra* note 11, para. 71.

13 United Group Rail Services, *supra* note 11.

14 United Group Rail Services, *supra* note 11, para. 72.

15 Nagla Nassar, Sanctity of Contracts Revisited, Dordrecht, Boston, London 1995, at 150, *available at* www.trans-lex.org/105700/_/nassar-nagla-sanctity-of-contracts-revisited-dordrecht-boston-london-1995/.

16 Nassar, *supra* note 15. In international practice, non-disclosure of information amounts to breach of good faith and liability to the extent that it results in a misrepresentation of a fact perceived to be material for the conclusion of the contract. Nassar, *supra* note 15; see ICC Case No. 3572, 14 Y.B. Comm. Arb. 111, 114, 1989 (concerning non-disclosure of information to the government relating to an oil and gas concession contract).

17 ICDR Case No. 50 110 T 00731 11, Feb. 28, 2014, para. 71 (Arbitrator Intelligence Materials, Kluwer Law International).

18 ICDR Case No. 50 110 T 00731 11, *supra* note 17, para. 93.

doing or not doing under the contract"[19] would violate the duty of good faith in the performance of the contract under the applicable Greek law. Further, any kind of interference or failure to cooperate with the other contracting party in the performance of the obligations is deemed to be in violation of a duty of good faith.[20] Another arbitral tribunal held that a good faith standard in performance also refers to the way the parties' rights are exercised. For example, a party should not demand performance before such performance becomes due.[21] What is noteworthy, at least from a comparative perspective, is that the content of good faith is broader if civil law is applicable to the contract. Conversely, if common law occurs to be applicable, the arbitrator would be less liberal to imply an obligation of good faith into the contract – which was not otherwise bargained for by the parties – or read it inconsistently with the express contractual terms.[22]

3.2.2 Variations of Normative Good Faith: From Opportunism to Loyalty

Should the arbitrator draw a line between self-interested and opportunistic conduct? How far should they go in allowing self-interested behavior? The arbitral tribunal faces a travesty of justice, where, on the one hand, one is mandated to respect the parties' autonomy and let parties pursue their self-interests and, on the other, they are obliged not to let them take more than their agreed share, otherwise the equilibrium of the contract may be disturbed. First, what has to be explained is the notion of opportunism. *Muris* described opportunism as follows:

> A major problem occurs when a performing party behaves contrary to the other party's understanding of their contract, but not . . . contrary to the agreement's explicit terms, leading to a transfer of wealth from the other party to the performer – a phenomenon that [is] known as opportunistic behavior.[23]
> (alteration to original)

Quite often, an opportunistic behavior is subtle rather than explicit. *Muris* provides an example. A construction company hires an architect for $15,000 a month for a

19 ICC Case Nos. 6515 and 6516, 1994 24 Y.B. Comm. Arb., para. 64 (A. J. Van den Berg ed., 1999).

20 ICC Case No. 17052/VRO, Nov. 25, 2011, para. 120 (Arbitrator Intelligence Materials, Kluwer Law International).

21 ICC Case No. 20910/ASM/JPA (C-20911/ASM), Partial Award, Sept. 21, 2020, para. 2160, *available at* https://jusmundi.com/fr/document/decision/en-autoridad-del-canal-de-panama-v-1-grupo-unidos-por-el-canal-s-a-2-sacyr-s-a-3-salini-impregilo-s-p-a-and-4-jan-de-nul-n-v-ii-partial-award-on-merits-saturday-26th-september-2020.

22 See ICC Case No. 16982/JRF/CA/ASM (C17336/JRF), Apr. 14, 2014, para. 292 (Arbitrator Intelligence Materials, Kluwer Law International) ("[T]he covenant of good faith and fair dealing cannot be construed so broadly as to effectively nullify express terms of the contract. Nor should the tribunal re-write the terms of the Parties' contracts") (quoting Exhibit RL-7, Fesseha v. TD Waterhouse Inv. Servs., Inc, 193 Misc.2d 253, N.Y. Sup. Ct. 2002, aff'd, 305 A.D.2d 268, N.Y. App. Div. 2003).

23 Timothy J. Muris, *Opportunistic Behavior and the Law of Contracts*, 65 Minn. Law Rev. 521, 521 (1981).

two-year term project. The architect, after becoming familiar with the details of the project, advises the construction company that the project will be finished for $20,000 instead.[24] Provided that the company cannot replace the architect requesting the increased monthly salary with another one, and apart from the question of whether the court is going to enforce such an increase by taking into account the circumstances of the case, the company may end up paying the additional sums of money on the basis of the familiarity of the architect with the project; otherwise, a new architect might require a higher salary in order to catch up, especially when other architects of the market would not be available straightaway.[25] It would be unwarranted to penalize such opportunistic conduct often disguised as legitimate, not to mention that it would incur particularly high costs, notably litigation costs, to prove its opportunistic nature, especially when the actor has invoked unanticipated conditions.[26] Good faith may promote a party's self-interested conduct to the degree acceptable. At the same time, it operates as an anti-opportunism measure. Provided that the inner system of positive law cannot sufficiently regulate the legal uncertainty resulting from opportunistic conduct, the open-ended concept of good faith may be used as a last resort rule to confine new forms of opportunistic conduct.[27] Given the argument that international arbitrators can dynamically contribute to the body of international commercial law, such an open-ended concept assists in "meet[ing] the demand of newly created rules . . . that curtail opportunism at an international level."[28] On the other side of opportunism, however, lies the rigorous duty of loyalty. In Nordic law, for example, good faith manifests through the duty of loyalty, the effect of which is the obligation to take into account the interests of the other party.[29] Provided that the duty of loyalty, especially in principal-agent relationships, requires the fiduciary (agent) to subordinate their interests to the beneficiary's (principal) interests, it becomes evident that in sophisticated international transactions of parties with a relatively high negotiating leverage, the parties' right to serve their own interests overshadows any sort of loyalty to the other. However, once it is ascertained by the decision-making authority (*in casu* the tribunal) that pursuant to the applicable law and the nature of the transaction, a fiduciary duty is applicable, that means a "duty of the finest loyalty . . . . Not honesty alone, but the punctilio of an honour the most sensitive"[30] (like to joint venturers), the standard

24 Muris, *supra* note 23, at 522–23.

25 Muris, *supra* note 23.

26 Muris, *supra* note 23, at 525.

27 Santiago Dussan Laverde, A Commentary on the Meaning of Objective Good Faith in the Translex Principles through International Arbitration – A Law & Economics Approach, 13 Rev. Estud. Const. Hermeneut. Teor. Direito No. 2 (2021), at 171, *available at* www.trans-lex.org/131150.

28 Dussan Laverde, *supra* note 27, at 177.

29 Jori Munukka, *The Contractual Duty of Loyalty: Good Faith in the Performance and Enforcement of Contracts*, *in* The Nordic Contracts Act: Essays in Celebration of its One Hundredth Anniversary 203–4 (Torgny Håstad ed., 2015), Faculty of Law, Stockholm University Research Paper No. 49.

30 ICC Case No. 19134/CA/ASM, Aug. 5, 2014, para. 118.3 (Arbitrator Intelligence Materials, Kluwer Law International).

of good faith automatically encompasses a stringent duty of loyalty, which must be understood as the attempt of the law to create a modality incentivizing the fiduciary to align their self-interests with the best interests of the beneficiary.[31] Depending on the agreement of the parties, a good faith obligation does not necessarily imply a duty of loyalty. If it does, its intensity would be ascertained based on the contract and the law.

3.2.3 Importation of Extra-contractual Standards?

Mapping out the scope of good faith arguably requires identifying the boundaries of its existence. *ICC Case No. 11760* illustrated the point. The tribunal invoked article 1796 of the Federal Civil Code of Mexico that parties should not only perform their obligations pursuant to what they have expressly agreed to in the contract, "but also to the consequences which according to their nature result from good faith, custom and usage of the law."[32] It may be the case that an international contract, regardless of the level of sophistication of the contracting parties, cannot be regarded as a self-contained risk allocation device. The immediate reaction would be that good faith must have the capacity to import additional substantive obligations for the parties. However, the importation of further obligations, or limitations, should not be accepted as it manifestly violates the party autonomy principle and leads to doubtful results. It would be thus more appropriate to analogize the scope of good faith to *the pool of reasonable means* that the parties may resort to in order to achieve the *purpose of the contract*.

Interestingly, the ICC case *Marubeni v. Medivas* confirmed that every contract under Californian law imposes upon the parties a duty of good faith in the performance of contractual obligations.[33] All the more, the tribunal reasoned that the implied covenant of good faith requires that the party will do everything resulting *from the purpose of the contract*.[34] It can be validly proposed that the mission of good faith in the performance of obligations is not to make the contract perfect by importing additional extra-contractual standards but to reveal the true purpose of the contract, which can only be achieved by reasonable means.[35] Recent English

31 Robert Cooper & Bradley J. Freedman, *An Economic Model of the Fiduciary's Duty of Loyalty*, 10 Tel Aviv U. Stud. L. 297, 314 (1990).

32 ICC Case No. 11760/KGA/CCO/JRF, Dec. 23, 2011, para. 184 (Arbitrator Intelligence Materials, Kluwer Law International).

33 ICC Case No. 17052/VRO, Nov. 25, 2011, para. 120 (Arbitrator Intelligence Materials, Kluwer Law International).

34 ICC Case No. 17052/VRO, *supra* note 33.

35 Citigroup Inc. v. Abu Dhabi Investment Authority, ICDR Case No. 50 2013 000782, Dec. 12, 2016, para. 288 (Arbitrator Intelligence Materials, Kluwer Law International) ("Commercially reasonable efforts denote an obligation of diligence as opposed to an obligation of result. The notion of efforts refers to the *processes and decisions taken by the Parties, as opposed to the end result*") (emphasis added) [hereinafter *Citigroup award*].

case law confirms this position.[36] An arbitrator should determine by reference to good faith whether any exercise of discretion by one party in the performance of its obligations was within the pool of acceptable and legitimate solutions connected to the purpose of the contract as originally shaped by the parties and for which purpose such discretion was granted.[37]

3.2.4 Positive Tests

Depending on the applicable law and the facts of the case, a number of positive behavioral standards of good faith are effectively generated, the violation of which might constitute a breach of contract and justify damages, specific performance or other equitable remedy. The following list is not exhaustive since there are various specific duties of good faith (*i.e.*, the duty to cooperate, the duty of confidentiality, non-competition or the duty of transparency, all of which seem to be fact-driven). Instead, the purpose of the following section is to construct various *tests* for ascertaining compliance with good faith.

3.2.4.1 Minimum Loyalty

The meaning of loyalty cannot be explained from the viewpoint of semantics since it is principally of contextual nature. A *CAM award* reasoned that good faith indicates the obligation of mutual loyalty and correctness to each other and the obligation to cooperate and inform the contracting party.[38] A more rigorous duty of loyalty is often omnipresent in long-term contractual undertakings. An SCC tribunal reasoned that in *long-term contracts,* the duty of loyalty is rigorous and the consequence that flows from the joint venture agreement *implied* that a failure to correct a previously given – yet misleading – information comprised an independent breach, even if the respondent had been in good faith when providing such information.[39] This is important, especially in such long-term contracts where the duty of good faith is perceived as a *continuous* duty of loyalty of one party to the other in *regard to the purpose of the contract* because a failure to rectify misleading

36 See, e.g., Faulkner v. Vollin Holdings Ltd. [2022] EWCA Civ 1371, [205] ("[A]lthough judges have, on occasions, used the expression 'the spirit of the contract' in the context of a good faith clause, I do not read that as an open invitation to the court to interpret a good faith clause as imposing additional substantive obligations (or restrictions on action) outside the other terms of the contract").

37 Wastech Services Ltd. v. Greater Vancouver Sewerage and Drainage District, 2021 SCC 7, para. 75 (Can.) ("Good faith does not eliminate the discretion-exercising party's power of choice. Rather, it simply limits the range of legitimate ways in which a discretionary power may be exercised in light of the relevant purposes") (citation omitted).

38 CAM Case No. 10915, Nov. 14, 2016, 42 Y.B. Comm. Arb. 280, [58] (A. J. Van den Berg ed., ICCA & Kluwer Law International 2017).

39 First National Petroleum Corporation (FNP) v. OAO Tyumenneftegaz (TNGZ), SCC Case No. 196/2011, Dec. 9, 2013, paras. 11.47, 11.60 (John Kadelburger, A Contribution by the ITA Board of Reporters, Kluwer Law International).

information would entail abstention from the continuation of the project and thus incur losses, which would not have happened had the wrongdoing party corrected the misleading information in the first place. The caveat is that such duty should be distinguished from a different yet more stringent duty. That could be the fiduciary duty owed by the agent to the principal or by the director to the company. In that sense, good faith reflects a minimum loyalty standard predicated on the duty to "recognise and have due regard to the legitimate interests of both the parties in the enjoyment of the fruits of the contract as delineated by its terms."[40]

3.2.4.2 Honesty

The standard of transactional honesty is recognized as another pillar of good faith, forming a behavioral criterion and, hence, a rule of law.[41] Notwithstanding the myriad interpretations of honesty under national laws and the subtlety of its construction, honesty oils the wheels of cross-border transactions and establishes, therefore, what is broadly understood as decency and credibility in international dealings. A CCIR award elucidated that in complex areas of international business, credibility is founded on notions of honesty, honorable dealing, keeping one's word and other moral values, "without which the world of business is unthinkable."[42] From the perspective of an individualistic conceptualization of good faith, one is permitted to seek opportunities even if that means that they would be indifferent to the interests of others insofar as such behavior does not prove to be deceptive.[43] Contracting may be a mechanism of allocating risks and costs between the parties to the benefit of one's interests and often at the expense of the other, but such a mechanism would be useless absent the subjective element of the merchants' genuine belief that they transact truthfully and are consistent with such belief.[44] The relevant standard of 'honesty in fact' does not effectively ensure that one should share his fortune with others or be caring toward them, but such standard aims at ensuring that one should not misinform the other and profit from the other's misinformed decision and that any arrangements made shall be honored.[45] It may become particularly relevant when, under the surrounding circumstances, some sort of reliance and dependency between the contractors exists.[46] This is the case of a party that did not obviously cause the other party's ignorance, but due to the other party's ignorance and the failure to disclose

40 *Overlook v. Foxtel* [2002] NSWSC 17, ¶ 67 (Austl.).
41 Areios Pagos, Case No. 1116/2019.
42 CCIR Case No. 33, Sept. 30, 1993, 23 Y.B. Comm. Arb. 113, [11] (A. J. Van den Berg ed., ICCA & Kluwer Law International 1998).
43 Nassar, *supra* note 15, at 144.
44 Nassar, *supra* note 15.
45 Nassar, *supra* note 15.
46 Nassar, *supra* note 15, at 145.

information they possessed, they eventually enjoyed a benefit that would not have been received otherwise.[47]

The systemic importance of honesty for the ascertainment of good faith is so immense that *Mr. Justice Teare* reiterated that

> good faith connoted both honesty and the observance of reasonable commercial standards of fair dealing. Where a party clearly fails to honour such standards of conduct judges and commercial arbitrators will have no particular difficulty in recognising and identifying such failures.[48]

However, the notion of honesty should not be conflated with the more stringent test of reasonableness that requires some sort of diligence.

To illustrate, the facts of *ICC Case No. 6490/1993* concerned a charter party for the provision of tug services by the claimant, a Netherlands Antilles company, to the respondent, a Venezuelan one.[49] The charter party was suspended by the respondent due to government restrictions, which the respondent considered it to be a *force majeure* frustration. The claimant sought damages for losses. The tribunal found that the respondent did not comply with its duty of good faith with respect to its representations and promises to the claimant that the charter party could be concluded and operate regardless of any government interference.[50] Although the respondent had the power to do so, it rather sought to excuse itself from its obligations toward the claimant. The tribunal, having carefully examined the facts of the case, remarked:

> *The . . . legislator preferred to reserve the expression "good faith" . . . for . . . the state of mind of a person who in all honesty errs about a legal situation*, and to use the expression "reasonableness and equity" . . . for the normative description of how participants in a given social context . . . ought to behave.[51]
>
> (emphasis added)

The HKIAC award in *Intel Capital v. Airway Communications* likewise reasoned that subjective honesty should be contrasted with

> *an objective standard of any kind, whether reasonableness, care, or objective fair dealing* [and that] [t]he decision maker is not required to do more than

47 Nassar, *supra* note 15, at 144.

48 Emirates Trading Agency LLC v. Prime Mineral Exports Private Ltd [2014] EWHC 2104 (Comm) [53].

49 ICC Case No. 6490 of 1993, *available at* https://jusmundi.com/en/document/decision/en-icc-case-ndeg-6490-final-award-in-case-6490-extract.

50 ICC Case No. 6490 of 1993, *supra* note 49, para. 10.7.

51 ICC Case No. 6490 of 1993, *supra* note 49, para. 11.6.

> make an honest decision and is perfectly entitled to consult only his own interests in doing so.[52]
>
> (alteration to the original) (emphasis in original)

However, a logical reaction would be that pegging good faith to the innermost, mind-residing honesty of a person would naturally disregard what the counterparty expects from the party – in light of their contractual commitments – and render the establishment of a standard of good faith an esoteric effort of seeking the hidden honesty of one's psyche. This view may not produce tangible results, nor can it tell when a standard of good faith in the form of honesty is breached. Instead, to determine whether the standard of honesty has been met, a more holistic formula pegged to the common intentions of the parties may better serve the parties' interests. A preferred standard of *inter*-subjective good faith would suggest that the credibility that honesty implies should be ascertained by a degree of mutuality, trust and confidence among the parties targeted to serving the very purpose of the contract.[53]

3.2.4.3 Reasonableness

The content of reasonableness, both at the level of semantics and mechanics of international arbitration, is closely connected to rationality. Even so, the attempt to equate reasonableness with rationality creates a penumbra of unresolved questions pertaining to what constitutes a rational conduct. It is true that the twentieth century shifted away from the nineteenth century's obsession with freedom and sanctity of contracts to more fairness and ideas of trust and cooperation between parties.[54] This was necessary to restore the economic equilibrium between parties, as well as to revisit the elusive idea that the freedom of contract presupposes that parties know exactly what best serves their interests.[55] The chimera of unbridled freedom of contract can no longer be sustained by virtue of the proliferation of monopolies and standardized contracts to which parties of low leverage are compelled to acquiesce.[56] Thus, almost all legal systems have increasingly focused on promoting *contractual justice*, best described as "restrict[ing] the freedom of the parties to fix the terms of their contracts by considerations of fairness *as to the means and ends*

52 Intel Capital (Cayman) Corp. v. Airway Communications Int'l Holding Co., Final Award (Corrected), HKIAC Case No. 13043, Nov. 17, 2014, para. 152 (Arbitrator Intelligence Materials, Kluwer Law International).

53 Klaus Peter Berger, *The International Arbitrator's Dilemma: Transnational Procedure versus Home Jurisdiction: A German Perspective*, 25(2) Arbitr. Int. 217, 233–34 (William W. Park ed., 2009) (citing Nassar, *supra* note 15, at 143).

54 K.M. Sharma, *From "Sanctity" to "Fairness": An Uneasy Transition in the Law of Contracts?* 18 N.Y.L. Sch. J. Int'l & Comp. L. 95, 112. *Sharma* explains that this shift was achieved through legislation regulating commercial activity and the judicial process construing the contractual terms in such a way as to minimize the abuse of the stronger party's bargaining power against the weaker.

55 Sharma, *supra* note 54, at 113.

56 Sharma, *supra* note 54.

of contracting."[57] (emphasis added). The notion of contractual fairness *vis-à-vis* contractual freedom is not newfangled. English law Professor Collins supported the idea that the modern law of contracts is premised on the societal notion of interdependence and reliance, which is best known as the duty of cooperation.[58] Understanding contracting as a unity between parties of different and adverse interests and commitment to cooperation instead of merely allocating risks is gathering momentum because it perfectly integrates the pragmatic effect of social control upon contracting.[59] The epitome of a restored contractual equilibrium is the resurrected idea of the "social vision of fairness,"[60] from which the formulation of rationality[61] and reasonableness derives as a standard that incarnates social justice and commercial sense. However, such perception of reasonableness suggests traveling beyond the four corners of the contract to find patterns of parties' commitments "in the underlying relation of the contractual realities itself."[62] The surrounding circumstances of the case may form an integral part of the contract either before or after its conclusion. The standard of reasonableness, therefore, requires that the 'social environment' of the contract is duly respected. Amalgamations of the standard of reasonableness are found in uniform international instruments, such as the CISG,[63] where it "can appropriately be determined by ascertaining what is normal and acceptable in the relevant trade."[64] Further, arbitral institutions have

57 Sharma, *supra* note 54, at 114.

58 Stewart Macaulay, *The Reliance Interest and the World Outside the Law Schools' Doors*, 1991 Wis. L. Rev. 247, 289 (1991) (quoting Hugh Collins, The Law of Contract 45 (CUP 1986)).

59 Sharma, *supra* note 54, at 123. Sharma explains that the example of the dynamic interrelationship between the contracting parties is more common in relational contracts, long-term contractual undertakings or a series of short-term contracts that have to be examined as one economic project. For example, with respect to long-term international contracts, the parties will not be able to contractually specify from the outset all possible contingencies or circumscribe the network of lawyers, accountants, financiers, engineers, executives and other major players given the longevity of these contractual arrangements and any (necessary) changes that might occur along the way. Sharma, *supra* note 54, at 122. Put simply, the classical contract theory fails in that the parties cannot incorporate the future into the contract. The latter is not frozen in amber but a lively organism which, if statically seen, cannot absorb the effects of unwelcome contingencies.

60 Sharma, *supra* note 54, at 140.

61 Despite the numerous variations of the understanding of rationality in law and economics, it suffices for the purpose of this monograph to resort to the following understanding of rationality as the "the capacity of making accurate assessments of oneself in one's surroundings and of using the tools of reason to make the best decisions possible in a given situation . . . [which effectively reflect] the pursuit of a selected purpose, the adherence to understood concepts of morality . . . habit or custom" (alteration to original) Stephen Michael Sheppard, The Wolters Kluwer Bouvier Law Dictionary: Desk Edition (Wolters Kluwer 2012).

62 Sharma, *supra* note 54, at 153.

63 See, e.g., CISG, art. 8(2), 16(2)(b), 34, 35(2)(b), 39(1), 48(1), 48(2), 63(1), 75, 79(1), 79(4), 86(1), 86(2), 88(1) and 88(2).

64 John O. Honnold, Uniform Law for International Sales under the 1980 United Nations Convention 101 (3rd ed., 1999), *available at* https://iicl.law.pace.edu/sites/default/files/bibliography/honnold_0.pdf.

acknowledged over time the need to elevate this pattern to a rule. For instance, the CIETAC once provided a rule that:

> The arbitration tribunal shall independently and impartially make its award on the *basis of the facts*, in accordance with the law and the terms of the contracts, *with reference to international practices* and in compliance with the principle of *fairness and reasonableness*.[65]
>
> (emphasis added)

Measuring reasonableness in international commercial practice is not straightforward but depends on its constituents. In doing so, it is rightly claimed that reasonableness is comprised of "what is rational and informed behavior, given all available 'knowledge' and the 'intended purpose' of the agreement"[66] (citation omitted). It is thus constituted of the knowledge of the surrounding circumstances to determine whether the parties have *voluntarily* undertaken any changes in the contract, and that is because a rational individual who, notwithstanding their awareness of the changed circumstances, chooses not to object to them as they should have done so, is deemed to have accepted and acquiesced to such changes voluntarily.[67] Not perceiving such a conduct as a *de facto* modification of the contract by virtue of a subsequent conduct would be irrational, hence, unreasonable.[68] The element of knowledge is the yardstick to discover what reasonable conduct is in a *force majeure* scenario. For example, resorting to one's knowledge can determine whether the *force majeure* event was foreseeable because the party who relies on *force majeure* to be excused from performance must prove that they had no knowledge of the *force majeure* event. The same is true with the knowledge of new information that renders contractual obligations obsolete or unsatisfactory to fit in the reality of the new information, in which case a duty might be imposed upon the parties to renegotiate the contractual terms.[69] Another limb of reasonableness is presumed to be the intended purpose of the agreement. Sharma eloquently supported the idea that the originally intended purpose of the agreement must be fervently pursued.[70] Reasonableness is thus the net force of two components: the knowledge of the new contingencies that occurred and the originally intended purpose of the transaction.[71]

65 CIETAC, Arbitration Rules (1998), art. 53 (1998).
66 Sharma, *supra* note 54, at 162.
67 Sharma, *supra* note 54.
68 Sharma, *supra* note 54.
69 Sharma, *supra* note 54, at 163.
70 Sharma, *supra* note 54, at 165 (quoting The American Independent Oil Company (AMINOIL) v. The Government of the State of Kuwait, Ad Hoc Award, Mar. 24, 1982, para. 101, *available at* https://jusmundi.com/en/document/decision/en-the-american-independent-oil-company-v-the-government-of-the-state-of-kuwait-final-award-wednesday-24th-march-1982.
71 Sharma, *supra* note 54.

Reasonableness is inherent in every contract. That is because "only reasonable contracts are binding."[72] Given that the contract must be reasonable in order to be binding and effectively enforceable, the process of "deciding what is reasonable is not an exact science but an exercise in judgment."[73] It is, therefore, of cardinal importance to explain what reasonable is by reference to contractual discretion. Such discretion is generally construed as the state where one has certain leeway to decide upon an act or omission or choose one course of things over a pool of other alternatives, potentially under a cost-benefit analysis, and in the belief that it is the best solution[74] at that moment. Absent this interrelation, reasonableness would be trimmed down to a deterministic outcome of just the two components mentioned previously. However, the contractual discretion, for instance, the "freedom of a lender to set interest rates in financial agreements,"[75] is not unfettered as both civil and common law traditions have well cemented the idea that constraining discretion is necessary to control any misuse of discretionary powers.[76] The claimant in an ICDR case submitted, to the satisfaction of the sole arbitrator, that when the contract provides one party with the absolute discretion to determine whether the counterparty's performance was satisfactory, such discretion has to be exercised in good faith, thus by reference to an objective reasonableness test.[77] Along these lines, the English High Court in *MSC Mediterranean* reasoned that "contractual discretion must be exercised in good faith for the purpose for which it was conferred, and must not be exercised arbitrarily, capriciously or unreasonably (in the sense of irrationally),"[78] as a result it requires that parties should take into consideration the legitimate interests of each other.[79]

The conclusion to be drawn is that the standard of reasonableness suggests an exercise of discretion that takes into account the informed conduct of the parties, the latter being demystified by reference to the surrounding circumstances, the legitimate interests of the parties and, of course, the purpose that the parties originally intended to attach to the contract.

The assumption that the originally intended purpose of the contract cannot be but reasonable is corroborated by the firm belief that the more unreasonable or

72 Company (Finland) v. Consultant (nationality not indicated) (Final Award), SCC Case No. 2018/084, June 25, 2019, 45 Y.B. Comm. Arb., para. 307 (Stephan W. Schill ed., ICCA & Kluwer Law International 2020).

73 ICC Case No. 15082, 2 ICC Disp. Res. Bull., 2016, para. 89, *available at* https://jusmundi.com/en/document/decision/en-icc-case-ndeg-15082-final-award-in-case-15082.

74 It is not the best solution *stricto sensu* that is required but rather a less absolute standard of the most workable or beneficial solution.

75 Jonas Rosengren, *Contract Interpretation in International Arbitration*, 30(1) J. Int'l Arb. 1, 10 (Kluwer Law International 2013).

76 Rosengren, *supra* note 75.

77 American Partner Group, S.A. v. T-Rex Engineering and Construction LC, ICDR Case No. 01-14-0001-0759, May 20, 2015, paras. 16–17 (Arbitrator Intelligence, Kluwer Law International).

78 MSC Mediterranean Shipping S.A. v. Cottonex Anstalt [2015] EWHC 283 (Comm) [97].

79 Klaus Peter Berger & Thomas Arntz, *Good Faith as a 'General Organising Principle' of the Common Law*, 32 Arb. Int. 171 (2016), at 178.

absurd the result of the contract is, the more unrealistic it is that the parties have intended such a result.[80] This is because, in commercial arbitration, the standard of reasonableness is inevitably cloaked in commercial practice. It is for arbitrators to direct their attention to commercial norms in order to determine whether parties have acted in accordance with good faith.[81] The grandiosity of commercial reasonableness that permeates the matrix of trade and business is embedded in what was earlier discussed as social fairness. Arbitral decision-making does not replace business judgment, nor are arbitrators expected to adopt Pontius Pilate's stance by washing their hands of the case. They are destined to be commercially fair-minded; otherwise, the alignment of commercial law and commercial practice[82] would be a midsummer night's dream. Reasonableness as a core pillar of the UNIDROIT Principles "encourages a reorientation toward what constitutes proper conduct in the international marketplace".[83]

UNIDROIT Article 5.1.3 stipulates that "each party shall co-operate with the other party when such co-operation may reasonably be expected for the performance of that party's obligations." That is a profound expression of good faith. Indeed, had good faith not been the backbone of commercial reasonableness, the latter would have been reduced to sterilized rationality stripped of parties' expectations and context. It suffices to note that when one is speaking of commercial reasonableness as a standard of commercial conduct, they have to bear in mind it indicates

> an obligation of diligence as opposed to an obligation of result [which attaches to] processes and decisions taken by the Parties [that have to be judged by reference to the] surrounding circumstances and the information known at the time, not in hindsight.[84]
>
> (alteration to the original)

The standard is objective and "requires comparison of the [party]'s acts with how other similar businesses faced with the same circumstances would act"[85] (alteration to the original). It is immaterial whether the parties have acted according to what they honestly believed, but what matters is due diligence in performing their obligations and the vindication of common contractual objectives.[86]

80 Joshua Karton, *The Arbitral Role in Contractual Interpretation*, 6(1) J. INT. DISPUT. SETTL. 4, 37 (Thomas Schultz ed., OUP 2015) (citing L Schuler AG v. Wickman Machine Tool Sales Ltd [1974] AC 235, 251 (Lord Reid)).

81 Christopher R. Drahozal, *Commercial Norms, Commercial Codes, and International Commercial Arbitration*, 33 VAND. J. TRANSNAT'L L. 79, 84 (2000).

82 Drahozal, *supra* note 81.

83 Sharma, *supra* note 54, at 166.

84 *Citigroup award*, *supra* note 35, para. 288.

85 *Citigroup award*, *supra* note 35, para. 289.

86 Nassar, *supra* note 15, at 145–46.

3.2.5 Negative Tests

The negative tests refer to those standards, the ascertainment of which leads to a finding of breach of the rule of good faith. This analysis does not include concretizations of specific negative standards, such as the prohibition of participation in negotiations with third parties without disclosure. The focus is on the perimeter of such impermissible conduct by referring to the following negative tests: (a) abuse of right, (b) inconsistency, (c) unconscionability and (d) bad faith.

3.2.5.1 Abuse of Right

BGB Section 226, which establishes the prohibition of chicanery, stipulates that the exercise of a right is prohibited if it is targeted at inflicting damage to a party. German courts have confirmed such conceptualization of the doctrine of abuse of right by applying it in those cases where the exercise of a right disregards the other parties' legitimate interests, especially when such exercise is conducted in a mischievous way.[87] The French Court of Cassation, on the other hand, had adopted a much more liberal stance by ruling that "even the legitimate exercise of the rights of ownership will generate liability if the resulting inconvenience to third parties goes beyond the ordinary obligations toward neighbors."[88] As far as the common law jurisdictions are concerned, the failure to codify abuse of rights has not impaired the ability to affirm the indicia for the ascertainment of a breach of the rule. The doctrine of unclean hands is employed *inter alia* to guard against abusive conduct.[89] In the sphere of international commercial arbitration, the negative test of abuse of rights is not quite different. In particular, the tribunal in *ICC Case 10977* held that the claimant failed to support their abuse of rights submissions under the applicable state law, which requires, for an abuse of right, the existence: (a) of a legal act, (b) that violates the good morals, good customs or public policy and (c) an intention to cause harm coupled with the knowledge about the harmful effect.[90] As Oldenstam explained at a symposium on abuse of process in arbitration, at least from the perspective of the civil law tradition, different criteria might be used to fathom abuse of right, including "(i) intention to harm, (ii) lack of a legitimate interest, (iii) disproportionality, and (iv) exercising a right contrary to its intended function."[91] However, such firm tests for the ascertainment of abuse of

87 John David Branson, *The Abuse of Process Doctrine Extended: A Tool for Right Thinking People in International Arbitration*, 38(2) J. of Int'l Arb. 187, 190 (Maxi Scherer ed., Kluwer Law International 2021).

88 Branson, *supra* note 87. (quoting Vera Bolgár, Abuse of Rights in France, Germany, and Switzerland: A Survey of a Recent Chapter in Legal Doctrine, 35 Louisiana L. Rev. 1016, 1021–22 (1975)).

89 Branson, *supra* note 87.

90 ICC Case No. 10977, 24 ICC Bull. No. 1, 49, para. 485 (2013).

91 Ileana M. Smeureanu, *Symposium on Abuse of Process in International Arbitration*, ICC Disp. Res. Bull. No. 2 (ICC 2017). Although abuse of rights "more generally refers to improper exercise of any legal right, abuse of process narrowly focuses on the improper exercise of procedural rights." Branson, *supra* note 87, at 188.

rights should not be adopted irrespective of the circumstances of the case and the requirements set out in the applicable law.

3.2.5.2 Inconsistency

Inconsistency in parties' conduct refers to any contradictory act resulting from the transgression of the rule of good faith. The *CAM Case No. 115* vividly portrayed the inconsistent behavior that violated the principle of estoppel of UNIDROIT Article 1.8, pursuant to which "a party cannot act inconsistently with an understanding it has caused the other party to have and upon which that other party reasonably has acted in reliance to its detriment."[92] The rule of *estoppel* should not be viewed as another rule that adds more and distinct legal obligations under the contract. On the contrary, it only furthers the original purpose that the parties intended. The award in *ICC Case 15453* highlighted that "estoppel does not change or affect in any way the terms of the contract. Estoppel by representation operates outside of the contract to preclude a party from relying upon a construction of the contract inconsistent with the representation made."[93] It would be educative to flesh out the elements of estoppel. An ICDR tribunal adopted the four-prong test that the Nevada courts applied:

> (1) the party to be estopped must be apprised of the true facts; (2) he must intend that his conduct shall be acted upon, or must so act that the party asserting estoppel has the right to believe it was so intended; (3) the party asserting the estoppel must be ignorant of the true state of the facts; (4) he must have relied to his detriment on the conduct of the party to be estopped.[94]

The components of *knowledge* and *intent* of the offending party on the one hand and *ignorance*, *reliance* and *detriment* of the injured on the other are decisive in showing a lack of good faith on the part of the party to be estopped. The tribunal further explained that not only words, but it is also silence which can establish an estoppel situation.[95] However, there is no uniformity in the application of estoppel as the proper test will depend each time on the applicable law and particulars of the case. One would remark that estoppel should not be readily identified with abuse of rights. The reason is that, as *ICC Case No. 6330* affirmed, *estoppel* is of a highly exceptional nature and will be triggered when a long time has passed

92 CAM Case No. 115, Feb. 11, 2016 (Stefano Azzali & Benedetta Coppo, A contribution by the ITA Board of Reporters).

93 ICC Case No. 15453, Partial Award, 2 ICC Disp. Res. Bull. 113, para. 120, 2016.

94 Abdulkareem A. Al Mutawa v. Andrew S Kanigowski, ICDR Case No. 50 180 T 0030110, June 24, 2011, para. 26 (Arbitrator Intelligence Materials, Kluwer Law International) (quoting Mahban v. MGM Grand Hotels Inc. 100 Nev. 593, 691 P. 2d 421, 423, Nev. 1984).

95 Abdulkareem A. Al Mutawa, *supra* note 94, para. 25 (quoting NGA No. 2 Ltd. Liab. Co. v. Rains, 113 Nev. 1151, 946 P2d 163, 169, Nev. 1997).

after the option of asserting a claim, thus violating good faith.[96] Second, estoppel specifically concerns a good faith reliance of a party on the offending party's prior statement or conduct, the latter not necessarily being *contra legem*.[97]

Third, there is a difference in scope. *Estoppel* has a narrower scope in that it focuses on "*consistency* in dealing which creates confidence in international commerce"[98] (emphasis added). On the contrary, abuse of rights has a broader scope, including the detrimental effect on good morals and public policy. Whether common law or civil law applies, the flexibility of good faith lies in that it forms the bedrock of estoppel. Abuse of right eventually encompasses the improper conduct of acting inconsistently or, as *ICC Case No. 7421* explained, the conduct pursuant to which a party openly contradicts its prior conduct that the other party relied upon in good faith to take an action to which it was entitled.[99] In an ICC case between a Dutch and a Turkish company, parties had to observe in their contractual undertakings the general principle of good faith embodied in Article 2 of the Turkish Civil Code. Given that the Turkish respondent denied that the share purchase agreement had been concluded and thus had failed to act in good faith in the sense that it prevented parties by obstruction from proceeding to the closing of this agreement, it would have been a manifest abuse of right and a blatant violation of good faith on the part of the respondent if the latter had been permitted to rely on the expiration that it provoked by obstruction.[100]

3.2.5.3 Unconscionability

The doctrine of unconscionability is suffused with almost the same fundamental philosophy as good faith. Seemingly, it implies certain limitations to the conduct of the parties, yet it is not aimed at restricting the contractual freedom. Unconscionability is not an exception to the parties' autonomy but an expression of it.[101] Despite the fact that judges of common law countries are afforded much greater latitude to affirm

96 ICC Case No. 6230 of 1990, 17 Y.B. Comm. Arb., para. 27 (A. J. Van den Berg ed., ICCA & Kluwer Law International 1999).

97 Gavin Dingley, Estoppel, Jus Mundi Wiki Notes, *available at* https://jusmundi.com/en/document/publication/en-estoppel (last updated Jan. 2, 2023); see also D.W. Bowett, *Estoppel before International Tribunals and Its Relation to Acquiescence*, 33 BRIT. Y.B. INT'L L. 176, 202 (1957).

98 PAUL BOWDEN, *L'interdiction des se contredire au détriment d'autrui (estoppel) as a Substantive Transnational Rule in International Commercial Arbitration, in* TRANSNATIONAL RULES IN COMMERCIAL ARBITRATION (Emmanuel Gaillard ed., ICC Publication No. 480, 1993), at 135, *available at* www.trans-lex.org/110600.

99 ICC Case No. 7421, 21 ICC Bull. No. 2, 64, 2010.

100 ICC Case No. 13856/AVH/EC/GZ, Jan. 15, 2007, paras. 348, 371, *available at* https://jusmundi.com/en/document/decision/en-sonera-holding-b-v-v-cukurova-holding-a-s-partial-award-monday-15th-january-2007.

101 See State v. Wolowitz, 96 A.D.2d 47, 68 (N.Y. App. Div. 1983) ("The doctrine of unconscionability, with its emphasis on the contract-making process, is really an expression of, rather than an exception to, this principle [of contractual freedom]. By focusing on the manner in which a contract is entered into and the status of the parties, the doctrine is designed to insure [sic] freedom of contract and not to negate it") (citation omitted) (alteration to original).

unconscionability, contrary to their civilian counterparts where the examination of what is oppressive or unfair is dictated by very specific statutes,[102] the notion is understood by both worlds quite similarly.[103] To grapple with the very essence of unconscionability in the commercial setting, the US Revised Uniform Arbitration Act provides for a number of indicia, including the right of the weaker party to withdraw from arbitration, the existence of "unequal bargaining power," whether the weaker party was forced to arbitrate, whether the arbitration agreement falls within the scope of weaker party's reasonable expectations or whether the stronger party employed trickery.[104] There is indeed a wealth of various concretizations of unconscionability. A series of decisions have deemed arbitration agreements invalid because they reserved disproportionate rights in the selection of the arbitral tribunal, prevented the weaker party from accessing legal representation, imposed prohibitions with regard to statutory remedies or even "impose[d] grossly unfair terms regarding substantive rights or remedies";[105] or finally they were entered into under "procedurally unfair circumstances."[106] Other decisions have held arbitration agreements unconscionable on the basis that their terms reserved an unbearable economic burden for a party[107] or entailed important disincentives that prevented a party from pursuing their legal rights.[108]

Despite the many variations of the test of unconscionability, the notion of fairness as a core element of unconscionability remains unaltered. What constitutes unfairness might be subject to different interpretations and sometimes lead to inhomogeneous results. Despite the lack of hard rules or a uniform understanding of what fairness entails, many legal traditions tether contractual fairness to attitudes of good faith in reciprocal obligations.[109] Given that the link of good faith and conscionability is somewhat clear, it must be noted that not every unfair conduct is unconscionable. The threshold is relatively high. An *ad hoc* tribunal reaffirmed the high threshold of unfairness for the determination of unconscionable conduct by referring to Australian Consumer Law. It reasoned that unconscionable conduct is more than just harsh or simply unfair; it requires an element of bad conscience or a high level of moral condemnation.[110] In this respect, to ascertain the

102 Paul Bennett Marrow, *Policing Contracts for Unconscionability: Guidelines for International Arbitrators Subject to the Scrutiny of US Courts*, 73(4) INT'L J. OF ARB. MED. & DISP. MAN. 382–83 (CIArb; Kluwer Law International 2007).

103 However, this does not come without reservations. For example, a US court held that "[i]t is doubtful that there exists a precise, universal definition of the unequal bargaining power defense that may be applied effectively across the range of countries that are parties to the [NYC] Convention, and absent any indication to the contrary, we decline to formulate one." Bautista v. Star Cruises, 396 F.3d 1289, 1303 (11th Cir. 2005) (alteration to the original) (footnote omitted).

104 United States Revised Uniform Arbitration Act (Dec. 13, 2000) § 6 cmt. [7].

105 BORN (3rd ed.), *supra* note 2, at 927.

106 BORN (3rd ed.), *supra* note 2, at 928.

107 BORN (3rd ed.), *supra* note 2, at 925.

108 BORN (3rd ed.), *supra* note 2.

109 Bennett Marrow, *supra* note 102, at 392.

110 Who Ya Gonna Call Bark Busters Pty v. Dingo, Inc. (Partial Award), Dec. 20, 2012, para. 223 (Arbitrator Intelligence Materials, Kluwer Law International).

unconscionability of the conduct, many factors will be considered, including lack of good faith, inequality of bargaining power and undue influence.[111] Moreover, and despite the variety of unconscionability tests adopted by different legal systems,[112] an agreement will only be held unconscionable not on the grounds of some showing of inequality between the contractual parties but on the grounds of "an absence of meaningful choice on the part of one of the parties together with contract terms which are unreasonably favorable to the other party"[113] (footnote omitted). As a result, the conduct would be unconscionable if the stronger party could "surprise" the weaker party with some kind of particularly oppressive term.[114]

3.2.5.4 Bad Faith

A finding that a party has acted in bad faith surely leads to the breach of a good faith standard and may entail the non-enforcement of the contract (or part of it) and give rise to damages. The ICC tribunal in *PDV Sweeny v. ConocoPhillios* held that to find a breach of good faith there has to be a showing of bad faith, notably "trickery, misconduct, an intention to deceive or evidence that one party is taking advantage of the other party's ignorance."[115] What is particularly decisive is the element of intent. It is not just about deceit; there has to be some kind of awareness around such deceit. The arbitral tribunal in *ICC Case No. 5694* referred to the Egyptian Cour de Cassation to explain that bad faith consists of an "unjustified and deliberate refusal on the part of the debtor to perform his obligation while being aware of the damage."[116] The said intent might be evidenced either through active conduct, *i.e.,* in a party's lying or through a passive attitude and silence, that is, by retention of information.[117] Further, to establish bad faith, one has to prove the connection of bad faith with "an element which is crucial for the other party's consent to the agreement, in such a way that the latter would not have entered into the contract if it had been aware of these facts or would have done so only on different terms."[118]

111 Who Ya Gonna Call Bark Busters Pty, *supra* note 110, para. 222.

112 For example, the civilian legal systems will establish unconscionability by close reference to the detailed provisions of their codes, whereas the English common law tradition defined unconscionability as early as 1750 as a bargain "such as no man in his sense and not under a delusion would make on the one hand, and as no honest and fair man would accept on the other; which are unequitable and unconscientious bargains; and of such even the common law take notice." Richard A. Eastman, *Rent-A-Center v Jackson*, 77(2) Int'l J. of Arb. Med. & Disp. Man. 280, 281 n.7 (Michael O'Reilly ed., Chartered Institute of Arbitrators (CIArb); Sweet & Maxwell 2011) (quoting *Earl of Chesterfield v. Sir Abraham Janssen* [1750] 28 E.R. 82 (Ch) 100).

113 Williams v. Walker-Thomas Furniture Company, 350 F.2d 445, 449 (D.C. Cir. 1965).

114 Gary B. Born, International Commercial Arbitration: commentary and materials 222 (2nd ed., Kluwer Law International 2001).

115 ICC Case No. 16982/JRF/CA/ASM (C-17336/JRF), Apr. 14, 2014, para. 296 (Arbitrator Intelligence Materials, Kluwer Law International).

116 ICC Case No. 5694, 3 ICC Bull. No. 1, 17, 1992.

117 ICC Case No. 14235, 24 ICC Bull. No. 1, para. 225, 2013.

118 ICC Case No. 14235, *supra* note 117, para. 226.

However, it is the opinion of the author that bad faith and good faith should not be used interchangeably for the purpose of ascertaining a violation of a good faith standard. Bad faith requires more than mere transgression of a good faith standard. A tribunal held that the conduct of the respondent gave rise to a breach of its duty of good faith pursuant to the applicable Bolivian law, yet the conduct was not malicious in the sense that bad faith requires *mens rea* and that was not proven in that case.[119] This is of particular importance since it may be possible to act "not in bad faith"[120] but at the same time "not in good faith."[121] Whether agreeable or not, such argumentation raises uncertainty in the sense that it becomes difficult to distinguish between a conduct which is "not in bad faith" yet "not in good faith" from a conduct "not in bad faith" though in line with good faith.[122] In arbitral practice, liability for breach of good faith by virtue of a duty to inform will attach regardless of bad faith or intention to conceal information.[123] In *Wintershall/Qatar arbitration*, the Qatari government was not in bad faith with respect to the disclosure of information, yet such omitted details led the government to be held liable for breaching a duty to inform on the grounds that Wintershall's exploration venture was affected.[124]

3.3 Contract Termination

The ubiquitous influence of good faith should not be absent from the stage of contractual termination. The practice of international commercial arbitration reveals that, irrespective of whether the contract is terminated for just grounds or not, the validity of termination depends on compliance with the principle of good faith. The ICC award in *Devon Robotics v. Health Robotics* is illustrative. It held that, under the applicable Swiss law, a long-term agreement could only be terminated for just grounds.[125] In so doing, the well-versed arbitrator reasoned that "just ground is defined as any circumstance, under which it cannot be reasonably expected from a party according to the principle of good faith to continue to perform an agreement

119 Compania De Inversiones Mercantiles S.A. v. GCC Latinoamérica, S.A. DE C.V., Final Award on Damages, IACAC Case No. 50 180 T 00867 11, Apr. 10, 2015, 60 n.118 (Arbitrator Intelligence Materials, Kluwer Law International).

120 Pat Andriola, *Leap of Faith: Determining the Standard of Faith Needed to Violate the Implied Covenant of Good Faith and Fair Dealing for Delaware Limited Liability Companies*, 58 B.C. L. REV. 1, 4 (E. Supp., 2017).

121 Andriola, *supra* note 120.

122 Andriola, *supra* note 120. Although Delaware courts have not taken a clear stance on the concept of neutral faith and have consistently ruled that there should be no distinction between "bad faith" and "failure to act in good faith," they have still endorsed the view that in some instances the previous notions do not necessarily share an identical function. Andriola, *supra* note 120. *See, e.g.*, Lyondell Chem. Co. v. Ryan, 970 A.2d 235, 240 n.8 (Del. 2009).

123 Nassar, *supra* note 15, at 155.

124 Nassar, *supra* note 15.

125 ICC Case No. 17522/FM/MHM/EMT, Jan. 24, 2013, para. 211 (Arbitrator Intelligence Materials, Kluwer Law International).

until its term,"[126] and such would be those "circumstances mak[ing] the performance of the agreement unbearable for the party who terminates the agreement"[127] (alteration to original). Eventually, the tribunal found that the parties' mutual trust had been damaged to such an extent that the respondent was not expected to continue performing under the agreement.[128] Conversely, *ICC Case No. 13730* explained that in long-term contractual dealings of definite duration, no compelling reasons are required for validly terminating the continuous agreement at the end of its term, pursuant to the applicable Japanese law.[129] Instead, the arbitral tribunal, by citing a series of Tokyo court decisions, held that what is only required is whether the termination or non-notification of renewal was done in breach of the principle of good faith or public policy, the effect of which would be that only a breach of public policy would invalidate the termination, whereas a breach of good faith will only form the basis of a compensation claim.[130] At any rate, it seems that adherence to the principle of good faith safeguards against arbitrariness in commercial transactions, the latter being apparent when a terminating party succumbs to abusing its right to terminate.[131]

3.4 Damages

The impetus of good faith in the phase of assessment of damages is traced back to the motives of the parties to choose arbitration over litigation, those being closely related to arbitrators' commercial acumen and commitment to fairness.[132] By the same token, the decision to award damages may be grounded on equitable considerations, including good faith. True, actual practice has revealed that arbitrators may limit the applicable national law to liability, whereas equity constructions of good faith are reserved for the measurement of damages.[133] Provided that good faith in terms of equity and *ex aequo et bono* decision-making is not central to the purpose of this monograph, the focus of this section is the examination of a substantive standard of good faith, which not only informs the aggrieved party's more specific

126 ICC Case No. 17522/FM/MHM/EMT, *supra* note 125, para. 212.
127 ICC Case No. 17522/FM/MHM/EMT, *supra* note 125.
128 ICC Case No. 17522/FM/MHM/EMT, *supra* note 125, para. 226.
129 ICC Case No. 13730, 38 Y.B. Comm. Arb., para. 39 (ICCA & Kluwer Law International 2013).
130 ICC Case No. 13730, *supra* note 129.
131 See ICC Case No. 16240/GZ, Dec. 7, 2010, para. 344 (Arbitrator Intelligence Materials, Kluwer Law International). The tribunal tested whether the right to terminate is consonant with the overriding good faith principle as enshrined in the applicable Turkish law.
132 Felix Praendl, *Measure of Damages in International Commercial Arbitration*, 23 STAN. J. INT'L L. 263, 273 (1987).
133 Praendl, *supra* note 132, at 274. The rationale for such an inhomogeneous approach lies in that the arbitrators "feel that they serve the cause of justice better by taking account of day-to-day business realities than by applying the law, which may be designed to further goals other than international commerce." Praendl, *supra* note 132, at 265 (citing Kuwait v. AMINOIL, 21 I. L. M. 976, 1016 (1982), summary in 1984 Y.B. Comm. Arb. 71, 78).

duty of mitigation of damages, but a breach of such a duty may as well trigger punitive damages.

3.4.1 Good Faith and Determination of Damages

The fabric of a substantive good faith standard hailed in the applicable law constitutes the blueprint for calculating damages. The valuation of the harm shouldered by the aggrieved party is not always an easy task for the tribunal. First, as a matter of evidence, arbitrators are not always familiar with accounting and finance and often find themselves entangled in conflicting expert determinations with respect to the valuation of the harm.[134] Second, the measure that the tribunal will apply is interwoven with a degree of precision.[135] As speculation of damages should be precluded, the proper test to ascertain whether damages are speculative certainly includes good faith. For example, the breach of a contract by a government, under which the contractor expected to generate profit, may result in damages or not "depending on whether the business was reasonably likely to be profitable in the future in the absence of the [government]'s conduct."[136] (alteration to the original). Such an assessment by the tribunal should take into account the parties' good faith conduct as evinced in their prior dealings, their negotiations, the course of the performance and whether the breaching party "knew and understood the consequences of a failure by it to perform as agreed."[137] *A fortiori*, the assessment of whether the failure to mitigate is within or "outside of the *bona fide* expectation of the non-performing party"[138] (emphasis in original), militates in favor of the usefulness of such good faith standard in the assessment of damages. The *Himpurna* tribunal employed the standard of good faith to explain that claiming damages resulting from investments not yet made in "a situation where [the] benefit [for the investor] will clearly exacerbate the already great losses of the [host state], strikes the Arbitral Tribunal as likely to constitute an abuse of right inconsistent with the duty of good faith which is fundamental to the Indonesian law of obligations."[139] (alteration to the original). As a matter of fact, the principle of proportionality, as a special manifestation of a standard of good faith, may also be resorted to, especially when the market price and currency fluctuations, inflation or other risks of

134 Jeffrey Maurice Waincymer, Procedure and Evidence in International Arbitration 1040–41 (Kluwer Law International 2012).

135 Waincymer, *supra* note 134, at 1159.

136 CPR Protocol on Determination of Damages in Arbitration, International Institute for Conflict Prevention & Resolution (2010), at 2, *available at* https://static.cpradr.org/docs/CPR-Protocol-on-Determination-of-Damages-in-Arbitration-fnl.pdf [hereinafter *CPR Protocol*].

137 *CPR Protocol*, *supra* note 136.

138 Yasuhei Taniguchi, *The Obligation to Mitigate Damages*, *in* 4 Evaluation of Damages in International Arbitration 79, 85 (Yves Derains & Richard Kreindler eds., ICC Dossiers 2006).

139 Himpurna California Energy Ltd. v. PT. (Persero) Perusahaan Listruik Negara, Final Award, 4 May 1999, 25 Y.B. Comm. Arb., para. 318 (A.J. Van den Berg ed., ICCA & Kluwer Law International 2000).

government intervention are extant.[140] Interestingly, the CPR Protocol on Determination of Damages in Arbitration avows that arbitrators may require the claimant to specify the theory based on which it will advance the damages claim and "a good faith estimate of such damages."[141]

3.4.2. Mitigation of Damages

The doctrine of mitigation of damages is decisive in determining the damages to be awarded. Several national laws[142] and international instruments[143] equip arbitrators with robust rules on the mitigation of losses. The rationale is that an aggrieved party should take reasonable action to mitigate the damage resulting from the breach, including loss of profits.[144] A comparative analysis shows that different jurisdictions understand and apply the doctrine of mitigation quite dissimilarly. *Lando* and *Beale* have analyzed three scenarios: (a) the conduct of the aggrieved one partly itself caused non-performance; (b) the conduct of the aggrieved party increased the losses, although it was not liable for non-performance; (c) the aggrieved party could – or should – have reduced or annihilated the losses by taking suitable steps.[145] They support that English law perceives situations (a) and (b) as resembling the notion of contributory negligence, whereas (c) is treated as a failing-to-mitigate-damages case.[146]

On the contrary, civil legal systems do not make such a distinction, yet they obtain similar results by resorting to the concept of causation.[147] Even if the applicable national law does not *per se* recognize the doctrine of mitigation of damages, there are certain mechanisms producing the same results. For instance, French law does not require the injured party to minimize its losses.[148] However, what French law recognizes is the doctrine of *faute de la victim*, pursuant to which the passivity on behalf of the aggrieved party that results in a "break in the causality"[149] and contributes to increasing the damages by failing to take proper action is considered to be bad faith.[150] Most importantly, and notwithstanding national law disparities, it is firmly understood that a duty of a party to behave in good faith, in the sense that one should abstain from aggravating losses which would have been prevented

140 Himpurna California Energy, *supra* note 139, para. 294.
141 *CPR Protocol, supra* note 136, at 4.
142 See, e.g., BGB § 254(2); see also Codice Civile [C.C.], art. 1227(2) (It.); Restatement § 350 (1981); U.C.C. § 2–712(2).
143 See, e.g., CISG, art. 77; see also UNIDROIT Principles, art. 7.4.8. The duty to mitigate damages is admitted as part of the *lex mercatoria*: *accord* WAINCYMER, *supra* note 134, at 1179.
144 WAINCYMER, *supra* note 134, at 1179.
145 TANIGUCHI, *supra* note 138, at 85.
146 TANIGUCHI, *supra* note 138.
147 TANIGUCHI, *supra* note 138.
148 HERFRIED WÖSS ET AL., DAMAGES IN INTERNATIONAL ARBITRATION UNDER COMPLEX LONG-TERM CONTRACTS, para. 4.214 (OUP 2014).
149 WÖSS ET AL., *supra* note 148.
150 WÖSS ET AL., *supra* note 148.

in other respects, is a key consideration for the tribunal in measuring damages.[151] The sole arbitrator in *ICC Case No. 17730*, where Californian law was applicable, found that the respondents failed to prove that the claimant did not reasonably mitigate its damages.[152] The court emphasized that the mitigation doctrine does not require taking disproportionate or impractical measures but only reasonable, with due diligence and in compliance with good faith.[153] A relatively old case decided by the Society of Maritime Arbitrators augments the proposition that a good faith standard is inextricably related to the doctrine of mitigation of damages. In *Pollux Marine Agencies v. Louis Dreyfus Corp.*, the defaulting charterer (respondent) advanced that the shipowner (claimant) failed to reasonably minimize its losses resulting from the breach of the charter party.[154] The tribunal held that the defaulting party failed to discharge its burden of proof in showing that the shipowner's efforts to mitigate the loss were unreasonable.[155] The tribunal specified: "[t]he [injured party] is required only to use good faith and reasonable diligence in so doing. He is not required to use the best judgment possible or adopt the wisest course which hindsight might have dictated"[156] (alteration to the original).

3.4.3 Punitive Damages

Awarding punitive damages in international arbitration may periodically cause systemic uncertainty. It may even result in an existential crisis for arbitrators as they may feel that their mandate to resolve disputes and remediate a private wrong conflicts with the state-imposed power of the judge to grapple with public interests and penalize a certain conduct.[157] However, what this monograph aspires to examine is whether punitive damages or moral damages with a punitive element can be awarded as a natural consequence of a breach of a contractual duty of good faith. There is substantial criticism on whether punitive damages can be awarded as a result of a breach of the contract, even if there is an intentional breach of the duty of good faith.[158] The criticism is justified. First, as *ICC Case No. 5946* explained, punitive or exemplary damages, which punish the wrongdoer, contravene Swiss public policy,

151 See Jorge Oviedo-Albán, *Mitigation of Damages for Breach of Contract for the International Sale of Goods*, VNIVERSITAS No. 137 (2018), *available at* www.redalyc.org/articulo.oa?id=82556549010.
152 ICC Case No. 17730/CYK/RD, Mar. 18, 2014, paras. 249, 255 (Arbitrator Intelligence Materials, Kluwer Law International).
153 Royal Thrift and Loan Co. v. County Escrow, Inc. (2004), 123 Cal. App. 4th 24, 33 (Cal. Ct. App. 2004) (quoting Green v. Smith (1968) 261 Cal. App. 2d 392, 396–97).
154 Pollux Marine Agencies Inc., as Agents for the Owners of the M/V Captain Demosthenes v. Louis Dreyfus Corp., Charterer, Award, AAA Case No. 1569, Aug. 3, 1981, 8 Y.B. Comm. Arb. 171, 171 (Pieter Sanders ed., ICCA & Kluwer Law International 1983).
155 Pollux Marine Agencies Inc., *supra* note 154, at 179.
156 Pollux Marine Agencies Inc., *supra* note 154, at 178 (quoting Ellerman Lines Ltd. v. The President Harding, 187 F. Supp. 948, S.D.N.Y. 1960, aff'd 288 F. 2d 288 (2d Cir 1961)).
157 CLAUDIA SALOMON, *Damages in International Arbitration*, *in* INTERNATIONAL COMMERCIAL ARBITRATION IN NEW YORK, para. 10.27 (James H. Carter & John Fellas eds., 2nd ed., 2016).
158 SALOMON, *supra* note 157.

which should be respected by the arbitral tribunal having its seat in Switzerland, even though the applicable law to the dispute may allow for awarding such damages.[159] Second, other than the ensuing uncertainty at the annulment or enforcement stage, punitive damages awards can become highly unpredictable "in the absence of applicable guidelines, caps, or appellate bodies that greatly control the circumstances and the amounts of awards."[160] Moreover, the arbitral practice reveals that even though awarding punitive damages does not *per se* violate public policy, considering punitive damages as a means to give the principle of good faith a tangible content ('legal teeth') so that it can remediate the breach of an express or implicit duty of good faith may render an award arbitrary.[161] In *Mammoet v. Pico Mexico*, it was alleged that good faith had been transgressed, yet the tribunal did not grant punitive damages.[162]

Nonetheless, it may generally be argued that the objective of the law is to do justice, which is not always served by regulating the contractual relationships of the parties in the most equitable fashion but by deterring certain conduct that is seemingly undesirable.[163] In that sense, punitive damages could be exceptionally employed by arbitrators as a tool to remediate a breach of a duty of good faith, which is either expressly or impliedly provided in the contract. For instance, the US federal courts upheld the arbitrator's power to award punitive damages.[164] More specifically, the 1981 decision of the United States Court of Appeal for the First Circuit in *Raytheon v. Automated Business Systems* abstained from vacating an award of punitive damages, which was based on the laws of California and was a consequence of a violation of good faith and fair dealing.[165] This may be necessitated by policy considerations that punitive damages can deter deliberate and unjustifiable breach of contract, "especially if there is no sensible commercial rationale for such misconduct."[166] Effectively, it is advocated that the "introduction of punitive

159 ICC Case No. 5946 of 1990, 16 Y.B. Comm. Arb. 97, para. 51 (Van den Berg ed., ICCA & Kluwer Law International 1991).

160 J.Y. Gotanda, *The Unpredictability Paradox: Punitive Damages and Interest in International Arbitration*, 7(1) TDM 1, 10 (Apr. 2010).

161 Naimeh Masumy, *Punitive Damages in the Context of Maritime Arbitration: Myth or Reality? Lessons Drawn from the American Perspective and the Existing Practice of the Society of Maritime Arbitrators*, 18(1) TDM 1, 15 (Jan. 2021).

162 Masumy, *supra* note 161, at 17; see also ANDRÉ PEREIRA DA FONSECA, *SMA Arbitration*, *in* INTERNATIONAL ARBITRATION IN THE UNITED STATES 759, 787 n.201 (Laurence Shore et al. eds., 2017) (supporting that the Society of Maritime Arbitrators (SMA) requires a high threshold of a "*showing of bad faith*" as well as "*clear evidence of wrongdoing*" in order to award punitive damages).

163 Sciences Po Mayer Brown Arbitration Lecture, *Pierre Mayer: Must Justice Be a Goal for the Arbitrator?* YOUTUBE, Oct. 30, 2020, *available at* https://youtu.be/OlUFkR_m32Q (last visited Apr. 8, 2022).

164 E. ALLAN FARNSWORTH, *Punitive Damages in Arbitration*, *in* 16 ARBITRATION INSIGHTS: TWENTY YEARS OF THE ANNUAL LECTURE OF THE SCHOOL OF INTERNATIONAL ARBITRATION, SPONSORED BY FRESHFIELDS BRUCKHAUS DERINGER, para. 5.23 (Julian D.M. Lew & Loukas A. Mistelis eds., 2007).

165 Raytheon Co. v. Automated Business Systems, Inc., 882 F.2d 6, 10 (1st Cir. 1989).

166 Masumy, *supra* note 161, at 15; *accord* Niccolò Pietro Castagno, *International Commercial Arbitration and Punitive Damages*, 4(3) ARBITRAJE: REVISTA DE ARBITRAJE COMERCIAL Y DE

damages into the arsenal of contractual remedies serves to regulate commercial behavior by incentivizing the parties to behave properly."[167] The bottom line should be that the exceptional remedy of punitive damages will depend upon the arbitrator's assessment of whether a breach of the contractual duty of good faith is able to justify such damages.[168] On the other hand, and insofar as the applicable law permits, so, adhering to good faith may prevent the adoption of unfair solutions, especially when awarding punitive damages is *disproportionate* to awarded compensatory damages.

3.5 Conclusion

This chapter attempted to reveal the content of the normative standard of good faith at the stages of contract formation, execution, termination and damages. It has been shown that national law considerations primarily influence the content of good faith, with a relative degree of variance between civil law and common law. However, the arbitrator's commercial acumen and idea of fairness will also be of decisive relevance, especially with respect to damages. Given that the substance of good faith is not static but rather plastic and dependent on the unique set of facts this chapter attempted to deduce specific behavioral standards anchored in the duty of minimum loyalty, reasonableness and honesty. Similarly, the negative standards of abuse of rights, unconscionability, the prohibition of inconsistency (*estoppel*) and bad faith operate as good faith safeguards. Importantly, this chapter underscored that good faith is not aimed *per se* at extending or restricting parties' substantive rights and obligations but determining them based on the parties' intent and the reasonable and lawful purpose of the contract. More contested is whether a breach of contractual good faith could be utilized as a foundation for awarding punitive damages. The criticism is justified since the risk of contravening the public policy of the arbitral situs and producing an arbitrary award further precipitates the overall unpredictability of punitive damages unless arbitrators are properly authorized by the parties and the applicable rules to employ good faith to regulate an unjustifiable and deliberate misconduct.

Inversiones 729, 737 (2011) ("[B]elieving that deterrence is the ultimate aim of punitive damages – that is the possibility by awarding them to prevent such misbehavior in future – there is really no reason why an arbitrator could not possibly undertake such role").

167 Castagno, *supra* note 166; see Areios Pagos, Case No. 17/1999, where the court ruled that punitive damages do not necessarily contravene the Greek public policy as such, unless they are disproportional.

168 In the United States, the traditional rule adopted in Section 355 of the Restatement (2nd) of Contracts holds that punitive damages are available when the breaching conduct also constitutes "a tort of bad faith breach". Castagno, *supra* note 166, at 732. A second theory adopted by the Supreme Court of Canada advanced that "a breach of the contractual duty of good faith is independent of and in addition to the breach of contractual duty to pay the loss. It constitutes an 'actionable wrong' . . . which does not require an independent tort", therefore making punitive damages available as a result of a breach of contract. Castagno, *supra* note 166, at 733 (quoting Vid. Whiten v. Pilot Insurance Co., 2002 SCC 18, [2002] 1 S.C.R. 595, para. 79).

4 Corrective Good Faith when National Law is Applicable to the Merits

4.1 The Sword and Shield Theory

4.1.1 The Sword

The observance of a good faith standard quite often impliedly[1] bestows upon the aggrieved party the right to claim damages insofar as the aforesaid standard is breached. Good faith functions then as a *sword*, a cause of action rooted either directly or indirectly into the contract. A similar rationale of a cause of action predicated on the autonomous breach of good faith is embedded in the Fair and Equitable Treatment (FET) standard in investment arbitration. It is widely accepted there that a failure to act in accordance with a good faith obligation gives rise to a claim under the FET provision.[2] However, a careful distinction should be made as the source of a duty of good faith in the first instance is detected in national law, whereas investment arbitration draws upon public international law.

From the perspective of commercial arbitration, Cremades, Reisman and Robertson eloquently conveyed a cause of action theory based on good faith. The ICDR award reasoned, based on the applicable New York law, that a claim for breach of the implied covenant of good faith can be sustained provided that it is

1 Civil law jurisdictions might imply good faith into the contract more often than common law jurisdictions, the latter being more skeptical to endorse a deviation from the literal meaning of the contractual agreement. Gary B. Born, International Commercial Arbitration 2960 (3rd ed., Kluwer Law International 2021).

2 Emily Sipiorski, Good Faith in International Investment Arbitration, para. 9.13 (OUP 2019). This, of course, requires that the FET standard embodies the duty to act in good faith, which is a rather contested area of law. Some tribunals have decided that FET does not require a bad faith conduct. See, e.g., Mondev International Ltd v. United States of America, ICSID Case No ARB(AF)/99/2, Award, ¶116 (Oct. 11, 2002) ("To the modern eye, what is unfair or inequitable need not equate with the outrageous or the egregious. In particular, a State may treat foreign investment unfairly and inequitably without necessarily acting in bad faith"). However, others have found that FET entails a duty to act in good faith. See, e.g., Waste Management v United Mexican States, ICSID Case No. ARB(AF)/00/3, Award, ¶138, Apr. 30, 2004 ("A basic obligation of the State under Article 1105(1) of the NAFTA is to act in good faith and form, and not deliberately to set out to destroy or frustrate the investment by improper means").

DOI: 10.4324/9781003527596-5

not "duplicative of an express breach of contract claim"[3] and that a separate action for breach of the implied covenant of good faith is precluded in case it "rests on the same factual predicates as the claim for breach of contract."[4] However, it was interestingly held that pursuing alternative claims based on a breach of the implied duty of good faith and breach of contract as such, albeit founded on the same facts, is acceptable.[5] The effect of such observation is of cardinal importance as it enhances the argument of a progressive liberal application of good faith not only as an alternative foundation for pursuing a claim but also as an independent cause of action. Extending the perimeter of good faith beyond what is necessary may open the floodgates of legal uncertainty. It may also result in an abuse of process by giving rise to frivolous claims triggered by an unspecified breach of contractual provisions that were never truly negotiated for by the parties.

4.1.2 The Shield

Just as good faith constitutes the foundation of a claim, it can also be used as a *shield*. The objective of this defense mechanism is either to bar a claim as inadmissible or invalidate the contract. Once the award is made, good faith may be invoked as a public policy defense against the enforcement of the award.[6] But even prior to that stage, an arbitrator should be able to consider public policy considerations and examine with care whether such public policy defenses hailed in good faith are meritorious, often in light of the motive of one party to "avoid sharing its benefits with the other party or otherwise to escape the consequences of its own contractual non-performance."[7] Even if not pleaded for, a serious public policy offense, such as fraud or bribery, should be examined by the arbitrator *sua sponte* in order to ensure

3 Citigroup Inc. v. Abu Dhabi Investment Authority, ICDR Case No. 50 2013 000782, Dec. 12, 2016, para. 281 (Arbitrator Intelligence Materials, Kluwer Law International).

4 Citigroup Inc., *supra* note 3 (*quoting* Miller v. HSBC Bank USA, 2015 WL 585589, at *5, S.D.N.Y., Feb. 11, 2015).

5 Citigroup Inc., *supra* note 3, para. 282 ("A party is only precluded from recovering on both theories at the same time") (quoting Fantozzi v. Axsys Techs. Inc., 2008 WL 4866054, at *7, S.D.N.Y., Nov. 6, 2008).

6 *Lalive* correctly observed that a party should not attempt to enforce "an international contract which would be against *bonos mores* by its object" (emphasis in original). Pierre Lalive, *Transnational (or Truly International) Public Policy and International Arbitration*, *in* 3 Comparative Arbitration Practice and Public Policy in Arbitration, para. 186(6) (Pieter Sanders ed., ICCA Congress Series, 1987). The Highest Regional Court of Bavaria affirmed pursuant to the NYC art. V(2)(b) that "the principle of contractual good faith [*Vertragstreue*] would be violated in a manner that is irreconcilable with the [German] legal system if the claimant obtained enforcement." Germany No. 71, Seller v. Buyer, Bayerisches Oberstes Landesgericht [Higher Court of Appeal of Bavaria], 4Z Sch 17/03, Nov. 20, 2003, 29 Y.B. Comm. Arb. 771, [6] (2004) (A.J. Van den Berg ed., ICCA & Kluwer Law International 2004).

7 Bernardo M. Cremades & David J.A. Cairns, *Trans-national Public Policy in International Arbitral Decision-Making: The Cases of Bribery, Money Laundering and Fraud*, *in* Arbitration – Money Laundering, Corruption and Fraud, 65, 84 (Kristine Karsten & Andrew Berkeley eds., ICC Dossiers I, 2003).

the enforceability of the award and overall systemic integrity.[8] However, more central to this study is the examination of the changed circumstances defense, which constitutes the restrictive mechanism of good faith.

4.2 Restrictive Good Faith: Exceptions to Normative Good Faith in Changed Circumstances

It has been hitherto argued that the principle of good faith is endemic to every contract. This principle behaves as a rule that imposes certain standards of conduct upon the contracting parties. However, the rule of sanctity of contracts is not rigid because of the volatility of circumstances. Exceptions to the rule of sanctity are possible in light of a change in circumstances that disrupts the contractual equilibrium and renders non-performance excusable. This solution is well-established in the theory of law and derives from the Roman law principle *impossibilium nulla obligatio est*. The financial crisis of 2008, the outburst of pandemics, wars, increased energy prices and inflation have shocked the modern model of market function and progressively led to the idea of a restricted capitalism requiring revisiting the balance between party autonomy and regulatory heteronomy.[9] This limitation to freedom is associated with the general public interest embedded in the optimal social value of justice.[10] An act of God, a war, sabotage, a curfew, embargo, a government action, a labor disturbance and other events may qualify as a *force majeure* defense and subsequently relieve the party from its obligation to perform, regardless of whether such impediment occurred prior to or after the conclusion of the contract.[11]

The normative function of good faith is 'bended' in situations where the rights and obligations of the parties have to be adjusted so that the contractual framework can be adapted to a change of circumstances, which the parties did not previously foresee or could not have foreseen. The concepts of *rebus sic stantibus* and *force majeure* become the manifestations of the restrictive impact of good faith upon the sanctity of contracts.[12] These doctrines necessitate an excuse from performance because a change of circumstances can cause an "excessive disproportion between performance and counter-performance [and] the insistence of a party on the

8 Cremades & Cairns, *supra* note 7, at 85.

9 charalambos pambouKis, *Introduction in* International Transactions Law, para. 64 (Charalambos Pamboukis ed., 2009) [ΧΑΡΗΣ ΠΑΜΠΟΥΚΗΣ, *Εισαγωγή στο* ΔΙΚΑΙΟ ΔΙΕΘΝΩΝ ΣΥΝΑΛΛΑΓΩΝ παρ. 64 (Χ. Παμπούκης επιστημ. επιμ., 2009)].

10 pambouKis, *Introduction*, *supra* note 9, para. 58.

11 See *ICC Force Majeure Clause 2003 and ICC Hardship Clause 2003*, ICC Publication No. 650, Feb. 2003, *available at* https://iccwbo.org/wp-content/uploads/sites/3/2017/02/ICC-Force-Majeure-Hardship-Clause.pdf. Such clauses were modified as of 2020 to reflect modern practice and be more user-friendly. However, the substance of the earlier versions is not significantly altered. The old versions may still be incorporated into the parties' contract.

12 ICC Case No. 1512 of 1971, 1 Y.B. Comm. Arb. 128, 129, 1976 (Pieter Sanders ed., ICCA & Kluwer Law International 1976). Strictly speaking, *force majeure* is distinguished from *rebus sic stantibus* in that performance in *force majeure* is impossible, not just onerous as *in rebus sic stantibus*.

performance by the aggrieved party strictly in accordance with the terms of the contract may be contrary to the principle of good faith"[13] (alteration to the original). However, such risky exceptions could easily be taken advantage of by one party to further its own interests, distort the carefully negotiated equilibrium and adversely prejudice the other party's interests. In that regard, the tribunal in *ICC Case No. 1512* correctly stated that these exceptions do not apply without limitation.[14] The flexibility of good faith is not unrestrained. It is controlled by predictability and legal certainty. A limitation of *pacta sunt servanda* should only occur where 'compelling reasons' are justified by the nature of the change, the specific type of the contract and circumstances, as well as the requirements of equity and fairness.[15]

A comparative analysis of the legal systems worldwide reveals that the doctrine of *clausula rebus sic stantibus* varies since its application is subject to the specific requirements that the applicable national law sets out. Even though a national law does not always provide for strong regulation of the *force majeure* concept, as opposed to the detailed terms of a *force majeure* (or hardship) clause inserted into the contract, it is undoubtedly instrumental in terms of contractual interpretation,[16] especially where the principle of good faith has inspired the development of such concept in the respective law.

Many domestic law approaches have been expressed on the definition and consequences of changed circumstances, all of which seem to converge rather than diverge. However, it should not be overlooked, especially while crafting *force majeure* or hardship clauses, that considerable differences exist among various legal traditions, which in turn determine if, and to what extent, good faith can be used to (re)formulate the duties of the parties in light of changed circumstances and how much freedom is bestowed upon the arbitrator to interpret the changed circumstances requirements through the lens of good faith.

4.2.1 Impossibility of Performance

Under *Swiss law*, a hard rule on *force majeure* is not recognized as a basis for cancellation of a contract, except for the doctrine of impossibility of performance, which dictates, according to Articles 97 and 119 of the Swiss Code of Obligations, that an obligation to perform is 'frozen' as long as such impossibility is in effect.[17]

13 Christoph Brunner, Force Majeure and Hardship under General Contract Principles: Exemption for Non-performance in International Arbitration 394 (International Arbitration Law Library 18, Kluwer Law International 2008).

14 ICC Case No. 1512, *supra* note 12, at 129.

15 ICC Case No. 1512, *supra* note 12.

16 Christoph Brunner, *Rules on Force Majeure as Illustrated in Recent Case Law*, *in* 17 Hardship and Force Majeure in International Commercial Contracts: Dealing with Unforeseen Events in a Changing World 82, 106 (Fabio Bortolotti & Dorothy Ufot eds., ICC Dossiers, 2018).

17 F.R. German Engineering Company v. Polish buyer, Ad Hoc Interim Award, Sept. 9, 1983, 12 Y.B. Comm. Arb. 63, 67 (A.J. Van den Berg ed., 1987).

However, Swiss case law has developed the concept of *clausula rebus sic stantibus*, pursuant to which a party may be discharged of an obligation to perform if circumstances taking place after the contract was made render performance unacceptable by reason of good faith provided that the occurrence of such circumstances is not imputed to the party's fault.[18]

4.2.2 Frustration of Purpose

English law does not recognize *per se* the concept of *force majeure*,[19] yet the equivalent notion of frustration of purpose has long been established since *Taylor v. Caldwell*. The English judge, in that case, reasoned that there is an implied condition in the contract, although not explicitly provided in the contract, which requires that non-performance should be excused if it depends on the existence of a thing or person and such thing or person no longer exists.[20] A typical example of frustration of contract is reflected in the *Coronation* cases, where an English aristocrat rents an apartment for the purpose of viewing the coronation of his king Edward VII, but unfortunately, two days before the coronation, the king fell ill, the celebration was postponed and the contract was rendered void on the grounds of frustration of purpose.[21] The philosophical rationale for frustration is different from what a civil lawyer would consider as a *force majeure* excuse. The rationale is that the purpose of the contract has changed radically owing to an act of God; as a result the performance of the contract has now become impossible. On the other hand, a continental judge would likely enforce the contract.[22] The aristocrat would have to pay the rent and if he wanted to see his king's coronation, a second agreement would have to be signed.[23] This stark comparison shows that resorting to good faith may be able to add more stability and flexibility to international contracts, as opposed to a cynical black letter interpretation and the stiff consequences of frustration, pursuant to which the contract is automatically ended without any regard to the intentions of the parties.[24] Indeed, courts are frequently reluctant to enforce the doctrine of frustration of purpose on the basis that it may produce inequitable results for the parties. Enforcing the harshness of the lack of alternative relief, along with a full discharge of all contractual obligations, may be deemed as in violation of a requirement of good faith or abuse of rights.[25] Good faith would necessitate a flexible solution allowing the frustrated party to get back their security given or recover

18 F.R. German Engineering Company, *supra* note 17.

19 Alfons H. Puelinckx, *Frustration, Hardship, Force Majeure, Imprévision, Wegfall der Geschäftsgrundlage, Unmöglichkeit, Changed Circumstances: A Comparative study in English, French, German and Japanese Law*, 3(2) J. Int'l Arb. 47, 54 (Kluwer Law International 1986).

20 Puelinckx, *supra* note 19, at 49.

21 Puelinckx, *supra* note 19, at 50.

22 Puelinckx, *supra* note 19, at 51.

23 Puelinckx, *supra* note 19.

24 Brunner, *Rules on Force Majeure as Illustrated in Recent Case Law*, *supra* note 16, at 84.

25 T.W. Chapman S.Ed., *Contracts-Frustration of Purpose*, 59 Mich. L. Rev. 98, 118 n.119 (1960).

expenses incurred by them to the degree that the other party enjoyed a benefit from the venture originally agreed upon.[26] It would echo the approach of equitable adjustment of the contract that urges the arbitrator to arrange the parties' rights and obligations in such a way that the parties themselves, being reasonable persons, would have done so had they known of the supervening event.[27] As already advocated, it is precisely that equitable adjustment that preserves the sanctity of the contract and helps parties attain their initial contractual purpose rather than the complete termination.[28]

4.2.3 Impracticability

American law follows a multi-level approach. It distinguishes between a change of circumstances that renders performance absolutely impossible (impossibility), burdensome (impracticable) and fruitless in the sense that the purpose of the contract is frustrated (frustration).[29] The scope of impracticability under US Restatement (Second) Section 261 on *Discharge by Supervening Impracticability* is broader than the standard of impossibility so that it can also cover situations where the supervening impediment makes performance unworkable, unfair or unprofitable[30] or where the strict impossibility standard is not broad enough to capture the "required extent of the impediment to performance."[31] Good faith has a special role in the interpretation of the requirements of commercial impracticability under American law. U.C.C. Section 2–615(a) provides that

> delay in delivery or non-delivery in whole or in part by a seller . . . is not a breach of his duty under a contract for sale if performance as agreed has been made impracticable by the occurrence of a contingency the non-occurrence of which was a basic assumption on which the contract was made or by compliance in *good faith* with any applicable foreign or domestic governmental regulation or order whether or not it later proves to be invalid.
>
> (emphasis added)

Further, if under U.C.C. Section 2–103(b) good faith has the meaning of "honesty in fact and the observance of reasonable commercial standards of fair dealing in the trade," then recourse to good faith may determine whether the disruptive event

26 Chapman S.Ed., *supra* note 25, at 120.

27 Chapman S.Ed., *supra* note 25, at 119 ("'The gap filling doctrine clearly warrants equitable adjustment of the rights and duties of the parties short of discharge, if prevailing notions of good faith and fair dealing so require'") (quoting Smit, Frustration of Contract: A Comparative Attempt at Consolidation, 58 COLUM. L. REV. 287, 314 (1958)).

28 Chapman S.Ed., *supra* note 25.

29 Félix J. Montero, *International Arbitration and Changed Circumstances in Contract Performance: An Overview*, 2008(1) SPAIN ARB. REV. 85, 87 (2008).

30 BRUNNER, *Rules on Force Majeure as Illustrated in Recent Case Law*, *supra* note 16, at 84–85.

31 BRUNNER, *Rules on Force Majeure as Illustrated in Recent Case Law*, *supra* note 16.

was reasonably foreseeable because if it is, the impracticability defense cannot be invoked.[32] In addition, an imprudent use of impracticability to relieve a party of a contract must be restrained in case a contracting party shows bad faith in their efforts to avoid a bad deal. The arbitrator, as much as courts, should be granted the power to protect a party from the counterparty's bad faith.

4.2.4 Unmöglichkeit

The theory of the impossibility of performance (*Unmöglichkeit*) in the evolution of *German* contract law is firmly established on the principle of good faith. A broad construction of this doctrine fuses to the *Opfergrenze* doctrine, according to which an insistence that the debtor should perform their obligations, despite the occurrence of an unforeseen event that is not imputed to their fault, would be against the reasonable undertakings of the parties and the principle of good faith.[33] By the same token, Berger and Behn advocate that the doctrine of *Wegfall der Geschäftsgrundlage* (suggesting that any contract is founded on implied grounds, the disturbance of which may lead to the termination or the amendment of it) is hailed into the moral foundation of the principle of good faith.[34] This German case law approach was later codified in BGB Section 313 ("Disturbance of the Foundation of the Transaction").[35] It was the same principle of good faith requiring that one

32 Stephen G. York, *Re: The Impracticability Doctrine of the U.C.C.*, 29 DUQ. L. REV. 221, 223 n.14 (1991) ("The question is . . . was the contingency which developed one which the parties could *reasonably be thought to have foreseen* as a real possibility which could affect performance?") (emphasis added) (quoting Mishara Construction Co. Inc. v Transit-Mixed Concrete Corp., 365 Mass 122, 127, 310 NE2d 363, 367, Mass. 1974).

33 Puelinckx, *supra* note 19, at 65; see BGB § 275(2), Civil Code in the version promulgated on Jan. 2, 2002 (Federal Law Gazette [*Bundesgesetzblatt*] I, p. 42, 2909; 2003 I, p. 738), last amended by Article 1 of the Act of Aug. 10, 2021 (Federal Law Gazette I p. 3515), Translation provided by Langenscheidt Übersetzungsservice, updated by Neil Mussett. The translation has most recently been revised and updated by Samson Übersetzungen GmbH, Dr. Carmen v. Schöning, *available at* www.gesetze-im-internet.de/englisch_bgb/englisch_bgb.html#p0849 ("The obligor may refuse performance to the extent that performance requires an expenditure of time and effort that, taking into account the subject matter of the obligation and the requirement of acting in good faith").

34 Klaus Peter Berger & Daniel Behn, *Force Majeure and Hardship in the Age of Corona: A Historical and Comparative Study*, 6 MJDR, No. 4, 79, 122 (2019–2020).

35 Berger & Behn, *supra* note 34, at 123; See, e.g., BGB § 313(1), Civil Code in the version promulgated on Jan. 2, 2002 (Federal Law Gazette [*Bundesgesetzblatt*] I page 42, 2909; 2003 I, p. 738), last amended by Article 1 of the Act of Aug. 10, 2021 (Federal Law Gazette, I p. 3515). Translation provided by Langenscheidt Übersetzungsservice, updated by Neil Mussett. The translation has most recently been revised and updated by Samson Übersetzungen GmbH, Dr. Carmen v. Schöning, *available at* www.gesetze-im-internet.de/englisch_bgb/englisch_bgb.html#p1180 (holding that in case circumstances that were the foundation of the contract have been materially disturbed to the effect that parties would not have concluded it had they been aware or would have entered the contract on different terms, "adaptation of the contract may be demanded to the extent that, taking account of all the circumstances of the specific case, in particular the contractual or statutory distribution of risk, one of the parties cannot reasonably be required to uphold the contract without alteration"); *accord* GCC 2:388 (Greece). ("If circumstances based on which, by virtue of good

should not "enrich itself at the expense of the other in scenarios of unforeseen and changed circumstances and [has] to cooperate with the other side when such events arise"[36] that imported into the German jurisprudence the justification of the remedy of contractual adaptation as an alternative to termination. However, and this is in line with the view supported herein, the corrective use of good faith should be made by tribunals cautiously, almost in a restrictive fashion, as there is a grave concern that a liberal use of good faith may open the floodgates of parties' escaping their initial commitments under the contract.[37] Despite the reasonable criticism, it is evident that German law has been at the forefront of a paradigm shift where good faith is heavily relied on to provide flexible solutions guaranteeing the survival of the contract in lieu of its premature termination.[38]

4.2.5 Imprévision

In *French law*, the evolution of the theory of *imprévision* or the *hardship* doctrine – pursuant to which performance is still possible, yet relief may be granted if changed circumstances have rendered performance for one party excessively onerous – is closely connected to the principle of good faith. For a long time, the French legal system resisted the recognition of the hardship doctrine since such relief would allegedly constitute a pretext for parties to avoid their contractual commitments, thus undermining legal certainty.[39] In the famous case of *Canal*

faith and fair dealing, the parties founded the conclusion of the bilateral agreement, changed as a result of reasons that were supervening and could not have been foreseen, and that change renders the performance of the debtor by reference to the counter performance excessively burdensome, the court may at its own choice and at the debtor's application adjust the performance of the debtor to the extent appropriate and decide the termination of the agreement either in whole or for the part that has not yet been performed"). It is maintained that this article is a more specific manifestation of the bedrock art. 288 ("The debtor has the obligation to perform the contract as good faith requires, taking into consideration the fair dealing"). As such, it echoes the principle *lex specialis derogat legi generali*. However, even in cases where the more specific art. 388 is applicable, recourse to art. 288 may be appropriate to regulate the *extent* of its application. According to Karampatzos, in the application of art. 288 the Supreme Court may take stock of the fact that, even if the risk was predicted and anticipated, the scope of the initial foreseeability of such risk was exceeded by its consequences. Eleni Kozmai, The Readjustment of Contracts on the Basis of Articles AK 388 and 288, Especially in Times of Financial Crisis [Ελένη Κοζμάϊ, Η αναπροσαρμογή των Συμβάσεων επί τη Βάσει των Άρθρων ΑΚ 388 και 288, Ιδίως σε Περιόδους Οικονομικής Κρίσης] (Athens, May 2018) (master's dissertation, National & Kapodistrian University of Athens), at 49 n.134, *available at* https://pergamos.lib.uoa.gr/uoa/dl/frontend/file/lib/default/data/2762789/theFile (citing Antonios G. Karampatzos, Economic Crisis and Re-adjustment of Contractual Obligations – Especially under the Prism of Recent Case Law of Courts of Substance on the Commercial Lease Agreement, CHRONIKA IDIOTIKOU DIKAIOU (CHRID), 92–105 2013 [Αντώνιος Γ. Καραμπατζός "Οικονομική Κρίση και Αναπροσαρμογή των Συμβατικών Παροχών – Ιδίως υπό το Πρίσμα της Νεώτερης Νομολογίας των Δικαστηρίων Ουσίας για την Εμπορική Μίσθωση," ΧρΙΔ, 92–105 (2013)]).

36 Berger & Behn, *supra* note 34, at 86.

37 Berger & Behn, *supra* note 34, at 124.

38 Berger & Behn, *supra* note 34, at 125.

39 Berger & Behn, *supra* note 34, at 118.

de Craponne, the court refused to adapt the fee agreed to by the parties for the maintenance of the canal on the grounds that *pacta sunt servanda* must be strictly observed and such adaptation is not allowed unless specifically authorized by law.[40] The novelty of the French law regime is portrayed in a new Article reading:

> If a change of circumstances that was unforeseeable at the time of the conclusion of the contract renders performance excessively onerous for a party who had not accepted the risk of such a change, that party may ask the other contracting party to renegotiate the contract. The first party must continue to perform his obligations during renegotiation.
>
> In the case of refusal or the failure of renegotiations, the parties may agree to terminate the contract from the date and on the conditions which they determine, or by a common agreement ask the court to set about its adaptation. In the absence of an agreement within a reasonable time, the court may, on the request of a party, revise the contract or put an end to it, from a date and subject to such conditions as it shall determine.[41]

The remedy of renegotiation is anchored to a standard of good faith. The French Court of Appeal enforced an obligation to renegotiate a supply contract in good faith because the new legislation that was introduced with a view to reducing greenhouse emissions disturbed the balance of the contract on the basis of unforeseen profits generated due to that legislation.[42] Even if a duty of renegotiation does not entail a mutual solution, it must be accepted that the judge will resort to the principle of good faith to assess whether renegotiations actually took place in accordance with, or contrary to, a standard of good faith.[43] Also, even if performance continues during the phase of renegotiation, the judge may also turn to good faith to assess whether any affected party is entitled to withhold their performance in case the other party abstains from renegotiation.[44] It can be supported that the spirit of the new article on hardship elevates good faith to a standard of cooperation for the reason that any threat of judicial intervention as a last resort – either in the form of adaptation or termination – actually incentivizes the parties to rely on themselves, seek a negotiated solution as opposed to a judicial one; thus, party autonomy is further enhanced.[45]

40 Berger & Behn, *supra* note 34, at 117.

41 Code civil [C. civ.] [Civil Code] art. 1195 (Fr.), translated in J. Cartwright et al., The Law of Contract, the General Regime of Obligations, and Proof of Obligations: The New Provisions of the *Code Civil* Created by *Ordonnance* No. 2016–131 of Feb. 10, 2016 and including revisions made to the text by *Loi* No. 2018–287 of Apr. 20, 2018, translation commissioned by the *Direction des affaires civiles et du sceau, Ministère de la Justice, République française, available at* www.textes.justice.gouv.fr/art_pix/THE-LAW-OF-CONTRACT-2-5-16.pdf.

42 Catherine Pédamon, *The Paradoxes of the Theory of Imprévision in the New French Law of Contract: A Judicial Deterrent?* 112 Amicus Curiae: Journal of the Society for Advanced Legal Studies 12 (2017) (discussing Cour d'appel de Nancy [CA] Sept. 26, 2007, D. 2008.1120).

43 Pédamon, *supra* note 42, at 13, 15, 17.

44 Pédamon, *supra* note 42, at 15.

45 Berger & Behn, *supra* note 34, at 120.

4.2.6 The Katsumoto Doctrine

Japanese law has been very successful in developing the doctrine of changed circumstances on the grounds of good faith. Building on German jurisprudence, Katsumoto produced a colossal treatise on the evolution of the doctrine throughout time and, most importantly, envisioned the changed circumstances doctrine as a tangible expression of the principle of good faith.[46] He further explained that the legal consequences of an unforeseeable change of circumstances not attributable to the parties "are to be adapted in equity and good faith,"[47] provided that their creation or continuation are "considered as unreasonable in the light of the rule of equity and good faith."[48] It was not paradoxical that the Japanese courts endorsed the Katsumoto rule, the requirements of which are: (a) a substantial change of circumstances, (b) which could not be reasonably foreseen by the parties, (c) was not attributable to them and (d) any continuance or execution of the original obligations, as a result of such change, transgresses the principles of fairness and good faith.[49] Based on the foregoing, it is ascertained that fairness is a vital component of good faith. True, any insistence on performing the original contractual obligations would disturb the equilibrium between the parties if execution is meaningless or performance proves to be exceptionally difficult.[50] Further, the vital role that good faith plays in the observance of the requirements of changed circumstances is evinced in Japanese court practice.[51] Receiving the profit of a higher price than the price originally agreed to, as a result of inflation in the aftermath of Japan's defeat, would transgress the principle of good faith – even if the change of circumstances was unforeseen – one reason being that it took place while one party was in delay of performance.[52]

4.3 A Comparative Overview of Changed Circumstances – Convergence of Cultures

Having sketched a comparison between different civil and common law jurisdictions regarding the role of good faith within the metes and bounds of the doctrine of changed circumstances, it is the time to explore whether a homogeneous reading of its requirements under the converging force of good faith is warranted. In spite of national law disparities, the discovery of a common formula for assessing those requirements can be sustained under the prism of good faith. This may be appropriate, especially on the international plane where international contracts are

46 Luke R. Nottage, *Economic Dislocation and Contract Renegotiation in New Zealand and Japan: A Preliminary Empirical Study*, 27 VUWLR 59, 83 (1997).
47 Puelinckx, *supra* note 19, at 66 (quoting K. Igarashi, KEIYAKU TO JIJOHENKO (3rd ed., Yuhikaku, 1983), 147–48).
48 Puelinckx, *supra* note 19.
49 Puelinckx, *supra* note 19.
50 Puelinckx, *supra* note 19.
51 Puelinckx, *supra* note 19, at 66 n.55.
52 Puelinckx, *supra* note 19, at 66.

more susceptible to opportunism and actors usually rely on *force majeure* defenses by virtue of political, climatological or health reasons to escape performance under the contract.[53] They might also do so by taking advantage of their own position *i.e.,* a state invokes its own law or enacts legislation to avoid performance. Save where the applicable law imposes a different solution, the three most characteristic crystallizations of good faith pertaining to changed circumstances are set out in what follows. Except for providing more stability in an environment of harsh competition among different laws, these tenets ensure that parties stand on an equal footing. Still, it is not tenable that maximum convergence is achieved across various legal systems. This is especially so if the common law skepticism toward good faith is added to the equation.

4.3.1 Good Faith Necessitating Reasonableness in Foreseeing Changed Circumstances

The first criterion is whether the change of circumstances was within the reasonable expectations of the parties upon entering the contract to the effect that the parties could have foreseen the unexpected event. Foreseeability is a core limb of the test.[54] What is not evident, though, is that in order to determine whether such risk is foreseeable, the arbitrator would employ good faith. If, for example, there is an unexpected change in the energy market, such as a state regulation, resulting in a price change, the reasonableness test would determine if – and to what extent – such change was different from what the parties expected when they entered the contract.[55] The objectively reasonable expectations constitute the "controlling mechanism"[56] of good faith. It is conceivable that a party may also invoke a *force majeure* defense even if the risk was foreseeable when they entered the contract. That scenario would be permissible if it is proven that the aggrieved party did not assume the risk of the unexpected event.[57] For instance, it may be the case that a natural disaster that would otherwise qualify as a *force majeure* event should have been foreseen by a party, yet the probability of the occurrence of such impediment may be so remote that the party "may not reasonably be expected to have assumed the relevant risk."[58] That, of course, requires a balancing exercise in

53 Prof Filip De Ly, *Analysing the ICC Force Majeure Clause 2003*, *in* Hardship and Force Majeure in International Commercial Contracts: Dealing with Unforeseen Events in a Changing World 113 (Fabio Bortolotti & Dorothy Ufot eds., ICC Dossiers 2018).

54 F.R. German engineering Company v. Polish buyer, Ad Hoc Interim Award, Sept. 9, 1983, 12 Y.B. Comm. Arb. 63, 68 (A.J. Van den Berg ed., 1987) ("[C]hanges should not have been foreseeable, nor have actually been foreseen by the parties").

55 ICC Case No. 13898 of 2009, para. 74, *available at* https://jusmundi.com/en/document/decision/en-icc-case-ndeg-13898-final-award-in-case-13898-extract.

56 ICC Case No. 13898 of 2009, *supra* note 55.

57 Brunner, Force Majeure and Hardship under General Contract Principles, *supra* note 13, at 157.

58 Brunner, Force Majeure and Hardship under General Contract Principles, *supra* note 13, at 156.

good faith where the arbitrator will weigh the "*foreseeable degree* of likelihood of the occurrence of the impediment [against the] conclusion that the [party] assumed the risk"[59] (emphasis in original) (alteration to the original).

Nonetheless, and this is invariably accepted in international arbitration practice, good faith is not a panacea. It is limited by the adjacent principle of sanctity of contracts to the extent that a carefully bargained-for contract does not leave room for ambiguous reading. This approach was well-endorsed in *Gujarat State Petroleum v. Republic of Yemen*. The tribunal held that the principle of good faith could not "enable arbitrators to second-guess what the Parties could have added to their common understanding,"[60] as reflected in their production sharing agreements governed by Yemeni law. Thus, the Respondent's argument that additional requirements of foreseeability should be imported into the contract by virtue of good faith failed as Yemeni law cannot "operate in a manner such that general principles of good will and good faith will apply to introduce additional requirements into carefully negotiated provisions."[61]

4.3.2 Good Faith Necessitating Cooperation and Renegotiation

The CISG Convention and UNIDROIT Principles, which both promote the adoption of uniform rules in international trade, prescribe almost in an identical manner that the non-performing party must provide notice to the counterparty of the *force majeure* impediment, the failure of which within a reasonable time after the non-performing party knew or ought to have known of such impediment may give rise to liability for damages.[62] It is accepted that such duty to duly notify the other party of the impediment and its consequences upon performance is a general application of good faith,[63] the latter being viewed as the "fulcrum of cooperation in cross-border trade."[64] Even parties from common law jurisdictions, which do not directly recognize the concept of *force majeure* unless expressly provided in the contract, will be mindful, while drafting their contract, of the good faith obligation to provide reasonable notice of the occurrence of it. Even though the notice requirement is perceived as a good faith obligation, one should not be short-sighted regarding its application. The notice requirement may not be relied upon by the performing party as a complete defense against the non-performing party invoking the *force majeure*, especially when it is evident from the *force majeure* clause that the good faith obligation of notice is not a condition precedent for the invocation

59 Brunner, Force Majeure and Hardship under General Contract Principles, *supra* note 13.

60 ICC Case No. 19299/MCP, Sept. 12, 2013, para. 156 (Arbitrator Intelligence Materials, Kluwer Law International).

61 ICC Case No. 19299/MCP, *supra* note 60.

62 CISG, art. 79(4); see also UNIDROIT Principles, art. 7.1.7(3).

63 Brunner, *Rules on Force Majeure as Illustrated in Recent Case Law*, *supra* note 16, at 102.

64 Lorena Carvajal Arenas & A.F.M. Maniruzzaman, *Cooperation as Philosophical Foundation of Good Faith in International Business-Contracting – A View Through the Prism of Transnational Law*, OUCLF 1 (2012).

of the *force majeure* defense or there is an indication that the performing party is not in good faith, particularly when it had prior knowledge of such impediment.[65]

Two recent ICC cases corroborate the previous finding. In *General Dynamics v. Libya*, the state of Libya, acting as a respondent, purchased a communication and information system from the claimant, General Dynamics, according to the contract, which was governed by Swiss law.[66] The Respondent identified a number of *force majeure* impediments that prevented its performance, notably international sanctions that imposed a freeze on the assets of Libya, the Gaddafi troops and military intervention.[67] General Dynamics asserted that Libya should not rely on *force majeure* because it had already defaulted prior to the *force majeure* impediment; as a result, the casual nexus to the *force majeure* event has been broken, pursuant to the Swiss Code of Obligations.[68] The tribunal agreed that the requirement to give notice of the *force majeure* event flows from the general obligation to act in good faith, the violation of which may give rise to damages, yet it disagreed that "an obligation to act in good faith necessarily precludes reliance on force majeure where notice is not given. This is so especially when the prevailing circumstances at the time militate against an inference of absence of good faith."[69] It held that the notice requirement was not a condition precedent to the invocation of *force majeure* and that the claimant cannot purport that they were not aware of the repercussions of the *force majeure* on the parties' performance.[70] Likewise, the tribunal in *Global Tungsten & Powders v. Largo Resources* applied a similar approach. It explained, based on the contract and the applicable Pennsylvanian law, that "clear language is required in order for a force majeure notice obligation to be construed as a condition precedent"[71] and that "whether or not the party complaining of lack of notice had actual knowledge of the circumstances giving rise to the force majeure event is a relevant consideration."[72] The takeaway is that resorting to good faith, as prescribed in the respective applicable law, can indeed be meaningful in terms of contract interpretation.[73] Nevertheless, such recourse should be discouraged when good faith becomes the trojan horse to import additional requirements into the reading of the *force majeure* clause that the parties did not want them to be part of their contract in the first place.

Finally, it would be remiss not to spotlight the existence of another standard of substantive good faith during a change of circumstances. It is the duty of the parties

65 Brunner, *Rules on Force Majeure as Illustrated in Recent Case Law*, *supra* note 16, at 102.

66 ICC Case No. 19222/EMT, Jan. 5, 2016, paras. 13–14 (Arbitrator Intelligence Materials, Kluwer Law International).

67 ICC Case No. 19222/EMT, *supra* note 66, paras. 199, 202.

68 ICC Case No. 19222/EMT, *supra* note 66, para. 263.

69 ICC Case No. 19222/EMT, *supra* note 66, para. 274.

70 ICC Case No. 19222/EMT, *supra* note 66, paras. 270, 278.

71 ICC Case No. 19566/AGF/RD, Nov. 24, 2014, para. 182, *available at* https://jusmundi.com/en/document/decision/pdf/en-global-tungsten-powders-corp-v-largo-resources-ltd-final-award-monday-24th-november-2014.

72 ICC Case No. 19566/AGF/RD, *supra* note 71.

73 Brunner, *Rules on Force Majeure as Illustrated in Recent Case Law*, *supra* note 16, at 106.

to renegotiate their agreement in good faith. An illustrative example is a trade sanction affecting the contract. Even if the sanction is later lifted, the resurrection of the contract might require a renegotiation in good faith, typically because of the greater onus upon the party to resume its operations.[74] It is confirmed as a matter of arbitral case law that the non-fulfillment of a duty to renegotiate the contract in good faith in light of a change of circumstances might give rise to damages.[75] When national law so requires, and guided where appropriate by international instruments such as the UNIDROIT Principles,[76] the arbitrator will assess the behavior of the parties by examining whether the renegotiation efforts were made in conformity with good faith prerequisites.[77] Such prerequisites will usually refer to a number of indicia, *i.e.* whether a party maneuvered the renegotiation process by being unresponsive to the harmed counterparty, by making unreasonable offers and turning down reasonable requests or even by trying to improperly leverage its position.[78]

4.3.3 Good Faith Necessitating Fairness

The typology of changed circumstances and, more specifically, the ensuing consequences upon the performance of the parties vary among jurisdictions.[79] For instance, in civil law countries, any *force majeure* relief may be implied into the contract on top of the contractual relief expressly provided for in the contract, and that is usually the result of a civil law statute, unlike in common law jurisdictions where such a mechanism in the absence of a *force majeure* clause is considered to be exceptional and rough.[80] Further, there might be conceptual differences among legal constructions of the notion of changed circumstances, as illustrated previously, which inevitably are accountable for disparate consequences and remedies. To illustrate, the effects of *force majeure* and hardship are very different. Unlike *force majeure*, which is raised to excuse non-performance or suspend the affected parties' obligations, the proof of hardship requires a showing that performance

74 Marc Blessing, Introduction to Arbitration – Swiss and International Perspectives, para. 819 (Helbing & Lichtenhahn 1999).

75 ICC Case Nos. 6515 and 6516, 1994 24 Y.B. Comm. Arb., paras. 50–53 (A. J. Van den Berg ed., 1999) (where the tribunal found that the contract was clear that the parties should renegotiate their agreement in good faith in case of changed circumstances and that obligation was consistent with applicable GCC articles 288 and 388).

76 See, e.g., ICC Case No. 8486, Y.B. Comm. Arb. 162, 164 (1999), *available at* www.trans-lex.org/208486 (where the arbitrator interpreted the doctrine of hardship not only in line with the applicable Dutch law, but also in line with the UNIDROIT Principles).

77 See Pascale Accaoui Lorfing, *Adaptation of Contracts by Arbitrators Realities and Perspectives*, *in* Hardship and Force Majeure in International Commercial Contracts: Dealing with Unforeseen Events in a Changing World 41 (Fabio Bortolotti & Dorothy Ufot eds., 2018).

78 Lorfing, *supra* note 77.

79 Todd Wetmore & Simon Elliot, *COVID-19 and Construction Disputes*, *in* International Arbitration and the COVID-19 Revolution 2.2 (Maxi Scherer et al. eds., 2020).

80 Reed Smith LLP, Force Majeure One Year Later, Global Commercial Disputes White Paper, May 2021, at 21, *available at* www.reedsmith.com/en/perspectives/2021/05/force-majeure-one-year-later (last visited Jan. 11, 2023).

became excessively burdensome in the sense that it resulted in an economic imbalance, yet the parties were still obliged to perform.[81] On the other hand, frustration requires a higher threshold, the consequence of which is the automatic termination of the contract, without the possibility of restoring the *status quo ante*.

Despite the inhomogeneous results of the application of changed circumstances across the globe, there is a common feature: The arbitrator, when mandated to resolve international disputes, should always be concerned about their mission to fairly resolve the dispute as a quintessential aspect of the contract and resulting from the law as well.[82] However, that is not tautological with the arbitrator's broad conscience. It is almost accepted that the duty of the arbitrator to do justice requires not only to respect and enforce the contractual commitments of the parties but also to make adjustments at any time the agreement is "apparently contrary to the basic logic in business and/or in the math."[83] The objective of deterring undesirable behaviors is not synonymous with regulating the contractual relationship in an equitable way.[84] Even so, arbitral tribunals' reluctance to intervene in the name of fairness subsists.[85] Yet, it would be mere casuistry to allege that fairness does not permit a deviation from the stiff compliance with *pacta sunt servanda*. Even the UK government, which represents a common law tradition that is traditionally skeptical toward explicitly authorizing the courts to interfere with the contract, has stressed that "[r]esponsible and fair behaviour [is advisable] where the relevant contract is materially impacted by Covid-19, so that fair and equitable outcomes can be achieved in contractual arrangements"[86] (alteration to the original). That behavior includes, *inter alia*, "making, and responding to, requests for contract

81 Wetmore & Elliot, *supra* note 79.

82 Sciences Po Mayer Brown Arbitration Lecture, *Pierre Mayer: Must Justice Be a Goal for the Arbitrator?* YouTube (Oct. 30, 2020), *available at* https://youtu.be/OlUFkR_m32Q (last visited Apr. 8, 2022) [hereinafter *Sciences Po Lecture]*.

83 Xiuming Tao, *Annual Review on Financial Dispute Resolution in China (2019)*, *in* Commercial Dispute Resolution in China: An Annual Review and Preview 259, 276 (Beijing Arbitration Commission ed., 2019).

84 *Sciences Po Lecture*, *supra* note 82.

85 See Producer v. Construction Company, Interim Award, NAI Case No. 1694, Dec. 12, 1996, 23 Y.B. Comm. Arb., para. 45 (A.J. Van den Berg ed., 1998) (The tribunal subscribed to the hesitance of the Dutch Supreme Court to apply BW Art. 6:258 in a liberal manner. The said article empowers the tribunal to adapt the contract if – due to unforeseen circumstances – the party cannot reasonably or fairly expect the contract to be maintained as originally bargained for. In the words of the tribunal, "[o]nly in highly exceptional circumstances is it permissible to deviate from [contractual predictability], which apply in particular in the international context. Under those circumstances, the Tribunal is prima facie disinclined to go beyond the four corners of the Contract") (alteration to the original); *Contra* Himpurna California Energy Ltd. v. PT. (Persero) Perusahaan Listruik Negara, Final Award, May 4, 1999, 25 Y.B. Comm. Arb., para. 188 (A.J. Van den Berg ed., ICCA & Kluwer Law International 2000) ("The Arbitral Tribunal is willing to accept that under Dutch as well as Indonesian law, there are situations in which the rule of good faith may operate to dissolve or transform contractual rights and obligations. On the other hand, it is quite clear that such a remedy is reserved for extreme cases").

86 UK Cabinet Office, Guidance on Responsible Contractual Behaviour in the Performance and Enforcement of Contracts Impacted by the Covid-19 Emergency (May 7, 2020), para. 16, *available*

changes and variations."[87] True, the corrective effect of a fair response would not be possible were it not for the principle of good faith. In case of changed circumstances, it may be against the principle of good faith to insist on the performance of contractual terms.[88] As the Swiss Supreme Court put it, a change of circumstances might constitute a ground for adaptation (or termination) of the contract as it may result in a great and manifest disproportion between the corresponding obligations of the parties and that would constitute a violation of good faith and fairness.[89] In that sense, the underlying principle of proportionality must be viewed as a substantive fairness criterion that has to be taken also into account in determining whether it would be contrary to good faith to maintain an excessive, unnecessary and unsuitable contractual situation resulting from a force majeure event. Just as a party is not allowed to withhold their essential performance by virtue of the counterparty's less significant non-performance, otherwise it would act contrary to good faith,[90] an unexpected change of circumstances must not justify a disproportionate (excessive) outcome resulting from the insistence on the original performance.

4.4 A Primary Rule of Corrective Justice

Good faith, as already explained, encompasses, *inter alia*, the notions of reasonableness and fairness, which imply that like cases should be treated alike and unlike cases in a different manner, as well as that the particular circumstances of each case should be paid due regard.[91] Generally, it is possible that a strict application of a legal rule might yield unacceptable results, especially from the perspective of the 'spirit' of the contested law, which reflects the purpose and values of the legal rule.[92] The same applies to a contractual term that is so strict that it produces

---

at https://assets.publishing.service.gov.uk/government/uploads/system/uploads/attachment_data/file/883737/_Covid-19_and_Responsible_Contractual_ Behaviour__web_final___7_May_.pdf.

87 UK Cabinet Office, *supra* note 86, para. 15(k).

88 Sebastiano Nessi, *Price Revision in Long-Term Energy Contracts: When Is It Possible to Adjust Prices or Modify the Terms of a Long-Term Energy Contract under Swiss Law?, in* 40 under 40 International Arbitration 385, 393 (Carlos González-Bueno ed., 2018).

89 Nessi, *supra* note 88. It is important to note that the Swiss Supreme Court has also highlighted that arbitral tribunals, as much as state courts, have the power to modify the terms of the contract or fill contractual lacunae even if the arbitration agreement does not explicitly provide so. Nessi, *supra* note 88, at 397 (citing Schweizerisches Bundesgericht [BGer] [Federal Supreme Court of Switzerland] 4P.114/2001, Dec. 19, 2001 in 22(3) ASA Bull. (2004), at p. 493 et seq.).

90 Emmanuel Gaillard & John Savage, Fouchard Gaillard Goldman on International Commercial Arbitration 1486 (Kluwer Law International 1999).

91 E.T. Feteris, *A Normative Reconstruction of Arguments from Reasonableness in the Justification of Judicial Decisions*, *in* Modern developments in linguistics and language teaching: II international conference proceedings (T. Dubrovskaya & Y. V. Kitayeva eds., Apr. 28–30, 2008) [Sovremennye napravlenija v lingvistike i prepodavanii jazykov: materialy II meždunarodnoj naučno-praktičeskoj konferencii, aprelja 28–30, 2008 (pp. 86–96) MNEPU].

92 Feteris, *supra* note 91.

undesirable results. The discretionary power of the arbitrator to provide an exception to such a strict rule is predicated on a teleological interpretation.[93]

4.4.1 Distinction from Supplementary Function and Ex Aequo et Bono Decision Making

One should be extremely careful not to conflate the corrective good faith with two distinct concepts. First, an interpretation of the contract would exceptionally entail the supplementation of an omitted term that the parties did not initially provide for, either because of an oversight or because they desired not to address that term[94] or because that particular obligation is needless to say. According to Article 4.8 of the UNIDROIT Principles, when the parties have not agreed to a particular term, which determines their rights and obligations, the arbitrator is vested with the discretion to fill in a contractual lacuna with an appropriate term under the specific circumstances by taking into consideration, *inter alia*, the intention of the parties, the nature and purpose of the contract, the principle of good faith and fair dealing, as well as reasonableness.[95] Good faith is a powerful tool in supplementing the omitted term, especially in long-term contracts, yet the arbitrator is not entitled to rewrite the contract or modify it whatsoever.[96] The interpretation principle of integration would be adhered to, pursuant to which the arbitrator may supplement any omitted terms in line with the principle of good faith and construct the language "in accordance with the nature of the contract as a whole"[97] (*interpretación integradora*). The capacity of the arbitrator to supplement the contract by virtue of good faith should be distinguished from the drastic effect of their capacity to interfere with the contract and correct it.

Second, in case of changed circumstances, the arbitrator acting as *amiable compositeur* or deciding *ex aequo et bono* may be able to adapt the contract due to circumstances which were unforeseen at the time of the conclusion of the contract and which have rendered the contractual terms onerous for one of the parties.[98] However, a line should be drawn. The power of the arbitrator to decide in consonance

93 *Cf.* Feteris, *supra* note 91 ("[W]hen a judge uses teleological-evaluative argumentation, he must justify his decision by arguing that . . . application in the strict literal meaning would have unacceptable consequences from the perspective of the goals and values the rule is intended to realize"). Although such a revision might be said to be associated with equity norms, it does not necessarily derive from those.

94 Eckart Brödermann, UNIDROIT Principles of International Commercial Contracts: An Article-by-Article Commentary 120 (Kluwer Law International 2018).

95 See UNIDROIT Principles, art. 5.1.2. ("Implied obligations stem from: (a) the nature and purpose of the contract; (b) practices established between the parties and usages; (c) good faith and fair dealing; (d) reasonableness").

96 Brödermann, *supra* note 94.

97 Andrés Jana Linetzky, *National Report for Chile (2018–2020)*, *in* ICCA International Handbook on Commercial Arbitration 1, 17 (Lise Bosman ed., ICCA & Kluwer Law International 2020, Supplement No. 113).

98 Jana Linetzky, *supra* note 97.

with equity, or otherwise with what is right, is not only broader than the notion of good faith but there is at least one fundamental difference. Good faith must be predicated on the law or body of rules applicable to the substance of the dispute. On the contrary, the arbitrator's power to decide *ex aequo et bono* may entail a deviation from a solution dictated by the applicable law to the extent the arbitrator finds it unjust and is urged to adapt the solution envisaged in the applicable law in order to make it compatible with equity.[99] As much as an arbitrator can moderate the stringent effect of contractual provisions by resorting to equity, they can also resort to good faith, with the exception that the latter power derives from and is subsequently restricted in the contract and applicable law.

4.4.2 Source of Power to Intervene

Arbitration as a method of resolving disputes is a creature of contract. The freedom of the arbitrator to deliver a judgment and shape the legal framework of their judgment is founded on Hart's established theory of authority, pursuant to which authority is conferred upon the adjudicatory body to produce legally binding rules of conduct.[100] In addition, the parties may determine the *method* of conferral of such authority in the sense that they can stipulate that their dispute should be resolved in accordance with a specific set of rules.[101] The primordial foundation of the theory of authority is, of course, the will of the parties. Yet, the arbitrator is equipped with a *presumption of freedom*, which means that if the parties have not explicitly provided for a specific term, the arbitral tribunal is vested with the power to fill in the gap[102] or adjust the consequences of the contract, both stemming from the authority granted to the tribunal as a result of the very agreement to arbitrate. Albeit contested, the exegesis resonates with the *theory of incompleteness* of the contract, pursuant to which the parties cannot, or will not, accede to every single aspect of the contract but instead focus on what is relevant.[103]

4.4.3 Practical Situations Justifying Correction

When dealing with a change of circumstances able to cause some sort of hardship to the performance of parties' contractual obligations, the Portuguese Civil Code provides that the contract may be adapted in case it is required by the principle

99 Laurence Kiffer, *Amiable Composition and ICC Arbitration*, 18 ICC Bull. No. 1, 51, 58 (2007).

100 Charalambos P. Pamboukis, Lex Mercatoria as Applicable Law in International Contractual Obligations, para. 128 (Sakkoulas 1996) [ΧΑΡΑΛΑΜΠΟΣ Π. ΠΑΜΠΟΥΚΗΣ, Η LEX MERCATORIA ΩΣ ΕΦΑΡΜΟΣΤΕΟ ΔΙΚΑΙΟ ΣΤΙΣ ΔΙΕΘΝΕΙΣ ΣΥΜΒΑΤΙΚΕΣ ΕΝΟΧΕΣ, παρ. 128 (ΣΑΚΚΟΥΛΑΣ 1996)].

101 Pamboukis, Lex Mercatoria as Applicable Law in International Contractual Obligations, *supra* note 100.

102 Pamboukis, Lex Mercatoria as Applicable Law in International Contractual Obligations, *supra* note 100, para. 133.

103 Cristiano de Sousa Zanetti, *Filling the Gaps: A Civil Law Tradition*, *in* 18 Legitimacy: Myths, Realities, Challenges 1006, 1011 (Albert Van Jan den Berg ed., ICCA Congress Series, 2015).

of good faith without resulting in a disruption of the contractual allocation of risks.[104] It is well-nurtured in the German law theory that a "doctrine [of good faith] explicitly authorize[s] courts in the name of fairness to revise contractual arrangements or to overturn them altogether"[105] (alteration to original). Although it is contested that arbitral tribunals may overturn parties' agreement altogether, good faith in international arbitration may indeed be employed as a corrective rule in case of changed circumstances.[106] It is explained in the literature that

> good faith can be deemed to provide for a duty to adjust such agreements upon . . . unforeseen events altering the relevant balance. Without such adjustment, it would . . . be impossible to *rebalance* the contract and . . . to *preserve* a profitable relationship and to *allow* the parties to achieve the scope pursued.[107] (emphasis added)

Having said that, insisting on performance or even termination without the contract being adapted would effectively be against good faith and the parties' intentions.[108] Long-term contracts in the construction and oil and gas industry are generally apt to change circumstances. Effectively, an adaptation or even a modification of the contract might be required. The *Quintette arbitration case* is an illustrative example. In 1980, a coal purchase agreement was concluded between Quintette Coal Ltd. and ten Japanese steel manufacturers, which resulted in the opening of a mine.[109] Infrastructure investments had to be made by Quintette, which were going to be mirrored in the coal price.[110] The contract determined a formula for the adjustment of the price on a quarterly basis.[111] The contract provided for an inequity review clause at any time significant changes took place that affected the price, pursuant to which a good faith discussion between the parties would determine the "fair and reasonable adjustment"[112] of the price. Arbitration proceedings were initiated by the Japanese manufacturers in order to readjust the price since the price of other coal in the market was lower, and Quintette was not willing to accede to further price

104 Código Civil [Civil Code], art. 437, para. 1 (Port.).

105 Klaus Peter Berger, *Adaptation of Long-Term Contracts by International Arbitrators in the Face of Severe Economic Disruptions: Three Salient Problems*, 37(5) J. Int'l Arb. 589, 597 n.40 (Maxi Scherer ed., Kluwer Law International 2020) (quoting Charles Fried, Contract as Promise: A Theory of Contractual Obligation 74 (2nd ed., OUP 2015).

106 Zanetti, *supra* note 103, at 1018.

107 Berger, *Adaptation of Long-Term Contracts by International Arbitrators in the Face of Severe Economic Disruptions: Three Salient Problems*, *supra* note 105, at 596 (quoting Pietro Ferrario, The Adaptation of Long-Term Gas Sale Agreements by Arbitrators 165, Wolters Kluwer 2017).

108 Berger, *Adaptation of Long-Term Contracts by International Arbitrators in the Face of Severe Economic Disruptions: Three Salient Problems*, *supra* note 105, at 596–97.

109 Lorfing, *supra* note 77.

110 Norbert Horn et al., Arbitrating Foreign Investment Disputes 432 (Kluwer Law International 2004).

111 Horn et al., *supra* note 110.

112 Horn et al., *supra* note 110, at 433.

decreases.[113] The arbitrators adjusted the price going forward, taking into account the "intention of the parties, the general decrease of coal price and the evolution of circumstances as expected by the tribunal."[114] The British Columbia Court of Appeal upheld the award and affirmed the decision of the tribunal to employ a creative adaptation.[115]

Lately, price review arbitrations are on the rise as a result of the volatility of natural gas as well as Liquefied Natural Gas (LNG) markets that agitate supply agreements of a long-term nature and result in price imbalances but also due to the severe economic consequences of the COVID-19 pandemic affecting demand and causing price decline.[116] Most recently, Russia's unforeseen, atrocious war against Ukraine torpedoed the energy crisis and contributed to the unprecedented inflation in Europe. Under that prism, the arbitrator's power to adjust the original contractual arrangements may be justified on the basis of good faith and, more particularly, on an ensuing standard of commercial reasonableness, which is tied to the nature of the contested transaction, surrounding circumstances and the protection of the legitimate expectations and interests of the parties. That solution is far from stale. Even if there is no adaptation clause and the arbitrators are not explicitly authorized by the parties to proceed to adaptation, it has been argued that adaptation founded on good faith is feasible in gas sale contracts.[117]

A 1975 ICC arbitral award adopted a similar reasoning – albeit indirectly. A French transportation company asserted a price increase despite the agreement with an English enterprise that only price adjustment "related to changes in sea freight tariffs"[118] would be admissible. The arbitrator ruled in favor of the French company on the grounds that

> [b]ehaving unreasonably . . . would have been tantamount to behaving in bad faith, in as much as a strict application of the contract terms – which would initially block the renegotiation of the price based on the French claims – would unjustifiably harm one of the parties.[119]
>
> (citation omitted)

113 Horn et al., *supra* note 110, at 433.

114 Lorfing, *supra* note 77.

115 Stefan Kröll & Thilo Kerkhoff, *Settlement Efforts and Contract Adaptation*, *in* 2 Cambridge Compendium of International Commercial and Investment Arbitration 946 (Stefan Kröll et al. eds., 2023).

116 Hagit Elul et al., Gas Supply and LNG Arbitrations, GAR, Nov. 10, 2020, *available at* https://globalarbitrationreview.com/guide/the-guide-energy-arbitrations/4th-edition/article/gas-supply-and-lng-arbitrations#footnote-041 (last visited Feb. 13, 2023).

117 Stefan Kröll & Thilo Kerkhoff, *Settlement Efforts and Contract Adaptation*, *in* 2 Cambridge Compendium of International Commercial and Investment Arbitration 951 (Stefan Kröll et al. eds., 2023) (citing Ferrario, *supra* note 107, at 165).

118 Santiago Dussan Laverde, A Commentary on the Meaning of Objective Good Faith in the Translex Principles through International Arbitration – A Law & Economics Approach, 13 Rev. Estud. Const. Hermeneut. Teor. Direito No. 2 (2021), at 176, *available at* www.trans-lex.org/131150.

119 Dussan Laverde, *supra* note 118.

Another example is the adjustment of contractual penalties. The way that contractual penalties are calculated in case of breach of contract may entail an excessive amount compared to the actual loss suffered.[120] Provided that the applicable law grants the power to the arbitrator to correct such result, as in the case of the French Civil Code, the arbitrator may do so.[121] Good faith confers upon the arbitrator the latitude to reduce the amount of the penalty clause agreed if that is "'extravagant and unconscionable' in relation to the 'greatest possible loss' that could be anticipated."[122] Despite the criticism that the nebulous content of good faith adds nothing to the requirement of 'imbalance' in assessing whether the enforcement of a penalty clause should be resisted and that its meaning is merely complimentary,[123] reference to good faith may be seen, where appropriate, as a criterion ensuring that the contractual penalty provision should not be disproportional, having regard to the parties' *legitimate interests*.[124]

4.4.4 Proposed Methodology

Upon the establishment of the (1) *procedural authority* of the arbitrator emanating from the *lex arbitri* and/or the (2) *substantive legitimacy* of such adaptation,[125] which derives from the *lex contractus*, the arbitral tribunal may be free to proceed to its adaptation decision. However, in case the substantive law of the contract is common law, the arbitrator will be most reluctant to adapt the contract if unexpected circumstances have a particular effect on the performance of parties' contractual obligations, mainly because the arbitral tribunal's powers under a stiff common law doctrine of frustration are solely reduced to imposing either the continuation of performance or the termination of the contractual obligation.[126] Of course, such an outcome will not exist if parties take the necessary steps to provide otherwise in their contract.

120 *Sciences Po Lecture*, *supra* note 82.

121 *Sciences Po Lecture*, *supra* note 82; see also GCC 2:409, providing the court with the power to reduce the penalty agreed if that is disproportional.

122 Antonias Dimolitsa, *Contractual Remedies: Clauses Pénales and Liquidated Damages Clauses*, *in* Interests, Auxiliary and Alternative Remedies in International Arbitration 13, 16 (Laurent Levy & Filip De Ly eds., ICC Dossiers 2008).

123 See, e.g., Lucinda Miller, *Penalty Clauses in England and France: A Comparative Study*, 53 ICLQ 79, 103 (2004).

124 *Cf.* Council Directive 93/13 of Apr. 5, 1993 on Unfair Terms in Consumer Contracts, 1993 O.J. (L 95) 29, 30 (EC) ("[W]hereas, in making an assessment of good faith, particular regard shall be had to the strength of the bargaining positions of the parties, whether the consumer had an inducement to agree to the term and whether the goods or services were sold or supplied to the special order of the consumer; whereas the requirement of good faith may be satisfied by the seller or supplier where he deals fairly and equitably with the other party whose legitimate interests he has to take into account").

125 Berger, *Adaptation of Long-Term Contracts by International Arbitrators in the Face of Severe Economic Disruptions: Three Salient Problems*, *supra* note 105, at 590.

126 Lorfing, *supra* note 77.

Next, the arbitral tribunal must examine (3) *a set of criteria* that determine the nature, scope and depth of the corrective intervention of good faith. First, the tribunal will ask for the parties' proposals regarding the contract adaptation since these proposals mirror the commercial and reasonable expectations of the parties that arbitrators, as legal experts, may not be familiar with. This way, justice will also be served for the reason that the right to be heard will have been satisfied, too.[127] Second, the nature of the contract will be decisive. For example, some contracts are riskier than others *i.e.*, the distribution agreement *vis-à-vis* an agency agreement.[128] Third, the length of the contract is also critical in terms of commercial and legal risks.[129] Fourth, the market oscillation will also have to be considered especially if a joint venture is at stake and involves parties from more than one jurisdiction.[130] Fifth, the foreseeability requirement should also be considered. In other words, whether – and to what degree – the parties have foreseen and accepted such a risk. Usually, such an inquiry is also related to the rarity of the unexpected event.[131] Sixth, whether the nature of the contract or the applicable law distributes and allocates the incurred losses between the parties.[132] Seventh, whether – and to what degree – the party receiving the performance of the contract may further obtain a benefit from a delayed performance.[133] Eighth, the fact that any good faith adaptation should not produce a more favorable deal for a party than the one originally agreed to.[134]

The last step in the process is that (4) arbitrators should be aware that a good faith adaptation should naturally have its *limits* for the very reason that the doctrine of party freedom implies party accountability.[135] That means the arbitrator cannot rewrite the contract in the name of good faith or in an effort to decide herself for, and instead of, the parties or protect them from their very own decisions.[136]

4.4.5 Analogy

Zanetti observed that analogy as a technique is distinguished from the function of good faith in that good faith may remodel the contractual framework guided by the

127 Berger, *Adaptation of Long-Term Contracts by International Arbitrators in the Face of Severe Economic Disruptions: Three Salient Problems*, *supra* note 105, at 602.
128 Zanetti, *supra* note 103, at 1024.
129 Zanetti, *supra* note 103.
130 Zanetti, *supra* note 103.
131 Zanetti, *supra* note 103.
132 Berger, *Adaptation of Long-Term Contracts by International Arbitrators in the Face of Severe Economic Disruptions: Three Salient Problems*, *supra* note 105, at 601.
133 Berger, *Adaptation of Long-Term Contracts by International Arbitrators in the Face of Severe Economic Disruptions: Three Salient Problems*, *supra* note 105.
134 Berger, *Adaptation of Long-Term Contracts by International Arbitrators in the Face of Severe Economic Disruptions: Three Salient Problems*, *supra* note 105, at 602.
135 Zanetti, *supra* note 103, at 1024.
136 Zanetti, *supra* note 103.

common intention of the parties, whereas analogy "could only provide an approximated answer, based on relations established among third parties."[137] The difference is that the methodology applied in the first case has an *endogenic* nature and is based on the internal contractual will, whereas in the second, it is rather *exogenic* by modeling the contract based on comparable facts.[138] However, the view that "one should only resort to analogy when no answer can be constructed based on good faith"[139] is ill-advised. Assuming *arguendo* that analogy replaces the corrective mechanism of good faith, such a proposition may lead to the circumvention of the limits imposed by party autonomy. Unless the arbitrator is mandated to decide *ex aequo et bono* or as *amiable compositeur*, in which case she enjoys greater freedom, the line between analogy and good faith shall not be blurry.

4.4.6 Limits

The corrective role of good faith should not be regarded as a panacea for the purposes of gap-filling. The reason is that the power of the arbitrator to intervene *always* faces three limits. First, the tribunal should respect and constantly uphold party autonomy. Party autonomy, which is the very foundation of the legitimacy of the corrective power of the tribunal, implies accountability; as such, arbitrators cannot protect parties from their own arrangements.[140] Second, the contractual terms as modified or supplemented by arbitrators, should not transgress the mandatory rules of *lex contractus*[141] or public policy. Third, the task of the arbitrator to adapt the contract does not simply require a legalistic approach. It is rather a dynamic process that involves "more commercial common-sense than legal knowledge"[142] given that parties' expectations are targeted more to commercial reasonableness "than a legally correct outcome."[143] Under this prism, the purpose of the arbitrator *grosso modo* is to debunk distributive justice that implies "broader political, social or economic ends and which often distributes resources to victims by reference to criteria of immediate need"[144] and do corrective justice which "eradicat[es] the ills of the past"[145] by "protect[ing] prior rights and restor[ing] the parties, as best as can be done, to their original normative positions"[146]

137 Zanetti, *supra* note 103, at 1021.
138 Zanetti, *supra* note 103.
139 Zanetti, *supra* note 103.
140 Zanetti, *supra* note 103, at 1024.
141 Klaus Peter Berger, *Power of Arbitrators to Fill Gaps and Revise Contracts to Make Sense*, 17(1) Arb. Int'l 1, 11 (William W. Park ed., OUP 2001).
142 Berger, *Adaptation of Long-Term Contracts by International Arbitrators in the Face of Severe Economic Disruptions: Three Salient Problems*, *supra* note 105, at 591.
143 Berger, *Adaptation of Long-Term Contracts by International Arbitrators in the Face of Severe Economic Disruptions: Three Salient Problems*, *supra* note 105, at 598.
144 Simone Degeling & Kit Barker, *Designing Reparation: Lessons from Private Law*, *in* New Directions for Law in Australia: Essays in Contemporary Law Reform 321, 322–23 (Ron Revy et al. eds., 2017).
145 Degeling & Barker, *supra* note 144, at 323.
146 Degeling & Barker, *supra* note 144.

(alteration to the original). That means that distributive justice compromises the parties' original rights for the sake of social policy, whereas corrective justice regulates the "bilateral relationship of right and duty."[147] In so doing, the requirement for predictability is also adhered to.

4.5 Conclusion

Various exogenous factors contribute to good faith becoming a primary rule of corrective justice. The new era calls for a re-conceptualization of good faith, particularly when adjusting the contract in a manner that is fair and consonant with business common sense is aligned with parties' expectations.[148] Notwithstanding the constellation of divergent concepts changed circumstances, a restrictive good faith could be premised on a homogeneous reading of the requirements and consequences of changed circumstances. Such a notion would safeguard the principle of *pacta sunt servanda* by upholding reasonableness in foreseeing the change of circumstances, necessitating party cooperation and renegotiation of the contract and finally instilling fairness and proportionality in measuring the consequences of such disruptive contingencies. This chapter examined the source of the arbitrator's power to adjust contracts, yet it emphasized that the arbitral freedom is not unrestrained. Instead, it must conform to party autonomy and to the mandatory rules applicable, and aim to restore the disturbed contractual equilibrium to the effect that both predictability and reasonableness under the contract are constantly upheld. Only then can good faith be elevated to a "central yardstick for the 'social control' of business behaviour and of the substantive fairness of any business agreement."[149]

147 Degeling & Barker, *supra* note 144, at 322.
148 Degeling & Barker, *supra* note 144, at 16–17.
149 Berger, *Power of Arbitrators to Fill Gaps and Revise Contracts to Make Sense*, *supra* note 141, at 16 (William W. Park ed., OUP 2001). This idea is not fresh. The arbitrators and parties involved in the process are human beings who are naturally prone to making mistakes. For this reason, arbitrators often resort to the principle of good faith and fair dealing to 'correct' prior actions of the parties and safeguard, when necessary, the integrity of the process. Derek Sharp, *The Arbitrator's Duty of Good Faith*, 66(3) Int'l J. of Arb. Med. & Disp. 226, 229 (Kluwer Law International 2000).

5 Transnational Good Faith

5.1 Legitimacy of Application

The arbitrator, in certain cases, is vested with the power to apply transnational rules instead of national law. Unless the parties have explicitly excluded the application of a-national rules as part of the applicable substantive law, and in the absence of a mandatory national rule otherwise applicable,[1] the tribunal is vested with the power to apply the default transnational rules. It is supported that arbitrators may *also* apply transnational rules, even if not explicitly authorized by the parties to do so.[2] Such a body of law, when governing the merits of the dispute, determines the content of the substantive good faith as a standard of conduct.

Regardless of whether transnational law or *lex mercatoria* forms a distinct legal order,[3] this body of law is interwoven with good faith given that the law applicable to international commercial transactions is grounded on the presumptive "expectations shared by rational business persons acting in good faith with one another."[4] Born advocates that such commercial players acting in good faith presumptively want to have their disputes resolved by an international, neutral and fair *forum*.[5] Pryles advanced that recourse to a substantive solution ingrained in the transnational environment "serves to avoid the uncertainties and unpredictable effects caused by the application of complicated conflict of laws-doctrines and

1 Julian David Mathew Lew, *Is There a "Global Free-standing Body of Substantive Arbitration Law"?, in* 17 International Arbitration: The Coming of a New Age? 53, 56 (Albert Jan Van den Berg ed., ICCA Congress Series, 2013).

2 Yves Derains, *International Commercial Arbitration in Civil Law Countries, in* 4 Arbitration in Settlement of International Commercial Disputes Involving the Far East and Arbitration in Combined Transportation 230, para. 30 (Pieter Sanders ed., ICCA Congress Series, 1989).

3 Derains reports that such transnational rules (or *lex mercatoria*) have been recognized by the Italian Supreme Court as an autonomous legal system. Derains, *supra* note 2; *accord* Emmanuel Gaillard, *Transnational Law: A Legal System or a Method of Decision-Making?*, 17 Arb. Int'l 59, 71 (2001) ("[I]f not a genuine legal order, transnational rules do perform, in actual practice, a function strikingly similar to that of a genuine legal system" in terms of "completeness, structured character, evolving nature or predictability").

4 Gary B. Born, International Commercial Arbitration: commentary and materials 2762 (2nd ed., Kluwer Law International 2001).

5 Born (2nd ed.), *supra* note 4.

DOI: 10.4324/9781003527596-6

of domestic substantive law rules, which are frequently inadequate to solve the manifold legal problems of contemporary international commercial law."[6] A classic example reflective of that legitimacy is UNCITRAL Article 28(3), authorizing the arbitrator to decide in accordance with the terms of the contract *and* the trade usages applicable to the transaction.

5.2 The Establishment of a Transnational Standard

Transnationality does not merely refer to an academic nomenclature. It principally points both to the *sources* and *status* of the free-standing substantive rule of good faith. It is boldly argued that "[g]ood faith was recognized as an incident of the law merchant."[7] It would not be a hyperbole to subscribe to this view, given that good faith is a core element of a number of international instruments that regulate and harmonize with the great virtuosity the international commerce.[8] It only suffices to examine the origin and current application of the substantive rule of good faith in international arbitral practice to recognize that the "maturing of an international legal order based on good faith"[9] is upon us.

5.2.1 Sources

The term *transnational arbitration* itself captures the idea that international commercial arbitration has evolved into a flexible dispute resolution method, surpassing the rigidity of domestic civil proceedings.[10] Two main characteristics comprise the foundation of the architecture of international arbitration: the convergence of laws, arbitration rules and decision-making methods, regardless of national boundaries that still trouble transnational litigation, and the divergence from any prevailing practice in international arbitration, which is still embedded in the party autonomy principle.[11] Bermann eloquently describes that the detachment of international arbitration from the national legal system (referred to as the "de-localization theory")[12] is a question of degree; however, that does not negate the fact that a "free-standing

6 Michael Pryles, *Application of the Lex Mercatoria in International Commercial Arbitration*, 18(2) MEALEY'S INT'L ARB. REP. 2 (2003).
7 James Allsop, *The Authority of the Arbitrator*, 30(4) ARB. INT'L 639, 655 (William W. Park ed., OUP 2014).
8 Allsop, *supra* note 7.
9 Allsop, *supra* note 7, at 659.
10 GEORGE A. BERMANN, INTERNATIONAL ARBITRATION AND PRIVATE INTERNATIONAL LAW, para. 45 (The Hague Academy of International Law, Brill 2017).
11 BERMANN, *supra* note 10, paras. 43–44.
12 BERMANN, *supra* note 10, para. 47. Bermann defends against the over-enthusiasm about a completely denationalized arbitration mode, by explaining that "something is systemically lost when no court can speak with authoritativeness to the question of whether an . . . award reflected" compliance with the notion of fairness and boundaries of arbitrator's mission. BERMANN, *supra* note 10, para. 53. He adds that freeing an arbitral award from the arbitral situs comes with costs; for instance, no court would be authorized to annul the award. BERMANN, *supra* note 10.

body of substantive arbitration law [as] a system of rules that may be directly applicable to international disputes by international tribunals"[13] is required to meet the needs of the modern world of international commerce.

The status of transnational good faith is thereby molded by reference to a plethora of sources inspired by the de-localization theory: (a) international binding instruments, such as the CISG Convention, (b) non-binding international rules, such as the UNIDROIT Principles, (c) model laws and arbitral rules, such as the UNCITRAL Model Law on International Commercial Arbitration and UNCITRAL Arbitration Rules, (d) trade usages,[14] including the ICC INCOTERMS 2020 grouping the material terms on the international sale of goods, (e) universal trade usages and customs,[15] (f) systemized collection of principles, such as the Trans-Lex Principles, (g) general principles of international law[16] and (h) arbitral awards. Irrespective of characterization and whether good faith is embedded in rules reflecting the *lex mercatoria* or whether such rules are labeled as "principles of international law,"[17] "customs and usages of international trade"[18] or "principles common to [state] and international law,"[19] to the extent they concern a commercial relationship, they form the same body of law that informs the content of transnational good faith.

*5.2.2 **Autonomy***

The transnationality of substantive good faith, albeit influenced by domestic law, imports, as Magnus had stressed back in 1998, an international standard defined and formulated by business actors in long-lasting commercial relationships and comparatists, and in case this standard is not yet existent, it is to be formulated

13 Lew, *supra* note 1, at 56.

14 See Miriam Goldby, *Enforceability of 'Spontaneous Law' in England: Some Evidence from Recent Shipping Cases*, *in* The Role of Arbitration in Shipping Law 3.05 (Miriam Goldby & Loukas Mistelis eds., 2016).

15 Their relationship with good faith is grounded on the fact that trade customs are considered to serve parties' commercial expectations. Goldby, *supra* note 14, n.70.

16 General principles of public international law can easily be conflated with transnational rules, although they are not strictly speaking a transnational body of law. It may, however, intersect with the latter. For example, an embargo which, as an act of public international law, has the capacity to affect private international business transactions offers evidence that public international law may govern in a nuanced way such business environment. Julian D. M. Lew et al., *Comparative International Commercial Arbitration* 68, paras. 18–71, 18–73 (Kluwer Law International 2003); *accord* David W. Rivkin, *Enforceability of Arbitral Awards Based on Lex Mercatoria*, 9 Arb. Int'l 67, 67 (1993).

17 Rivkin, *supra* note 16, at 68.

18 Rivkin, *supra* note 16, at 67.

19 Rivkin, *supra* note 16, at 70; *contra* Pierre-Yves Tschanz, *The Contributions of the Aminoil Award to the Law of State Contracts*, 18 Int'l L. 245, 262 (1984) (arguing by relying on the *AMINOIL* award that a blending of national and international law should not be conflated with *lex mercatoria* as "a transnational customary law in the making").

in practice by business circles, courts and arbitrators.[20] In fact, this very transnational standard in the form of contractual good faith governing the formation and execution of international contracts is what inspires *lex mercatoria* and affirms the convergence of municipal laws.[21] Relatedly, as practice has revealed, the transnational standard of good faith (at least as envisioned in UNIDROIT Article 1.7) is discussed in almost 70 arbitral and court cases.[22]

The critical question is whether such a standard is completely autonomous or instead must be determined by reference to a domestic legal system. Lando aptly noticed that courts or tribunals must be aware not to apply the principle of good faith to an international contract in the same fashion as in a domestic context[23] but only if the particular conduct is covered by "internationally recognized principles of honorable conduct."[24] The timeline of the evolution of good faith from a domestic concept to the subject of comparative analysis and finally to a rule imposing a transnational standard in international disputes has paved the way to its inclusion in the Trans-Lex Principles, an open-ended list of principles that reflects the progressive creeping codification of the *new lex mercatoria*.

Having construed the principle broadly, the current text reads, "[p]arties to international business transactions must act in accordance with good faith and fair dealing in international trade. This *standard* applies to the negotiation, formation, performance, and interpretation of international contracts."[25] (emphasis added). It is a dynamic rule, surely part of the *new lex mercatoria*, which is congenital to the arbitral process in the sense that counsel and arbitrators come up with arguments based not on national law idiosyncrasies but on comparative research, having regard to the nature of cross-border transactions.[26] As affirmed in arbitral case law, resorting to international principles has the advantage that they apply independently from the intricacies of domestic legal orders and in a uniform manner since they encapsulate the needs of merchants on the international plane and are tied to the fair and realistic resolution of the dispute.[27]

A landmark decision confirming the tenability of an autonomous standard is *Pabalk v. Norsolor*. The dispute arose under an agency agreement between the French company Norsolor and the Turkish company Pabalk, the termination of

20 Ulrich Magnus, *Remarks on Good Faith: The United Nations Convention on Contracts for the International Sale of Goods and the International Institute for the Unification of Private Law, Principles of International Commercial Contracts*, 10(1) Pace Int'l L. Rev. 89, 91 (1998).

21 ICC Case No. 3131, Rev. d. Arb. 1983, at 531, *available at* www.trans-lex.org/203131.

22 See UNILEX on UNIDROIT Principles of International Commercial Contracts, Selected Cases by Article & Issues, Article 1.7, *available at* www.unilex.info/principles/cases/article/109#article_109.

23 Ole Lando, *CISG and Its Followers: A Proposal to Adopt Some International Principles of Contract Law*, 53 Am. J. Comp. L. 379, 392 (2005).

24 Lando, *supra* note 23 (quoting English Commentary on the UN Convention on the International Sale of Goods (CISG) art. 7 n.18, Peter Schlechtriem ed., 1998).

25 Trans-Lex Principle I.1.1. (a), *available at* www.trans-lex.org/901000.

26 Klaus Peter Berger, The Concept of the "Creeping Codification" of Transnational Commercial Law, *available at* www.trans-lex.org/4.

27 ICC Case No. 8385, Clunet, 1997, at 1066, *available at* www.trans-lex.org/208385.

which urged Pabalk to resort to ICC arbitration for claiming damages and unpaid commissions.[28] Absent an express choice of law, the tribunal applied *lex mercatoria* instead of either French or Turkish law, the application of either of which could result in a completely different outcome for the case.[29] The importance of this decision lies in the fact that the tribunal recognized the international status of good faith as a rule of *lex mercatoria*. The tribunal further reasoned that good faith reflects a "required conduct which can be linked to the general principle of responsibility,"[30] based on which it determined whether the breach of the contract was imputable to the conduct of one of the parties and whether damage was caused.[31] It has been argued that the legacy of the Norsolor decision is "having directly connected liability to a general principle of transnational law,"[32] notably a rule of good faith imposing an autonomous international standard of conduct.

In addition, the *Sapphire* tribunal applied general principles of law. In the absence of parties' choice of law, the tribunal reasoned that "a failure by one party to a synallagmatic contract to perform its obligations in breach of contract releases the other party from its obligations and gives rise to a right to pecuniary compensation in the form of damages."[33] It explained that this general rule is "the inescapable and logical consequence of the principle of good faith, to which the parties intended to submit the performance of their agreement."[34]

As one tribunal decided, "good faith is recognized as part of the *lex mercatoria* and generally applies in international arbitration law, even *independently of the content of the law applicable to the merits of the dispute*"[35] (emphasis added). Whereas earlier in time, the transnational environment was fragmented and "at

28 ICC Case No. 3131 of 1979, 9 Y.B. Comm. Arb. 109–10 (1984) (Pieter Sanders ed., ICCA & Kluwer Law International 1984).

29 Bernardo M. Cremades, *Good Faith in International Arbitration*, 27 Am. U. Int'l L. Rev. 761–62 (2012).

30 ICC Case No. 3131 of 1979, 9 Y.B. Comm. Arb. 109–10 (1984) (Pieter Sanders ed., ICCA & Kluwer Law International 1984).

31 ICC Case No. 3131 of 1979, *supra* note 30.

32 Bernardo M. Cremades, *Good Faith in International Arbitration*, 27 Am. U. Int'l L. Rev. 761, 784 (2012) (quoting Philippe Kahn, Les principes généraux du droit devant les arbitres du commerce international [English translation], 116 J. Droit Int'l 305, 321 (1989)).

33 Sapphire International Petroleums Ltd. v. National Iranian Oil Company, Arbitral Award, Mar. 15, 1963, at 40, *available at* https://jusmundi.com/en/document/decision/pdf/en-sapphire-international-petroleums-ltd-v-national-iranian-oil-company-arbitral-award-friday-15th-march-1963 [hereinafter *Sapphire award*].

34 *Sapphire award*, *supra* note 33, at 41. Pamboukis reports that the binding nature of such transnational sources *i.e.*, *lex mercatoria*, the UNIDROIT Principles, INCOTERMS and others, ultimately derives from party autonomy in case the parties have selected such rules and principles, their persuasive value and appropriateness in commerce. Charis P. Pamboukis, Private International Law [Χαρης Π. Παμπουκης, Ιδιωτικο Διεθνες Δικαιο], paras. 112–14 and 492 (Nomiki Bibliothiki 2020).

35 ICC-FA-2020-005 of 2013, 2 ICC Disp. Res. Bull. 133, 2020, para. 265.

best . . . governed by legal provisions suited to domestic needs,"[36] the content of good faith in modern global disputes may be accorded a self-contained nature as a central feature of cohesion in transborder commerce.

5.2.3 Normative and Corrective Function

The *Norsolor* award explained that "[g]ood faith expresses not only a state of mind, but also 'reference to customs, to an ethical rule of conduct'"[37] (citation omitted). Admittedly, in such a transnational environment, good faith fosters predictability in transnational adjudication by reflecting the merchants' understanding and their ethics and code of conduct.[38] It further achieves greater substantive certainty by creating an "organized substantive framework for initiating principled adjudication which might yield more specific, fact-bound rules in particular cases."[39] Such specific rules include: (a) the duty to notify the other party of anything that can put the smooth performance of the contract at risk,[40] (b) the duty to cooperate[41] and refrain from any conduct that can hinder the performance of the contract even if such duty is against the short-term interests of the obliged party,[42] (c) the duty to renegotiate the contract, especially when changed circumstances necessitate an adaptation of the contract and the continuation of the contract is reasonably expected by the parties[43] and (d) the duty to mitigate damages, which requires that the aggrieved party relying upon a breach of contract should take all reasonable steps to mitigate the loss arising from the breach.[44] Further, (e) the duty to use "best efforts" or "best endeavors" in the performance of the contract, provided that such clause is incorporated in the contract. The latter only refers to "all efforts which can be expected

36 Thomas E. Carbonneau, *A Definition of and Perspective Upon the Lex Mercatoria Debate*, *in* Lex Mercatoria and Arbitration: A Discussion of the New Law Merchant 11, 17 (Juris Pub. rev. ed., 1998).

37 ICC Case No. 3131, *supra* note 28, at 109.

38 Carbonneau, *supra* note 36, at 17.

39 Carbonneau, *supra* note 36, at 18.

40 Trans-Lex Principle No. IV.6.9, *available at* www.trans-lex.org/936000; see also UNIDROIT, art. 1.10; UNIDROIT, art. 7.1.7 (3).

41 See UNIDROIT, art. 5.1.3.

42 Trans-Lex Principle No. IV.6.9, cmt. 2; see also State Joint Stock Holding Company Artem v. Gray Fox Aviation and Logistics, Inc., SCC Case No. V 2019/066, Final Award, Apr. 30, 2020, para. 450, *available at* https://jusmundi.com/en/document/decision/en-state-joint-stock-holding-company-artem-v-gray-fox-aviation-and-logistics-inc-final-award-wednesday-15th-july-2020 ("Claimant's delay did not reflect the level of cooperation to be expected under the standard of good faith").

43 Trans-Lex Principle No. IV.6.7, *available at* www.trans-lex.org/935000. A number of criteria are instrumental in determining whether such a duty is violated, including the making of reasonable suggestions for adjustment instead of vague statements, staying away from unnecessary delays, taking into account prior practice between the contractors, avoiding the creation of *fait accompli* in the negotiation process. See Trans-Lex Principle No. IV.6.7, cmt. [3]. Further, liability could potentially be attached if such a duty to renegotiate is violated. Trans-Lex Principle No. IV.6.7, cmt. [6].

44 Trans-Lex Principle No. VII.4, *available at* www.trans-lex.org/949000; see also UNIDROIT, art. 7.4.8.

from a reasonable party of the same kind in the same circumstances, taking into account the particular nature of the contract and the interests of the parties."[45]

Finally, the transnational rule of good faith informs certain negative standards, including but not limited to: (a) the duty of non-disclosure, pursuant to which it would be contrary to good faith to disclose information obtained in the course of the negotiations or use such information inappropriately,[46] and (b) the duty not to take advantage of one's wrongful conduct.[47]

Transnational good faith may also function as a corrective rule. In case of hardship, a party may urge the court or the tribunal to adapt the contract, or a term of it, in a bid to make it consonant with "reasonable commercial standards of fair dealing."[48] Arbitral case law confirms by resorting to CISG Article 79 and UNIDROIT Art. 6.2.3(4) that in case of unfairness, as a result of the occurrence of changed circumstances, and provided that neither party is willing to terminate the contract, the arbitrator is vested with the power to modify it.[49] Such power to restore the equilibrium may be predicated on good faith. To this effect, a tribunal cited the CISG Advisory Council's Opinion No. 7, explaining that:

> Even if one were not ready to stretch the principle of good faith buried in CISG Article 7(1) . . . CISG Article 79(5) may . . . open up the possibility for a[n] . . . arbitral tribunal to determine what is owed to each other, thus "adapting" the terms of the contract to the changed circumstances.[50]

Like in the case where national law is applicable to the dispute, one should be cautious not to envisage readily the option of adaptation. Potentially, there could be a creeping risk of vacating the award on the grounds of excess of power to the extent that the arbitrator's intrusion incurs re-writing of, and fundamental change to, the

45 Trans-Lex Principle No. IV.6.5, *available at* www.trans-lex.org/932000; see also UNIDROIT, art. 5.1.4.

46 Translex Principle No. IV.6.13, cmt. [1], *available at* www.trans-lex.org/936800.

47 See CISG, art. 80; *accord* SCC Case No. V 2019/066, *supra* note 540, para. 422 ("Article 80 CISG is said to be an example of the good faith principle. In simple terms, a party shall not be able to assert a claim based on non-performance from the other party, if he himself caused the non-performance") (citation omitted).

48 UNIDROIT, art. 3.2.7 (2).

49 National Joint Stock Company Naftogaz of Ukraine v. Public Joint Stock Company Gazprom, SCC Case No. V2014/078/080, Separate Award, May 31, 2017, para. 2926, *available at* https://jusmundi.com/fr/document/decision/en-national-joint-stock-company-naftogaz-of-ukraine-v-public-joint-stock-company-gazprom-separate-award-wednesday-31st-may-2017#decision_11143 ("Therefore, since neither Naftogaz nor Gazprom is seeking to terminate the Contract, the appropriate remedy is to adapt the Contract with a view to restoring its equilibrium").

50 National Joint Stock Company Naftogaz of Ukraine, *supra* note 49, para. 2566. However, the said tribunal hesitated to infer a general adaptation possibility for itself but only the option to "determine what is owed to each other." National Joint Stock Company Naftogaz of Ukraine, *supra* note 49, para. 2568.

parties' contract.[51] In support of the previous, the *AMINOIL* award, which applied transnational law to the merits of the dispute, reasoned that the arbitrators should always remember that their powers are confined and that they cannot substitute themselves in contract-making unless those powers are granted by their parties' consent or the law.[52]

David argued that arbitration is the proper route to adapt the contract where the cost-benefit analysis dictates that the long-term interests and cooperation of the parties are more important to the parties than the strict application of substantive law.[53] Lorfing articulated that even a serious error does not suffice to annul the arbitrator's adaptation decision if they act within their authority, and that reasoning also deterred the court from annulling the award in the *Quintette Coal arbitration* as the contract gave the power to the arbitrator to interpret the will of the parties.[54]

5.3 Critique and Support

5.3.1 Critique

One ICC tribunal held that "applying [the] *lex mercatoria* may present significant challenges given its general character."[55] Commentators highlight that the arbitrators risk facing criticism if they designate the *lex mercatoria* as applicable

51 Berger reports that the aggrieved party may want to challenge the award on the basis of such adaptation decision. Klaus Peter Berger, *Adaptation of Long-Term Contracts by International Arbitrators in the Face of Severe Economic Disruptions: Three Salient Problems*, 37(5) J. Int'l Arb. 591 (2020). See also Axia NetMedia Corporation et al. v. Mass. Tech. Park Corp., 2019 U.S. Dist. LEXIS 88549 at *18 (D. Mass. May 28, 2019) ("[I]n re-writing the contract, the arbitrator fundamentally altered the relationship between the parties to adhere to his own conception of fairness"). However, recent case law demonstrates that the court cannot review the award on the basis of factual or legal errors, especially when the arbitration agreement does not impose any restriction on adaptation; as a result, no excess of power can be justified. Stefan Kröll & Thilo Kerkhoff, *Settlement Efforts and Contract Adaptation*, *in* 2 Cambridge Compendium of International Commercial and Investment Arbitration 953 (Stefan Kröll et al. eds., 2023).

52 The American Independent Oil Company (AMINOIL) v. The Government of the State of Kuwait, Ad Hoc Award, Mar. 24, 1982, para. 74, *available at* https://jusmundi.com/en/document/decision/en-the-american-independent-oil-company-v-the-government-of-the-state-of-kuwait-final-award-wednesday-24th-march-1982.

53 Norbert Horn, *Procedures of Contract Adaptation and Renegotiation in International Commerce*, *in* Adaptation and Renegotiation of Contracts in International Trade and Finance 181 (Norbert Horn ed., 1985), *available at* www.trans-lex.org/130400.

54 Pascale Accaoui Lorfing, *Adaptation of Contracts by Arbitrators Realities and Perspectives*, *in* Hardship and Force Majeure in International Commercial Contracts: Dealing with Unforeseen Events in a Changing World 41 (Fabio Bortolotti & Dorothy Ufot eds., ICC Dossier XVII 2018).

55 ICC Case No. 23221/DDA (C-23222/DDA), Final Award, Mar. 24, 2021, para. 495, *available at* https://jusmundi.com/en/document/decision/pdf/en-mrs-holdings-ltd-v-societe-nationale-doperations-petrolieres-de-la-cote-divoire-petroci-award-thursday-25th-march-2021 (where the tribunal instead applied Panamanian law as the law having the closest connection to the agreement).

law, given that its legitimacy might not be obvious to domestic legal systems.[56] The criticism appears to be justifiable. First, an autonomous standard of good faith predicated on *lex mercatoria* would result in arbitrariness and insecurity among the parties in the sense that arbitrators tend to ascribe to *lex mercatoria* a content that reflects their own legal culture.[57] Even if an autonomous standard of good faith can be admitted by virtue of, for example, the UNIDROIT Principles, there is no evidence of understanding the concept uniformly across common and civil law traditions.[58] Further, the resistance to incorporating such transnational standards into the CISG, as well as the scarcity of arbitral awards applying and adequately explaining its content, render its existence rather disputable.[59]

Second, by applying an autonomous concept of good faith, the arbitrator might be criticized for deciding in equity.[60] The *ad hoc* committee in *Klöckner v. Cameroon* decided that "the Award's reasoning and the legal grounds on this topic . . . seem very much like a simple reference to equity, to 'universal' principles of justice and loyalty, such as amicable compositors."[61] Third, replacing all technical rules with a general rule of good faith is illusory.[62] Indeed, the eagerness of arbitrators to formulate specific rules justifies the insufficiency of *lex mercatoria* as a fully functional body of law with a complete account of detailed rules and further proves that state law is better suited to resolve international disputes.[63]

5.3.2 Support

An aphoristic attitude toward an autonomous good faith standard rooted in *lex mercatoria* should be addressed with skepticism. It is true that arbitrators might be influenced by their legal background; thus, a transnational standard of good faith – if any – is allegedly colored by domestic law biases. Nevertheless, one should not overlook the neutrality of solutions emanating from *lex mercatoria*. Pryles emphasized that such transnational rules "though not necessarily enshrined in any specific national legal system, are specially *adapted to the needs of international transactions like the Contracts and enjoy wide international consensus*."

56 W. Laurence Craig et al., International Chamber Of Commerce Arbitration 337–38 (3rd ed., Oceana TM 2001).

57 Pierre Mayer, Le Principe de Bonne Foi devant les Arbitres du Commerce International, Festschrift Pierre Lalive, Basel, Frankfurt a. M. 1993, at 549, *available at* www.trans-lex.org/115700.

58 Giuditta Cordero Moss, *International Contracts between Common Law and Civil Law: Is Nonstate Law to Be Preferred? The Difficulty of Interpreting Legal Standards Such as Good Faith*, 7(1) (Advances) (Article 3) Glob. Jurist 1, 30 (2007).

59 Moss, *supra* note 58, at 31–32.

60 Mayer, *supra* note 57, at 549.

61 Klöckner Industrie-Anlagen GmbH and others v. United Republic of Cameroon and Société Camerounaise des Engrais, ICSID Case No. ARB/81/2, Decision of the Ad Hoc Committee ¶ 77, Oct. 21, 1983 (Unofficial English Translation).

62 Mayer, *supra* note 57, at 555.

63 Mayer, *supra* note 57.

(emphasis added).[64] An autonomous transnational standard would reveal the convergence among heterogeneous legal traditions. Effectively, the standard's added value is not determined directly but indirectly in the sense that an objectionable conduct aiming to escape certain results under English law is incompatible with the appropriateness of the conduct under civil law.[65] The concretization of the standard effectively "assumes a clear consistency in the results that the various legal systems consider appropriate,"[66] albeit not entirely uniform.

Second, the argument that the application of transnational good faith can overlap with the decision-making power of the arbitrator to act as an amiable compositeur or decide *ex aequo et bono* is flawed.[67] Applying the a-national rule of good faith does not require that the arbitrator acts as an amiable compositeur. Derains explained that *lex mercatoria* "did not imply the exercise of powers of *amiable compositeurs,*"[68] whereas the amiable composition clause in the contract only serves as an *indication* to denationalize solutions, "thus opening the door to the intervention of the *lex mercatoria.*"[69] A leading practitioner supported the claim that a clear distinction exists between *lex mercatoria* and amiable composition since the amiable composition choice does not *per se* signify a choice of the law merchant.[70] It is effectively true that amiable composition choice frees the arbitrator from applying a particular law, while a choice of *lex mercatoria* obliges the arbitrator to apply obviously the *lex mercatoria.*[71] It can be inferred that notions of good faith in the context of decision-making in equity is markedly different from a denationalized standard of good faith predicated on *lex mercatoria*.

Third, all mechanical rules cannot be replaced by good faith since a transnational good faith "will not impose a pre-fabricated set of specific legal duties that need to be observed by the parties."[72] Instead, by acting as an *organizing rule*, it helps "develop the law in a more 'coherent and principled way' than under the

64 Pryles, *supra* note 6, at 24.
65 Moss, *supra* note 58, at 30.
66 Moss, *supra* note 58.
67 There is a difference between these two concepts. Park has eloquently stated: "Arbitrators who decide *ex aequo et bono* might begin and end with a private sense of justice, going directly to a personal view of the right result, while in *amiable composition* the arbitrators would start at rules of law, departing only if needed to achieve a just result." William W. Park, *The Predictability Paradox – Arbitrators and Applicable Law*, *in* The Application of Substantive Law by International Arbitrators 60, 66 (Fabio Bortolotti & Pierre Mayer eds., ICC Dossier XI, 2014); see also ICC Case No. 12772, 18 ICC Bull. No. 1, 112 (2007) ("An arbitrator applying 'ex aequo et bono' enjoys a wider area of authority, limited only by the principles of public policy") (citation omitted).
68 Yves Derains, *Possible Conflict of Laws Rules and the Rules Applicable to the Substance of the Dispute*, *in* 2 UNCITRAL's Project for a Model Law on International Commercial Arbitration, para. 40 (Pieter Sanders ed., ICCA Congress Series, 1984).
69 Derains, *Possible Conflict of Laws Rules and the Rules Applicable to the Substance of the Dispute*, *supra* note 68.
70 Rivkin, *supra* note 16, at 71.
71 Rivkin, *supra* note 16.
72 Klaus Peter Berger & Thomas Arntz, *Good Faith as a 'General Organising Principle' of the Common Law*, 32 Arb. Int. 171, 178 (William W. Park ed., OUP 2016).

traditional piecemeal approach."[73] Good faith reflects the common and cohesive aspiration that international merchants share in commerce.[74] An ICC tribunal held that *lex mercatoria* is the "law that best accords with the needs of the international commercial community, that is not in conflict with the reasonable expectations of the parties, that produces uniformity of results, and that provides for a reasonable solution of the problem."[75] Good faith, as a core rule of *lex mercatoria*, is therefore applied to manifest the parties' legitimate expectations, thus directing to a fair resolution of the dispute by reference to the parties' common and shared perspective of the contract. The source of such legitimate expectations is detected in the customary practices of the industry, which national judges are less likely to be familiar with.[76] Moreover, a general rule of good faith provides the required *flexibility* to refine the intolerable consequences that a rough solution rooted in national law may entail. In that case, the arbitrator may resort to good faith to "circumvent the inequitable consequences of such legal solution."[77] Such conceptualization contributes to the predictable concretization of the rule and prevents it from identifying it with some socio-political or moral principle of no concrete effect.

5.4 A Transnational Good Faith of Lex Metaverse

The emergence of the metaverse[78] elevates online arbitration and cross-border dispute resolution to a new dimension and is particularly intensified by the ongoing investment in technological advancements. The emergence of new models, such as blockchain technology, NFTs and smart contracts that have prompted new types of digital ownership, have propelled the rise of the metaverse as a virtual world of augmented physical reality that transcends borders and involves transactions

73 Berger & Arntz, *supra* note 72 (citing *Bhasin v. Hrynew*, *supra* note 85, para. 64).

74 Carbonneau, *supra* note 36, at 17.

75 Born (2nd ed.), *supra* note 4, at 2645 n.159 (quoting ICC Case No. 8385, in Collection of ICC Arbitral Awards 1996–2000 474, 476, J.-J. Arnaldez, Y. Derains & D. Hascher eds., 2003).

76 Marc Henry, *The Contribution of Arbitral Case Law and National Laws*, *in* Towards a Uniform International Arbitration Law? 39, 48 (Emmanuel Gaillard et al. eds., IAI Series No. 3, 2005).

77 François Dessemontet, *Use of the UNIDROIT Principles to Interpret and Supplement Domestic Law*, *in* Unidroit Principles Of International Commercial Contracts: Reflections On Their Use In International Arbitration 39, 47 (ICC, 2002).

78 'Metaverse' is best described as the evolution of the internet as we now know it. It is a 3D reality that converges physical and virtual worlds, enables people to possess virtual identities to transact and interact, offers an immersive experience provided by "augmented-reality technology" and is the playground of a fully functioning digital economy of digital assets, cryptocurrencies and non-fungible tokens (NFTs). This metaverse reality is here to stay because of (a) large infrastructures in the metaverse environment, a characteristic example of which is Meta's investment of USD 10 billion, (b) existing entertainment platforms, such as *Roblox*, *Decentraland*, Meta's *Horizon Worlds*, *Fortnite*, (c) the success of online commerce and (d) the natural inclination of humans to evolve and innovate. McKinsey Quarterly, Marketing in the Metaverse: An Opportunity for Innovation and Experimentation, May 2022, *available at* www.mckinsey.com/capabilities/growth-marketing-and-sales/our-insights/marketing-in-the-metaverse-an-opportunity-for-innovation-and-experimentation#/ (last visited Apr. 13, 2024).

akin to detachment from state law interference.[79] Facebook CEO Mark Zuckerberg characterized the metaverse as "the next generation of the internet – a more immersive, 3D experience. Its defining quality will be a feeling of presence, like you are right there with another person or in another place."[80]

A concept of a detached, truly a-national law would be potentially fit for resolving such immaterial digital transactions in the metaverse (*lex metaverse*).[81] One argument in favor of the suitability of a *lex metaverse* is the inherent difficulty in the choice of law. How should one be able to determine the applicable national law under traditional private international rules if the place of service provision is imaginary?[82] The decentralization of blockchain arbitration platforms[83] may warrant the appropriateness of the *lex metaverse* as a set of neutral rules governing such disputes or at least orchestrate the harmonization of territorial solutions. In that environment, the automatic enforcement of arbitral awards facilitated by smart contracts "programmed to partially or totally release funds in escrow, or transfer funds between digital wallets"[84] would materialize Lew's concept of an autonomous arbitration mechanism, free from national law idiosyncrasies.[85] Would a conceptualization of good faith of *lex metaverse* like its equivalent of *lex mercatoria* be employed by a metaverse arbitral tribunal applying the *lex metaverse*? A full-fledged notion of good faith in that virtual world is hard to specify. However, it would be useful in formulating the foundation of a standard of trust and cooperation and mitigating the adverse consequences of the anonymity of participants and the rise of fraudulent schemes. In that respect, it would constitute an anchor of expected behavior, transparency and accountability by and towards the participants involved, further weeding the tapestry of fair trade practices.

79 Sneha Vijayan, Autonomous Arbitration in the Era of the Metaverse, Kluwer Arbitration Blog, Mar. 11, 2022, *available at* https://arbitrationblog.kluwerarbitration.com/2022/03/11/autonomous-arbitration-in-the-era-of-the-metaverse/ (last visited Mar. 21, 2024); *accord* Vahid Rezadoost & Pragya Choudhary, Arbitration Tech Toolbox: Applicable Law, Choice of Courts and Enforcement Issues in Metaverse Disputes, Kluwer Arbitration Blog, Sept. 27, 2023, *available at* https://arbitrationblog.kluwerarbitration.com/2023/09/27/arbitration-tech-toolbox-applicable-law-choice-of-courts-and-enforcement-issues-in-metaverse-disputes/ (last visited Mar. 21, 2024) (arguing that the location of such dematerialized metaverse transactions for the purpose of determining the applicable law, absent parties' express choice, cannot be determined pursuant to traditional PIL connecting factors of habitual residence of the defendant or place of performance or closest connection).

80 Guardian, Mark Zuckerberg's metaverse vision is over. Can Apple Save It?, *available at* www.theguardian.com/technology/2023/may/21/mark-zuckerbergs-metaverse-vision-is-over-can-apple-save-it (last visited July 28, 2024).

81 Cécile Pellegrini, Conflict of Laws and the Metaverse, The EAPIL Blog, June 13, 2023, *available at* https://eapil.org/2023/06/13/conflict-of-laws-and-the-metaverse/ (last visited Mar. 25, 2024).

82 Pellegrini, *supra* note 81.

83 Examples include Kleros (https://kleros.io/), Aragon (https://aragon.org/) and Jur (https://jur.io/). See Vijayan, *supra* note 79.

84 Elizabeth Chan & Emily Hay, *Something Borrowed, Something Blue: The Best of Both Worlds in Metaverse-related Disputes*, 15(2) CONTEMP. ASIA ARB. J. 205, 217 (2022).

85 Vijayan, *supra* note 79. Albeit not completely plausible, because enforcement via domestic courts for non-digital compensation would still be relevant. Chan & Hay, *supra* note 84, at 218.

Further, the establishment of a regulatory notion of good faith would perhaps prevent the flaws of a metaverse award *i.e.,* enforcement of a decision against the other party's physical assets in the real world, especially when public policy in the place of enforcement is relevant.[86] Leveraging a regulatory principle of good faith with emphasis on due process and compliance with international public policy may prove to be invaluable in achieving increased harmonization across territorial laws, at least as far as the applicable substantive law in this new universe of disputes is concerned.[87] In fact, transnational instruments such as the CISG and the UNIDROIT Principles have both paved the way for a holistic global law (*droit global*). In that context, the *lex metaverse* would express the new regulatory geometry capable of surpassing the monopoly of the *forum* and the complications resulting from polycentrism.[88]

Even from a private international law perspective, the emergence of good faith of the *lex metaverse* would have a place in the choice of law in that "[a] harmonised PIL framework based on generally acceptable conflict-of-laws principles will thus protect users (and especially ensure weaker party protection), enable innovation, improve good governance, and strengthen the rule of law in the digital economy."[89] A more systematic recourse to the underpinnings of good faith could potentially mitigate the adverse effects of employing traditional connecting factors in an a-national setting, such as habitual residence, characteristic performance or the closest connection to the transaction, principally because these tools may prove to be ineffective in serving the parties' intentions, the nature of the dematerialized transaction and the parties' legitimate and reasonable expectations. Gaillard and Lalive had foreseen long ago the significance of a truly transnational public policy order envisaging the most universally accepted values as a safeguard of predictability and a safety valve against the risk of local mandatory laws overriding the parties' choice of law.[90] Similarly, a unified approach of a good faith standard would seem to guarantee the proper integration of international arbitration in the metaverse epoch.

5.5 Conclusion

It has been shown that the legitimacy of the application of transnational good faith is premised on party autonomy and, more precisely, on parties' joint expectations

86 See Jason Rix & Katrina Limond (A&O Shearman), Real-world Disputes in the Virtual World, *available at* www.aoshearman.com/en/insights/future-disputes-risks/real-world-disputes-in-the-virtual-world (last visited July 28, 2024).

87 R. Garnett, Substance and Procedure in Private International Law, para. 3.31 (OUP 2012).

88 Pamboukis, *supra* note 34, at 23.

89 Gérardine Goh Escolar, *The Role and Prospects of Private International Law Harmonisation in the Area of DLT, in* Blockchain and Private International Law 44 (2023).

90 Emmanuel Gaillard, *2018 LALIVE Lecture: The Myth of Harmony in International Arbitration,* 34(3) ICSID Review – Foreign Investment Law Journal 553, 566–67 (Kinnear & McLachlan eds., OUP 2019).

to have their dispute resolved in a neutral and even-handed way, where fair trade practices make more sense to them than the choice of domestic laws (and ensuing intricacies). Notably, arbitral case law, such as the *Norsolor* and *Sapphire* awards, confirms the elevation of good faith as a transnational rule imposing certain conduct upon the parties, independent of national law. Both the positive and negative standards of such rule are predicated on international instruments and soft law, such as CISG and the UNIDROIT Principles. It is worth mentioning that, despite the criticism, the support of a *lex mercatoria* version of good faith is justified on the basis that it mitigates the intolerable consequences of the strict application of domestic law and crystallizes the uniformity of solutions among otherwise conflicting national laws. Ultimately, it has been argued that a regulatory conception of good faith in the environment of metaverse disputes would concretize rules of expected behavior and increase accountability and transparency of all players, while its common DNA across jurisdictions would alleviate the straining monopoly of the *forum* in the choice of law and the enforcement of the award.

Part II

Interpretive Function of Good Faith

6 The Application of Interpretive Good Faith to the Contract and Arbitration Agreement

6.1 Interpretive Function of Good Faith in General

6.1.1 Interplay with Substantive Good Faith

Even if everyone accedes to a common understanding of good faith, they might fail in making "important distinctions in conduct,"[1] mainly because they might not have the training to "engage in the reflective process that arguably allows for extraction and justification of normative principles from vague phrases,"[2] notably standards deriving from the function of good faith as a rule of conduct. Herein lies the challenge of the normativity of good faith in the arbitrator's task: to determine a good faith standard after a careful exercise of interpretation and balancing. This is not, however, an easy task, as an expansive interpretation may produce different results from a restrictive interpretation. For example, an expansive interpretation may extend the commercial players' responsibilities further than what the parties bargained for or may preclude the actors from benefiting from a market downturn or even avoiding their bad bargains.[3] In that sense, an expansive interpretation minimizes the ability of a buyer to resort to the seller's breach for the purpose of canceling the contract and effectively obfuscates the legal consequences of conduct.[4] On the other hand, an expansive interpretation may prove justifiable when it is used to "prevent the waste inherent in the possibility of rejections for trivial defects."[5] The scope and extent of the substantive good faith largely depends on how elastic or rigid the interpretation may be. The latter would surely be a question of the substantive law of the contract. However, methodological issues may arise each time the substantive rules are detached from a national legal system within which the contract operates, and it befalls the arbitrator with no prior or little

1 Clayton P. Gillete, *Limitations on the Obligation of Good Faith*, 1981 Duke Law J. 619, 645 (1981).
2 Gillete, *supra* note 1, at 645 n.117.
3 Gillete, *supra* note 1, at 652.
4 Gillete, *supra* note 1.
5 Gillete, *supra* note 1, at 653.

DOI: 10.4324/9781003527596-8

experience of the applicable law[6] to determine the purpose and limits of a good faith interpretation.

6.1.2 Methods of Interpretation

Premised on Platonic and Aristotelian teachings, the science of hermeneutics nourished law, and, effectively, two main arguments were developed.[7] The Platonic school advanced the proposition that the purpose of interpretation was the esoteric, subjective will, whereas the Aristotelian school defended "the determination of an objective meaning of declarations"[8] by virtue of linguistics and logic. Both schools of subjective and objective interpretation have been employed over time,[9] with one question not being answered so far: what the relationship of good faith with these two interpretive methods is.

6.1.2.1 Subjective Interpretation

The method of subjective interpretation is targeted at revealing the parties' intentions; thus, it is a question of fact.[10] This was endorsed in the *ICC Case No. 9187/1999*, which held that CISG Article 8(1) establishes the subjective intent of a party's statement or conduct that was already known to the other party or of which the latter could not have been uninformed.[11] However, arbitrators have a contract in front of them that has to be understood in a rational way, literally.[12] As a result, before applying a subjective interpretation, what is first required is a 'naked' interpretation, which means that the pure wording of the contract precedes any interpretation method.[13]

Three are the more representative legal systems that embrace subjective interpretation. *Swiss law*, under which contract interpretation is guided by Articles 1 and 18 of the Swiss Code of Obligations (*Obligationenrecht*) and Section 2 Article 1 of the ZGB, provides that a commercial arbitrator should first discover the

6 Jonas Rosengren, *Contract Interpretation in International Arbitration*, 30(1) J. Int'l Arb. 1, 1 (Kluwer Law International 2013).
7 Ahmet Cemil Yildirim, Interpretation of Contracts in Comparative and Uniform Law 1, 3 (Kluwer Law International 2019).
8 Yildirim, *supra* note 7.
9 Yildirim, *supra* note 7.
10 Yildirim, *supra* note 7, at 131.
11 ICC Case No. 9187 of 1999, *available at* www.unilex.info/cisg/case/466. CISG art. 8(1) reads: "For the purposes of this Convention statements made by and other conduct of a party are to be interpreted according to her intent where the other party knew or could not have been unaware what that intent was."
12 Yildirim, *supra* note 7, at 126–27.
13 Yildirim, *supra* note 7. Technically, the proposition that the wording as such triumphs over any interpretation is misplaced, since it depends *a priori* on whether the arbitrator has determined that there is room for interpretation or whether the wording is so clear that any interpretation is otiose. That determination, in turn, depends on the applicable law and the arbitrator's training and thinking process.

parties' intentions, as envisaged in their contractual stipulations, the so-called "natural consensus."[14] *French law* has adopted the same approach, which is established on the parties' intentions, as a result of the great impact of liberalism on French literature and the direct effect of the freedom of contract (*liberté contractuelle).*[15] Indeed, the culmination of subjective interpretation in French law is portrayed in the revised Article 1188 (former Article 1156) of the French Civil Code: "A contract is to be interpreted according to the common intention of the parties rather than stopping at the literal meaning of its terms."[16] *Italian law* has similarly adopted a stance in favor of subjective interpretation, even though progress has been made toward striking a balance between subjective and objective approaches.[17] The rationale behind the prevalence of subjective interpretation is that interpretation should be guided by the "common intent of the parties,"[18] according to Article 1362 of the Italian Civil Code.

6.1.2.2 Insufficiency of and Limits to Subjective Interpretation

Within the perimeter of subjective interpretation, the rule holds that the ascertainment of the parties' common intent should not require the application of good faith. In essence, it can degenerate the original intent by employing a benchmark far off from the contract. Nonetheless, there is evidence that the subjective interpretation may not be pragmatic or workable. For instance, it is possible that there is a discrepancy between the parties' expressed intent and their subsequent conduct. In such case, pursuant to the principle *protestatio facto contraria non valet*, which is a natural consequence of the principle of good faith, the latter conduct should be considered.[19] In addition, it is the very principle of good faith that propels the

14 ICC Case No. 8240 of 1995, 10 ICC Bull. No. 2, 60 (1999).

15 Yildirim, *supra* note 7, at 27.

16 J. Cartwright et al., The Law of Contract, the General Regime of Obligations, and Proof of Obligations: The New Provisions of the *Code Civil* Created by *Ordonnance* No. 2016–131 of Feb. 10, 2016 and including revisions made to the text by *Loi* No. 2018–287 of Apr. 20, 2018, translation commissioned by the *Direction des affaires civiles et du sceau, Ministère de la Justice, République française, available at* www.textes.justice.gouv.fr/art_pix/THE-LAW-OF-CONTRACT-2-5-16.pdf. However, a limit to subjective interpretation is imposed by the principle *in claris non fit interpretatio*, which is also embedded in the revised art. 1192 of the French Civil Code reading that "[c] lear and unambiguous terms are not subject to interpretation as doing so risks their distortion." The same approach is followed in arbitral practice. Arbitrators denied relying upon extrinsic evidence, because the contract was clear. Joshua Karton, *The Arbitral Role in Contractual Interpretation*, 6(1) J. Int. Disput. Settl. 4, 11 (Thomas Schultz ed., OUP 2015); *contra* Lévy and Robert-Tissot, pursuant to whom, the clear wording is not decisive for the arbitrator, as the latter can take into consideration complementary interpretation means, such as the entire contract (systemic interpretation) or external and historical components. Laurent Lévy & Fabrice Robert-Tissot, *L'interprétation arbitrale*, 2013(4) Rev. Arb. 861, 896 (Comité Français de l'Arbitrage 2013).

17 Yildirim, *supra* note 7, at 42.

18 Yildirim, *supra* note 7, at 44.

19 Yildirim, *supra* note 7, at 72. Even if recourse to subsequent conduct is resisted in common law, Lord Denning recognized that recourse to subsequent conduct may be useful in understanding how

manifestation of the true intention of the parties, especially when a wrong term used does not reflect the parties' common intention (*falsa demonstratio non nocet*).[20] Further, the process of discovering the subjective will must not be unrestrained. That would be the case of an ambiguous contractual term. The less the parties have negotiated its incorporation into the contract, the more it is justified to interpret the term against the draftsman (*contra proferentem doctrine*).[21] This derives from the rationale that the drafting party should bear the risk of a possible unclarity[22] and effectively from the principle of good faith. It is clear, therefore, that there is some scope for involvement of good faith in aid of manifesting the true will of the parties.

6.1.2.3 Objective Interpretation

There are many reasons why the interpretive function of good faith has a more objective foundation. An ICSID award explained that any convention, including an agreement to arbitrate, shall be construed in good faith, that is to take into consideration "the consequences of the commitments the parties may be considered as having reasonably and legitimately envisaged."[23] *ICC Case No. 13585* affirmed the rule of reasonableness as a main interpretation rule that is internationally accepted, explaining that the parties to a contract want to achieve "reasonable aims,"[24] in other words, to "behav[e] rationally and striv[e] for the conclusion of contracts with which they can achieve their common purpose"[25] (alteration to the original).

English law reflects the objective theory. The aim of an objective interpretation is not what the parties understood or what they meant, that is, their real intention, but "what a reasonable third person in the same position with the parties would

---

the parties acted upon the contract or in clarifying the contract by giving rise to additional obligations. See Amalgamated Investment & Property Co. Ltd. v. Texas Commerce International Bank Ltd [1982] QB 84, 119.

20 See Translex Principle No. IV.5.5, *available at* www.trans-lex.org/928000 ("In case the parties have used the wrong term but mean the same thing, their common intention prevails ('*falsa demonstratio non nocet*')").

21 UNIDROIT Principles, art. 4.6 ("If contract terms supplied by one party are unclear, an interpretation against that party is preferred"); see also Translex Principle No. IV.5.4, *available at* www.trans-lex.org/926000 ("Where, after the interpretation of a contract term that has been supplied by one party, doubts remain as to the meaning of that term, an interpretation against that party is to be preferred ('*contra proferentem*')").

22 See UNIDROIT Principles, art 4.6, cmt.; see also UNIDROIT, art. 1.7 cmt. [1].

23 Ceskoslovenska Obchodní Banka, AS v. The Slovak Republic, ICSID Case No. ARB/97/4, Decision of the Tribunal on Objections to Jurisdiction ¶ 34, May 24, 1999.

24 ICC Case No. 13585, Partial Award on Jurisdiction, Aug. 31, 2005 [Enforcement of the award was sought and challenged in Germany. The German Supreme Court rendered a decision confirming that the Arbitral Tribunal had properly construed the arbitration agreement. See BGH III ZR 214/05 of Jan. 12, 2006, ASA BULL. 1/2013, p. 61.

25 ICC Case No. 13585, *supra* note 24.

have understood from the statements and conduct of the parties."[26] Emphasis is paid to the literal meaning of the contract because, as Lewison explains, the contracts "are written to be read by a third person in situations not predicted by the parties,"[27] thus there can be no intent that is independent of their literal meaning.[28] *German law* espouses a very similar position. First, the process of interpretation focuses on the true intent of the parties imprinted on their declaration pursuant to BGB Section 133. Then, the principle of good faith and fair dealing is utilized to ascertain what the addressee should have understood according to BGB Section 157 while examining all circumstances of the case.[29] The rationale is that the parties are *responsible* for the content of their declarations and how the recipient perceives them.[30]

6.1.3 The Objective Element of Good Faith Interpretation

The ascertainment of parties' intentions may not be feasible or the meeting of minds may not always be achieved. In such cases, it cannot be presumed that the contract does not exist. By resorting to the principle of good faith, and specifically to the principle of trust (*Vertrauensprinzip*), the arbitrator examines whether a party "requesting the interpretation of the contract is relying in good faith on the argument that a contract was validly formed"[31] so that a *normative consensus* can be established.[32] The principle of good faith is employed as an objective element of interpretation in case it is not possible to ascertain the parties' meeting of minds through subjective interpretation. In addition, even if the parties' intentions differ, their declarations should be construed in line with the principle of confidence (*confiance*), pursuant to which the arbitrator shall interpret the conduct and declarations of the party as they should have been understood in good faith by considering all surrounding circumstances.[33]

The consequence of a good faith interpretation is twofold. First, the objective meaning of the conduct or declaration of the party binds it even if it conflicts with an ostensible intent and second, the parties' consent generally depends on the *reasonable assumption* of the addressee that the other party had the intention to agree either to the arbitration agreement or the contract.[34] The *ICC Case No. 7929* adopted this approach. It highlighted that interpretation should be in line with good

26 Yildirim, *supra* note 7, at 99.
27 Yildirim, *supra* note 7.
28 Yildirim, *supra* note 7 (citing Kim Lewison, The Interpretation of Contracts, 191 et seq. (4th ed., Sweet & Maxwell 2007).
29 Yildirim, *supra* note 7, at 64.
30 Yildirim, *supra* note 7.
31 Yildirim, *supra* note 7, at 72.
32 Yildirim, *supra* note 7.
33 Daniel Girsberger & Nathalie Voser, International Arbitration: Comparative and Swiss Perspectives, para. 376 (3rd ed., Kluwer Law International 2016).
34 Girsberger & Voser, *supra* note 33.

faith and *confiance*, which means that "declarations of intent should produce the effect that the parties could or should have expected from them in the light of the circumstances surrounding their relationship."[35] The instrumentality of good faith interpretation is that, in case the natural consensus of the parties cannot be found, a normative or implied consensus should be constructed. At this point, the arbitrator will "discern what reasonable parties acting in good faith must have expressed as their common intentions at the moment of conclusion of the contract."[36] To achieve that end, the arbitrator will have to take into consideration the prior and later conduct of the parties, the contractual purpose and the backdrop of previously concluded contracts.[37]

Hence, the principle of good faith serves as the substratum of reasonableness in case the language is unclear and the intent of the parties cannot be revealed. Even more, good faith imports a rational standard of interpretation, pursuant to which the "reasonable expectations and purpose of the ordinary business person"[38] should be relied on to construe the intent of the parties, as a recent ICDR award suggests. Domestic courts dealing with the interpretation of arbitration agreements have used the principle of good faith in the same fashion as international tribunals. The Federal Supreme Court of Switzerland confirmed, according to the *principle of reliance*, that the "presumptive intention of the parties must be ascertained according to what the party receiving the statement could and should understand in good faith" (citation omitted)[39] in case there was no "concurring intention"[40] between the parties as to the meaning of the arbitration agreement. However, one should be very cautious not to conflate the interpretive mission of an international arbitral tribunal with the mission of a domestic court, mainly because of their various dissimilarities.

6.2 National Court Litigation vs International Arbitration

Provided that the scope of this section does not allow for an exhaustive comparison between a national court's mission and an arbitral tribunal's mission, it is advisable to reflect on why the application of the interpretative principle of good faith by an arbitral tribunal may produce different results from its corresponding application by a national court.

35 ICC Case No. 7929 of 1995, 25 Y.B. Comm. Arb. 11, [23] (A. J. Van den Berg ed., 2000). Indeed, a plethora of arbitral awards confirm this approach. See, e.g., ICC Case No. ICC-FA-2020-227, 45 Y.B. Comm. Arb. 1, [113] (Stephan W. Schill ed., 2020) (highlighting that the applicable Dutch law, like Swedish law, does not regard the "inner will" of the parties decisive but pursuant to BW art. 3:35, the "reasonable understanding of the other party" is the decisive criterion.)

36 ICC Case No. 8240 of 1995, 10 ICC Bull. No. 2, 60 (1999).

37 ICC Case No. 8240 of 1995, *supra* note 36.

38 Rohm And Haas Company v. Arkema France (Final Award), ICDR Case No. 50 154 T00532 10, Oct. 9, 2012, para. 44 (Arbitrator Intelligence Materials, Kluwer Law International).

39 Schweizerisches Bundesgericht [BGer] [Federal Supreme Court of Switzerland] 4A_244/2012, 1st Civil Law Chamber, Jan. 17, 2013, para. 4.2 (Georg von Segesser, A Contribution by the ITA Board of Reporters) (Switz.).

40 Schweizerisches Bundesgericht [BGer], *supra* note 39.

6.2.1 Diversity and Flexibility

It is highly common that an arbitral tribunal will be constituted of arbitrators of both civil and common law traditions. A common law jurist will likely be hesitant to go beyond a black letter interpretation even if the merits of the case necessitate otherwise.[41] On the other hand, a civil law jurist would be less hesitant to imply a term into the contract by virtue of a good faith interpretation. It would be a mistake to infer that such a mixed tribunal is more prone to an unrestrained interpretation. Rather, what this diversity suggests is that the mission of such a mixed tribunal draws upon common established principles and conceptions of good faith, which equip its diverse members with the agility "to make an award that reflects the merits, whilst giving the contract and the applicable law appropriate recognition."[42] The reasoning of a diverse arbitral tribunal might tend to be more holistic and effectively more balanced. At the same time, the reasoning of an arbitral decision-maker appears to be more flexible. According to a prominent practitioner, a French arbitrator, in case an interpretation in accordance with English law dictates a solution quite different from what they perceive as reasonable, will strive to "neutralise its effects"[43] and arguably will not feel bound by the strictness of the applicable rules.[44] This is precisely the case of giving more significance to the surrounding circumstances of the contract than what an English judge applying English law would typically do.[45] The only restriction imposed by modern statutes is that the arbitrator's interpretation should not be contrary to public policy.[46]

Further evidence of such flexibility is offered by the UNIDROIT Principles, which – albeit not a binding instrument – can be utilized by arbitrators as the law governing the dispute. They can also be used as a tool to interpret or supplement the chosen national law and the contract. Ultimately, the UNIDROIT Principles bolster the legitimacy of the adjudicator's reasoning in that they convince the parties that the solution suggested by the applicable national law is internationally accepted; thus such a solution can be considered just.[47] Given that the UNIDROIT Principles reflect the dominant standards of international trade, they harmonize party expectations with legal results. As such, they reflect pragmatism. Contrariwise, a

41 Jennie Wild, *Duties of Good Faith – The Challenge of a Mixed Civil and Common Law Tribunal*, *in* 40 under 40 International Arbitration 63, 72 (2018) (Carlos González-Bueno ed., Dykinson S.L. 2018).

42 Wild, *supra* note 41.

43 Pierre Mayer, *Reflections on the International Arbitrator's Duty to Apply the Law*, *in* 16 Arbitration Insights: Twenty Years of the Annual Lecture of the School of International Arbitration, Sponsored by Freshfields Bruckhaus Deringer, para. 15.16 (Julian David Mathew Lew & Loukas A. Mistelis eds., Kluwer Law International 2007).

44 Mayer, *supra* note 43.

45 Mayer, *supra* note 43.

46 Mayer, *supra* note 43, para. 15.12.

47 Andrea Carlevaris, *The Use of the UNIDROIT Principles and Other Transnational Principles of Commercial Law in Treaty Arbitration: Hazards and Opportunities*, 36(3) ICSID Review/filj. 592–616 (Kinnear & McLachlan eds., OUP 2021).

national court will be dissuaded from applying such flexible principles – among which good faith – since Rome I Regulation will normally repel the application of the UNIDROIT Principles as the governing law. If such principles are explicitly selected by the parties, these principles will normally be understood as mere provisos incorporated into the contract.[48] Absent the parties' choice, the national judge will only apply them to the extent they are compatible with the domestic law that the conflict-of-law rules will designate.[49]

6.2.2 Greater Freedom

One of the main advantages of arbitration over litigation is the relatively higher degree of freedom both for arbitrators and the parties. Arbitrators are free to consider a broader range of evidence, make any inquiries they deem suitable and craft solutions more tailor-made to the interests of the parties and the circumstances of the dispute.[50] They also enjoy ample discretion in deciding how strict the applicable evidentiary rules will be.[51] In addition, the parties can select arbitrators and experts who are well-educated in the specific industry. Admittedly, there is more freedom in arbitration to "exercise a measure of control over the proceedings and . . . determine both what is interpreted and who interprets it."[52] That freedom should be juxtaposed with the duty of a state judge as a state organ to uphold the law as is.[53] In contrast, the arbitrator is, in principle, bound by the wishes of the parties.[54]

6.2.3 Absence of Lex Fori

The difference from national court litigation is that the arbitrator is not bound by any *lex fori*. In particular, "the arbitrator does not belong to a national legal order."[55] By virtue of this disengagement from a national legal order, the arbitrator is more naturally familiar with comparative law principles, the recourse to which may prove to be practical in case a strict application of the substantive law does

48 Willem Calkoen, Perspectives in Practice of the UNIDROIT Principles 2016: Views of the IBA Working Group on the practice of the UNIDROIT Principles 2016, 21, 73, 80, 82, 97 (International Bar Association 2019).

49 Michael Joachim Bonell, *The UNIDROIT Principles as a Means of Interpreting and Supplementing International Uniform Law, in* Special Supplement 2002: UNIDROIT Principles of International Commercial Contracts: Reflections on their Use in International Arbitration 29, 32 (2002).

50 Catherine Mitchell, Interpretation of Contracts 162 (2nd ed., Taylor & Francis 2018).

51 Mitchell, *supra* note 50.

52 Mitchell, *supra* note 50.

53 Mayer, *supra* note 43, paras. 15–18.

54 Mayer, *supra* note 43, at 15–21.

55 Marc Henry, *The Contribution of Arbitral Case Law and National Laws, in* Towards a Uniform International Arbitration Law? 39, 59 (Emmanuel Gaillard et al. eds., IAI Series No. 3, 2005).

not offer a clear solution to the dispute.[56] Further, in case the law to be applied cannot be ascertained, the national judge will have a fallback option to resort to their *lex fori* to ascertain it and find the corresponding solution to the dispute.[57] On the contrary, an arbitrator is vested with absolute freedom to decide the applicable conflict-of-laws rules or determine directly which law or even which rules of law – including the *lex mercatoria* – apply in case of absence of choice of law.[58] An interpretive outcome anchored in the previous assumption should have its limits. The arbitral tribunal should not take the parties by surprise by construing a contract in such a way that the legal reasoning of the decision is remote from the submissions that the parties put forward.[59]

6.2.4 Lack of Coercive Powers

The prevailing axiom is that an arbitrator is deprived of coercive powers. For example, they cannot order an anti-suit injunction without the effective assistance of the supervisory court in the *arbitral situs*.[60] Contrary to the *imperium* reserved for a national judge as a public officer, the arbitrator is not authorized to impose sanctions of a public law nature.[61] However, the imposition of sanctions of a private law nature *i.e.,* monetary penalties, is justified even if the arbitration agreement or the arbitration rules are silent, as the ultimate goal of the arbitrator should be to deter any improper conduct affecting the swift and effective resolution of the dispute.[62] Indeed, the arbitrator's inherent power to levy such sanctions is premised on the parties' own voluntary assent to good faith arbitration, which could never have been achieved had it not been for the parties' own legitimate expectations to resolve their dispute fairly, effectively and swiftly. As such, the enforceability of the principle of good faith in international arbitration should rather be established on its persuasive value to incentivize parties and arbitrators to cooperate with each other during the arbitral process and urge the parties to comply with procedural orders, arbitration rules and decisions.[63] It is thus the consensual and persuasive

56 See generally Yves Derains, *Foreword* to 11 The Application of Substantive Law by International Arbitrators 6 (Fabio Bortolotti & Pierre Mayer eds., ICC Dossiers, 2014).

57 Derains, *supra* note 56.

58 Mayer, *supra* note 43, paras. 15–22.

59 Matthias Scherer, *The Recognition of Transnational Substantive Rules by Courts in Arbitral Matters, in* Towards a Uniform International Arbitration Law? 91, 100–2 (Emmanuel Gaillard et al. eds., IAI Series No. 3, 2005) (discussing the Swiss Fed. Trib., Sept. 30, 2003, 4P.100/2003/ech, 2004 ASA Bull. 574).

60 Faidon Varesis, Private International Law and Arbitral Jurisdiction 204 (Routledge 2023).

61 Varesis, *supra* note 60, at 206.

62 Varesis, *supra* note 60, at 207 (citing Reliastar Life Insurance v. EMC National Life Co, 564 F3d 81, 2d Cir. 2009).

63 Gary B. Born, International Commercial Arbitration) §8.02[B] (3rd ed., Kluwer Law International 2021).

value of good faith in arbitration that should be contrasted with the heteronomous application of it in court litigation.

6.3 Interpretive Function of Good Faith When National Law is Applicable

6.3.1 Source and Scope of Interpretive Good Faith

The national law applicable either to the contract or the arbitration agreement will typically govern issues of contract interpretation. National law would initially be the source of any rule of interpretation. It is, though, accepted *lato sensu* that substantial flexibility is reserved for arbitrators in their interpretative task by virtue of their entitlement to diverge their position concerning the meaning of the words reasonably.[64] Such divergence originally derives from the international status of the arbitrator and their comparative outlook. The scope of the interpretive principle of good faith is inexorably related to: (a) the determination of the meaning of the words, such as whether to deviate from the ordinary meaning of the words or narrowly construe general words and (b) the determination of a number of other issues, such as identifying the parties to the agreement, implying a term into the contract or whether termination of the contract or suspension of performance are validly made.[65] Essentially, the special role of good faith is to assist the arbitrator in answering the previous questions by balancing two conflicting objectives: the one is certainty dictating that full weight must be given to a literal construction of contractual terms which "maximize[s] the commercial certainty that the words permit,"[66] and the other is fairness.[67] The first gives priority to the text, whereas the second to the context. Balancing certainty and fairness will not always produce the same result, as the scope of the interpretive good faith depends on its source *i.e.*, the domestic law applicable to the contract. Depending on whether civil or common law is applicable, the scope and extent of interpretive good faith may significantly vary.

6.3.2 Concretizations of Interpretive Good Faith

It has been emphatically stated heretofore that good faith acts both as a principle and a rule. The analysis of the following expressions of the interpretive good faith is more consistent with the understanding of good faith as a general principle. The reason is that good faith guides and informs the arbitrator's decision-making. Such

64 James Jacob Spigelman, *The Centrality of Contractual Interpretation: A Comparative Perspective (Seventh Kaplan Lecture, Nov. 27, 2013)*, *in* International Arbitration: Issues, Perspectives and Practice: Liber Amicorum Neil Kaplan 176–77 (Hong Kong International Arbitration Centre ed., 2018).

65 Spigelman, *supra* note 64, at 176.

66 Spigelman, *supra* note 64, at 177.

67 Spigelman, *supra* note 64.

concretizations are (a) the prevalence of the true intent over literal meaning, (b) the contract efficacy and the *favor validitatis* principle, (c) the *contra proferentem* doctrine, (d) contractual systemicity and (e) the theory of confidence.

6.3.2.1 *Prevalence of True Intent over Literal Meaning*

The perception that the genuine intentions of the parties shall triumph over the grammatical meaning of their contractual undertakings lies in the significance of deterring a bad faith interpretation. A bad faith interpretation manifests when the contractual interpretation that a party adopts at the time of the dispute does not reflect the genuine intentions of the parties when signing the contract.[68] A series of awards support the supremacy of an interpretation that reveals the parties' true intent. *ICC Case No. 1434* held that the interpretation of the limitation of liability clause under French law should begin with a grammatical examination of the words used with an ultimate view to discovering the parties' real common intentions by considering the context of the words and the contract as a whole.[69] The tribunal in *ICC Case No. 13355* reasoned that its interpretive task under Brazilian law should be guided "by the general rule that the true intent of the parties at the time of signature should prevail over the literal meaning of the language; bearing in mind the principle of good faith . . ."[70] The recent award in *Copri & Aktor v. Albanian Road Authority* confirmed that the contractual wording is not *per se* conclusive.[71] What is decisive is that, under the applicable Albanian law, the literal interpretation should be given less weight than "the real and joint intention of the parties [which] must be assessed . . . in light of their conduct in general, prior to and following the conclusion of the contract."[72]

6.3.2.2 *Contract Efficacy and* Favor Validitatis

Another application is embedded in the *effet utile* interpretation pursuant to which, when the contract is inflicted with a defect, the arbitrator, guided by good faith, will usually render the contract effective. As the tribunal in *Petroci v. MRS Holdings* emphasized, good faith is decisive in interpreting arbitration agreements that refer to non-existing arbitral institutions, dictating that "under the principle of good faith a party should not be permitted to escape its obligations to arbitrate merely because

68 Emmanuel Gaillard & John Savage, Fouchard Gaillard Goldman on International Commercial Arbitration 1470 (Kluwer Law International 1999).
69 Gaillard & Savage, *supra* note 68.
70 ICC Case No. 13355, 23 ICC Bull. No. 1, 69, 2012, para. 97.
71 ICC Case No. 23988/MHM/HBH (c-24011/MHM/HBH), Final Award, Sept. 1, 2020, para. 233, *available at* https://jusmundi.com/en/document/decision/en-1-the-joint-venture-jv-copri-construction-enterprises-w-l-l-aktor-technical-societe-anonyme-2-copri-construction-enterprises-w-l-l-3-aktor-s-a-v-albanian-road-authority-under-the-authority-of-the-ministry-of-public-works-and-transport-final-award-tuesday-1st-september-2020.
72 ICC Case No. 23988/MHM/HBH, *supra* note 71.

a clause is poorly drafted."[73] Indeed, a derivative principle of good faith, which is used in the context of contextual interpretation, is the principle of *effectiveness*.[74] The principle ensures that the text of the contract is ascribed by its drafters a special weight. Pursuant to *ICC Case No. 1434*, if two interpretations conflict with each other, the arbitrator should give precedence to the one that renders the wording effective and not absurd or futile.[75]

Further, the *ad favorem arbitri* principle (deriving from the *favor validitatis* principle) equally reflects the interpretive good faith in the sense that the parties legitimately expect that an arbitration agreement must be valid. The Chinese Arbitration Association's interim award in *Clientron v. Devon* clarified that even if the defects of the arbitration agreement are such that the arbitral body it refers to does not exist or its name is inconsistent, the existence and validity of the arbitration agreement is not affected as a matter of good faith interpretation.[76] A pro-arbitration interpretation deters the multiplication of proceedings (thereby inconsistent decisions) and is based on the presumptive intentions of the parties to resolve their dispute in a centralized single *forum*.[77]

6.3.2.3 Contra Proferentem Doctrine

The *contra proferentem* doctrine expresses one of the core applications of the interpretive good faith. The ICC Award in *Gephar v. Danstar Ferment* explained that an unclear contractual provision will be interpreted against the party that initially drafted it, yet it underscored that its application is questionable in carefully negotiated contractual terms between arms-length parties, who are usually assisted by legal and other experts during the negotiation and drafting phase.[78]

73 ICC Case No. 23221/DDA (C-23222/DDA), Partial Award on Jurisdiction, Feb. 12, 2019, para. 199, *available at* https://jusmundi.com/fr/document/decision/en-societe-nationale-doperations-petrolieres-de-la-cote-divoire-petroci-v-mrs-holdings-ltd-partial-award-on-jurisdiction-tuesday-12th-november-2019.

74 Nobumichi Teramura, Ex Aequo et Bono as a Response to the 'Over-Judicialisation' of International Commercial Arbitration 96 n.154 (Kluwer Law International 2020) ("The principle of good faith contract interpretation (in other words, contextual contractual interpretation) may lead to other principles, such as the principles of effectiveness").

75 ICC Case No. 1434 of 1975, Clunet 1976, at 982, *available at* www.trans-lex.org/201434.

76 Clientron Co., Ltd. v. Devon IT, Inc., CAA Case No. 101-Zhong-Sheng-He-Zi-061, Interim Arbitral Award, Mar. 20, 2013, at [7], *available at* https://jusmundi.com/en/document/decision/en-clientron-co-ltd-v-devon-it-inc-interim-arbitral-award-wednesday-20th-march-2013.

77 Gary B. Born, International Commercial Arbitration: commentary and materials 1320–21 (2nd ed., Kluwer Law International 2001). A pro-arbitration mentality is also bolstered by the function of good faith and *estoppel* to compel arbitration and uphold the validity of the arbitration agreement in situations where the consent of both parties was clear, yet a formal requirement went missing (*i.e.*, signature), as illustrated by the practice of the Swiss Federal Tribunal in *Compagnie de Navigation et Transport v. MSC*. Andrea Marco Steingruber, Consent in International Arbitration, para. 6.48 (OUP 2012).

78 ICC Case No. 19890/EMT, Aug. 5, 2015, para. 218 (Arbitrator Intelligence Materials, Kluwer Law International).

Whereas this observation is justified, it ignores that in many cases, even at the level of highly sophisticated contracting parties, ambiguities and imbalances may occur. Interpreting the contract in good faith would reveal not what the parties actually intended or would have intended but what strategic conduct they would have desired to refrain from.[79] However, this theory is criticized as a last resort on the grounds that it can largely be substituted for the presumption that arbitration agreements are interpreted broadly, at least from the perspective of courts in the United States.[80]

6.3.2.4 Contractual Systemicity

Interpreting the contract as a whole or putting the individual contractual provision in its context, the so-called systemic interpretation prevents parties' tactical interpretations that give weight only to certain parts or terms of the contract while discarding others. The interpretive principle of good faith in the guise of systemic interpretation also helps resolve the conflict between two possible interpretations by drawing the attention of an arbitrator to the systemicity of the contract. As a CCIR award held, a tribunal should interpret all contractual clauses, systematically ascribing to each the meaning of the contract as a whole,[81] so that the full scope of the obligations of the parties[82] can manifest. Accordingly, it is ascertained that the guiding rationale behind a systemic good faith interpretation is that a fragmented interpretation grounded on specific terms or phrases should never prevail over a homogeneous and integrated interpretation focusing on the entire body of the contract. Interpreting the contract in a systemic way is the epitome of contextual interpretation. True, the tribunal in *ICC Case No. 1434* reasoned that it must not "fail to place [the words] in their *context* and to consider the contract *as a whole*, so as to discover the genuine common intention of the parties, referring in particular, if the terms are ambiguous, to *the principle of good faith*"[83] (alteration to the original) (emphasis added).

6.3.2.5 The Theory of Confidence

Failing to capture the true intentions of the parties, the arbitrator may be inclined to imply their intent. The implied consent is a derivative of the objective interpretation, which in turn pertains to the principle of good faith. These nomenclatures are not merely legal fictions "adapted as we wish in order to 'accommodate

79 Alan Scott Rau, *"Gap Filling" by Arbitrators*, *in* 18 Legitimacy: Myths, Realities, Challenges 935, 983 (Albert Jan Van den Berg ed., ICCA Congress Series 2015).

80 Gary B. Born, International Commercial Arbitration) 1430 (3rd ed., Kluwer Law International 2021).

81 CCIR Case No. 6 in Dossier No. 355/2007, Jan. 23, 2008, 11(3) Revista Română de Arbitraj 62, 66 (Radu Bogdan Bobei ed., Wolters Kluwer România).

82 CCIR Case No. 6 in Dossier No. 355/2007, *supra* note 81.

83 Gaillard & Savage, *supra* note 68.

commercial reality,'"[84] but reflect universal canons of contractual interpretation based on the theory of confidence, namely how a reasonable third party could have objectively understood the said statement or conduct.[85] Moreover, utilizing the reasonable interpretation of the arbitration agreement to extend its binding effect to non-signatories is a consequence of good faith. Whether good faith manifests through the doctrine of apparent authority, equitable estoppel or implied consent, the tribunal may justify the extension of the arbitration agreement to non-parties if *confidence* is generated that the non-signatory is indeed a contracting party to the agreement without regard to the theory of consent as such.[86] Although the art of implying the parties' intent is consistently resisted by common law traditions;[87] eventually, the effect of the notions of fairness and reasonableness is undisputed. Yet, one cannot ignore that differences will always exist since an application of the same theory in different cases will not always produce identical interpretive outcomes.[88]

6.3.3 Boundaries of Interpretation in General

It is critical to distinguish the interpretive principle of good faith applied for the purpose of identifying and explaining the meaning of the contract from the borderline instances of supplementation or correction. In such cases, the interpretive good faith *exceptionally* compels the adjudicator to take specific action *i.e.*, supplement or correct the contract. The suppletive effect focuses on the creation or identification of a rule that the contract has failed to supply in order to "solve a conflict in accordance with the parties' agreed common purpose."[89] From a common law

84 Nathalie Voser, *The Swiss Perspective on Parties in Arbitration: "Traditional Approach with a Twist regarding Abuse of Rights" or "Consent Theory Plus"*, *in* 37 The Evolution and Future of International Arbitration, para. 9.87 (Stavros Brekoulakis et al. eds., 2016).

85 Voser, *supra* note 84.

86 Stavros Brekoulakis, *The Polymorphic Concept of Consent to The Arbitration Agreement in International Arbitration*, *in* Arbitration (Ch. Pamboukis ed., Nomiki Bibliothiki 2024) [Σταύρος Μπρεκουλάκης, Η Πολυμορφική Έννοια της Συναίνεσης στη Διαιτητική Συμφωνία στη Διεθνή Διαιτησία]. Brekoulakis analyzes the case no. *4A_450/2013* of the Swiss Federal Tribunal, where the court overruled the arbitral award by reason of good faith, because the third party acted in such a way that it created the belief that it was indeed a contracting party. Brekoulakis, *supra* note 86. Further, a decision dated Jan. 29, 1996 (Saudi Butec Ltd et Al Fouzan Trading v. Saudi Arabian Saipem Ltd) clarified that the arbitration agreement could be extended to third parties under special circumstances if: (a) the third party created an appearance that it is bound by the arbitration agreement and (b) good faith necessitates the protection of the other party's reliance. Voser, *supra* note 84, para. 9.31.

87 Especially when such fictions are used to construct an implied consent of the non-signatory to the arbitration agreement. See Stavros Brekoulakis, *Parties in International Arbitration: Consent v. Commercial Reality*, *in* 37 The Evolution and Future of International Arbitration, paras. 8.12, 8.127 (Stavros Brekoulakis et al. eds., Kluwer Law International 2016).

88 Voser, *supra* note 84, para. 9.90.

89 Daniele Bertolini, *Toward a Framework to Define the Outer Boundaries of Good Faith in Contractual Performance*, 58 Alberta L. Rev. 596 n.150 (2021).

perspective, the suppletive function resembles the implied terms doctrine, pursuant to which the imposition of certain default rules will be ascribed to the parties' intent.[90] Implied terms are considered in English law as an exception to the parole evidence rule dictating that the court is not authorized to add to or contradict the contract by using extrinsic evidence, such as an oral communication.[91] On the other hand, the corrective effect of good faith entails deeper consequences for the contract. It infuses substantive fairness into the contract and cannot be derogated by the parties since it is founded on public policy considerations that are independent of the parties' intentions.[92] The suppletive effect is measured by the parties' common intentions, whereas the corrective effect is measured by external criteria employed to adjust the consequences of the contract.[93] Albeit heavily resisted in common law jurisdictions, these legal systems are slowly subscribing to the idea of corrective good faith, with the most profound example being the doctrine of unconscionability.[94]

6.3.4 Suppletive and Corrective Effect of Interpretive Good Faith in Arbitral Practice

The process of interpreting the contract is not restricted to merely explaining its terms; but is rather a dynamic process, the effects of which are inevitably extended to either supplementation or correction. The instances where a good faith interpretation would allow the arbitrator to supplement or correct parties' contractual arrangements are limited, though. Even so, the strong link between interpretation, supplementation and correction might be well justified. This is because the linguistic content of parties' expressions sometimes is not detailed enough and, effectively, their intentions seem to be rather incomplete. Having said that, the arbitrator's decision-making would be handicapped if they were based on the strictures of a parochial black letter interpretation. The arbitrators may want to rely on good faith interpretation to promote the parties' expectations when the applicable "commercial law lags behind standards shared by the business community."[95]

90 Bertolini, *supra* note 89.

91 RETO MARGHITOLA, DOCUMENT PRODUCTION IN INTERNATIONAL ARBITRATION 144 (Kluwer Law International 2015).

92 Bertolini, *supra* note 89, at 597.

93 Bertolini, *supra* note 89.

94 Bertolini, *supra* note 89; *accord* Bhasin v. Hrynew, 2014 SCC 71, [2014] 3 S.C.R. 494, [42] (Can.) ("Anglo-Canadian common law has developed a number of rules and doctrines that call upon the notion of good faith in contractual dealings . . . . It underlies doctrines that explicitly deal with fairness in contracts, such as unconscionability, and plays a role in interpreting and implying contractual terms") (citation omitted) (alteration to original); see also [43] ("Considerations of good faith are apparent in doctrines that expressly consider the fairness of contractual bargains, such as unconscionability. This doctrine is based on considerations of fairness and preventing one contracting party from taking undue advantage of the other") (citation omitted).

95 William W. Park, *Neutrality, Predictability and Economic Co-operation*, 12 (4) J. INT. ARBITR. 99, 107 (Kluwer Law International 1995).

A good faith interpretation would typically mirror the idea that the parties should abstain from exercising their rights in bad faith or invite the arbitrator to regulate the broad discretionary power of one of the parties.[96] That resonates with the idea that the interpretive principle of good faith equips the arbitrator with the power to fill in contractual lacunae by "assum[ing] [the parties] intended certain minimum standards of conduct commonly accepted in the contracting community to which the parties belong"[97] (alteration to the original). The compulsive and binding value of such suppletive effect of good faith derives from party autonomy as well as the persuasive value of the existing trade practices.

On the other hand, the interpretive principle of good faith may produce a corrective effect, giving the arbitrator the leeway to intervene and do justice, especially when the parties' intent, as soon as it is revealed, is found to be in direct opposition to mandatory rules or public policy. A highly contested issue where the freedom of the arbitrator, which was unequivocally granted by the parties, clashes with the parties' will is the case of parties' opting for the application of national law – the mandatory rules of which protect third innocent parties – yet the parties sought to "exclude the application of such a protective law to gain a benefit for themselves as against innocent third parties,"[98] the latter not having "consented to any commercial relationship purporting to avoid the laws' operation."[99] The arbitrators should not interpret the arbitration agreement in such a way as to affirm the validity of such consent. The reason is that "consent in arbitration must always be consent in good faith consistent with fair and reasonable arbitration as a dispute resolution methodology."[100]

The suggested solution may be that the arbitrator should sever from the general consent the part that negatively affects the third innocent parties' rights.[101] Not giving full effect to the interpretive effect of good faith may expose the award to the risk of enforcement challenges in accordance with Article V(1)(a) (invalidity of arbitration agreement) or NYC Article V(2)(b) (violation of public policy). Despite the previously mentioned *exceptional* effects, a good faith interpretation shall never "be used to amend a contractual clause which is clear."[102] This limitation is justified: the arbitrator should not pay lip service to the parties' intent. As a recent ICC tribunal has held, while

> good faith can have a role in the interpretation of contracts, the judge or arbitrator must always begin with the text of the contract, and good faith cannot

96 Park, *supra* note 95.

97 Bertolini, *supra* note 89, at 599.

98 Jeffrey Maurice Waincymer, Procedure and Evidence in International Arbitration 1035 (Kluwer Law International 2012).

99 Waincymer, *supra* note 98.

100 Waincymer, *supra* note 98, at 1036.

101 Waincymer, *supra* note 98.

102 ICC Case No. 22588/ASM/JPA, Final Award, Dec. 10, 2018, para. 516, *available at* https://jusmundi.com/en/document/decision/en-1-grupo-unidos-por-el-canal-s-a-2-sacyr-s-a-3-salini-impregilo-s-p-a-and-4-jan-de-nul-n-v-constructora-urbana-s-a-and-5-sofidra-s-a-v-autoridad-del-canal-de-panama-final-award-wednesday-12th-december-2018#decis.

be used to rewrite a contract or change the allocation of risks agreed by the Parties.[103]

6.3.5 Increasing Demand for Contextual Good Faith Interpretation

The tension between textual (formalistic) and contextual interpretation in international commercial arbitration rests on the rigid assumption that only one of these two opposites can survive an arbitrator's interpretive task. A contract governed by common law may be replete with duties that the parties act in good faith and cooperate with each other. Despite that the traditional English law approach dictates that these terms must be accorded merely a commercial morale rather than an enforceable content,[104] it is advanced that

> [t]he content of what is owed as a matter of good faith crucially depends upon the context and an objective assessment of the requirements of commercial conduct and reasonableness that operate between a particular body of contractors or within a particular market.[105]

It is critical to understand that contextual interpretation signifies that "the meaning of a legal text does not arise from the text alone, but rather reflects a holistic assessment of the text's relationship to a background context."[106] Importantly, contextual interpretation refers to concepts of "practical reasonableness"[107] and "practical rationality,"[108] which are both foundational for the contract. It is remarkable that contextual interpretation is even endorsed in common law. Californian courts have upheld that

> rational interpretation requires . . . a preliminary consideration of all credible evidence offered to prove the intention of the parties . . . . Such evidence includes testimony as to the "circumstances surrounding the making of the agreement . . . including the object, nature and subject matter of the writing . . ." so that the court can "place itself in the same situation in which the parties found themselves at the time of contracting."[109]
>
> (citations omitted)

There are at least three instances where a formalistic interpretation germane to a common law tradition fails to meet parties' expectations. First, sticking to the plain

103 ICC Case No. 22588/ASM/JPA, *supra* note 102.
104 CATHERINE MITCHELL, INTERPRETATION OF CONTRACTS 159 (2nd ed., Taylor & Francis 2018).
105 MITCHELL, *supra* note 104 (citing Gerard McMeel, Foucault's Pendulum: Text, Context and Good Faith in Contract Law, CLP 365, 393 (2017)).
106 JONATHAN CROWE, NATURAL LAW AND THE NATURE OF LAW 203 (CUP 2019).
107 CROWE, *supra* note 106.
108 CROWE, *supra* note 106.
109 Pacific Gas E. Co. v. G.W. Thomas Drayage Etc. Co., 442 P. 2d 641, 69 Cal.2d 33, 39–40 (Cal. 1968).

meaning of the text may sometimes lead to manifest injustice, such as inequality of bargaining power between the parties.[110] A paradigm shift toward contextualism is justified by virtue of an implied duty of good faith in the contract, the latter being also recognized by common law courts.[111] Second, good faith relies on the implied intention of the parties to the extent the contract fails to meet parties' expectations *ex post*. That is when a contingency takes place that the parties did not foresee *ex ante*. As Markovits put it, "[f]or imperfect planners, who cannot plan clearly for every contingency but whose plans inevitably involve haziness and have gaps, good faith is required to make joint planning possible."[112] In that instance, a good faith interpretation reveals the parties' implied intention by "attributing to them the purposes and values which reasonable people in their situation would have had."[113]

The consequence of the shift in this adamant view is that *both* the obligations that the parties expressly contracted for *and* those implicitly generated are enforceable, whereas the "presumed intention of the parties"[114] should not be seen as a prohibited limitation to the parties' freedom to advance their interests.[115] Third, contextual contractors may wish to supplement their contract with trade customs on the basis that market practices are important to merchants in understanding the different ways transactions work.[116] Following the parties' express or implied direction, the interpretive principle of good faith urges the arbitrator to make their contract complete. Fourth, a common law party may want to agree to an exhaustive regulation of parties' contractual relationship because it might expect that its contractor's choice of civil law and an ensuing principle of good faith would provide the arbitrator with greater latitude to interfere with the contract in case of hardship.[117] A principle of good faith within the applicable law may dictate a different result from the literal reading of the contract, such as imposing a restriction on the party's power to terminate the contract.[118] Is the arbitrator permitted to interpret the contract restrictively so that the governing law cannot prevail over the detailed contractual stipulations? Even though the solution directed by the governing law may

110 Mitchell, *supra* note 104, at 160.

111 Mitchell, *supra* note 104; see also Yam Seng Pte Limited v. International Trade Corporation [2013] EWHC 111 (QB) [138] [hereinafter *Yam Seng*] (Mr. Justice Leggatt emphasized that "there are . . . standards of commercial dealing which are so generally accepted that the contracting parties would reasonably be understood to take them as read without explicitly stating them in their contractual document. A key aspect of good faith, as I see it, is the observance of such standards").

112 Daniel Markovits, *Good Faith as Contract's Core Value, in* Philosophical Foundations of Contract Law 293 (Gregory Klass et al. eds., 2014).

113 *Yam Seng, supra* note 111, para. 144.

114 *Yam Seng, supra* note 111, para. 148.

115 *Yam Seng, supra* note 111.

116 Mitchell, *supra* note 104, at 145.

117 Giuditta Cordero Moss, *International Contracts between Common Law and Civil Law: Is Nonstate Law to Be Preferred? The Difficulty of Interpreting Legal Standards Such as Good Faith*, 7(1) (Advances) (Article 3) Glob. Jurist 1, 20 (2007).

118 Giuditta Cordero-Moss, *General Report on Jura Novit Arbiter, in* Iura Novit Curia in International Arbitration 463, 468 (Franco Ferrari & Giuditta Cordero-Moss eds., 2018).

not prevail over the parties' risk allocation, the same conclusion cannot be safely deduced in the case of mandatory rules.[119] In that instance, resorting to contextual good faith interpretation may shed light on whether – and to what extent – formalism should be compromised.

6.4 Interpretive Function of Good Faith When Transnational Law Applies

6.4.1 Source of Transnationality

The source of the interpretive good faith when transnational law is applicable to the contract and the arbitration clause is deeply associated with the delocalization theory of international commercial arbitration, according to which international commercial arbitration is rooted in an autonomous legal order able to deal with all questions that concern its subjects.[120] However, it is not always clear when – and to what extent – transnational law is applicable to the contract. That is because, apart from the cases where the parties have designated *lex mercatoria* as applicable law, which is rather a rarity in arbitral practice, sometimes the parties may not have chosen the governing substantive law. In that case, the absence of any reference to a national law will sometimes – but not always – direct the arbitrator to apply *lex mercatoria*,[121] thereby creating an autonomous interpretation that is detached from national law constraints. Even if a domestic law is specifically selected to govern the dispute, an autonomous good faith interpretation anchored in transnational law might assist in yielding the appropriate solution.

6.4.2 Paradigm Shift Toward Autonomous Good Faith Interpretation

In the eyes of counsel, arguments, constructions or interpretations in good faith seem to be a pleonasm or, even worse, an indicium of unconfident rhetoric.[122] However, the opinion that the good faith interpretation is amorphous and vague fails to capture the international angle of it. It is argued that the practice of arbitrators to follow territorial rules obtained from national legal systems during the interpretation process is rather parochial.[123] This theory is linked to the argument cultivated in France that international commercial arbitration as an order should be

119 Moss, *International Contracts between Common Law and Civil Law, supra* note 117, at 20.

120 George A. Bermann, International Arbitration and Private International Law, para. 267 (The Hague Academy of International Law 2017).

121 See, e.g., ICC Case No. 9875 of 1999, 12 ICC Bull. No. 2, 95–97 (2001), *available at* www.unilex.info/principles/case/675 (where the tribunal applied the *lex mercatoria* as enshrined, among other things, in the UNIDROIT Principles, because of the inadequacy of French and Japanese laws to govern the dispute absent an express choice of law).

122 See Ragnar Harbst, A Counsel's Guide to Examining and Preparing Witnesses in International Arbitration 59 (Kluwer Law International 2015).

123 Karton, *supra* note 16, at 35.

detached from any national law idiosyncrasies.[124] To further support this view, arbitrators often investigate commercial practices and trade usages to arrive at a fair and reasonable solution.[125] Even if a national law is applicable to the merits, they tend to downplay it when it comes to interpretation and put particular emphasis on the commercial context so that the desired solution comports with commercial sense.[126] According to an ICC publication based on a group of awards, contrary to state judges, "[a]rbitrators are not beholden to national legal systems. They enjoy greater freedom than state courts when engaging in contractual interpretation."[127]

6.4.2.1 Criticism

There is a great deal of criticism against an autonomous interpretation anchored in transnational law. First, it is highly unlikely that there are general contractual principles of interpretation, let alone uniform interpretation principles.[128] The majority of awards are inconsistent due to the variety of applicable national laws dictating very different interpretive outcomes; as such, it is mere sophistry to talk about an autonomous transnational legal order able to yield an autonomous contractual interpretation.[129] Second, even if there is a need to derogate from the applicable national law for the sake of an autonomous interpretive principle of good faith, which can better ensure reasonableness or avoid absurd solutions, there is a tenable argument that the more unreasonable the result is, the less likely that the parties actually intended that result.[130] Still, the sound argument that almost all national laws are highly developed and contain rules of interpretation that protect against absurd results, or at least necessitate commercially reasonable solutions, cannot be easily overcome.[131] Third, and most importantly, importing an autonomous interpretation regardless of the applicable national law may violate the utmost law of party autonomy. That is, the duty of the arbitrator is to act "within the limits of the law, whatever kind of justice the parties have chosen."[132]

6.4.2.2 Support

The previously stated contentions are not fully metabolized in the arbitral practice. First, even if a specific national law system is short-sighted enough to ignore the emergence of an autonomous interpretive principle of good faith, distinguished

124 Karton, *supra* note 16.
125 Karton, *supra* note 16, at 18.
126 Karton, *supra* note 16.
127 ICC Arbitral Awards on the Interpretation of Contracts, *in* 25(1) ICC Bulletin 39 (Andrea Carlevaris et al. eds., 2014), *available at* https://jusmundi.com/en/document/publication/en-icc-arbitral-awards-on-the-interpretation-of-contracts.
128 Karton, *supra* note 16, at 36.
129 Karton, *supra* note 16.
130 Karton, *supra* note 16.
131 Karton, *supra* note 16.
132 Karton, *supra* note 16, at 33.

arbitrators have recognized that a principle of good faith is "enshrined in the [New York] Convention's provisions."[133] That means that arbitrators while considering formal objections to the consent to arbitrate, must take into account the principle of good faith "with uniform international effect."[134] Born pleads for a pro-arbitration and uniform rule of construction of arbitration agreements, dictating that such agreements should be interpreted expansively in that, in case of doubt, all disputes shall fall under the agreement to arbitrate and such rule must be autonomous in the sense that it "applies without regard to the substantive law otherwise applicable to the interpretation of the arbitration agreement."[135]

Second, a number of arbitral awards have indeed applied transnational rules to the existence and validity of arbitration clauses on the basis that the most appropriate law to govern these issues is a-national law, including general principles of law, particularly good faith.[136] Support for such reasoning is also found in the *competence-competence* principle, according to which the arbitrator has the power to determine their own jurisdiction without having to apply a specific national law.[137] The Cour de Cassation in *Soerni v. Air Sea Broker* held that

> whether a company is bound to arbitration is not examined by reference to a national law but through . . . a material rule derived from the principle of the validity of the arbitration agreement based on the common intention of the parties, on good faith and on the legitimate belief in the power of the . . . signatory to . . . bind the company.[138]
>
> (alteration to original)

Likewise, in order to determine who is a party to an arbitration agreement, the tribunal in *Dallah v. Pakistan* reasoned that local law is not guiding, but such an inquiry is answered: "by reference to transnational general principles and usages reflecting the fundamental requirements of justice in international trade and the concept of

133 V.V. Veeder, *The 2001 Goff Lecture – The Lawyer's Duty to Arbitrate in Good Faith*, 18 ARB. INT'L 431, 440 (William W. Park ed., 2002).

134 BORN (2nd ed.), *supra* note 77, at 691.

135 BORN (3rd ed.), *supra* note 80, at 1510.

136 PIERO BERNARDINI, *Arbitration Clauses: Achieving Effectiveness in the Law Applicable to the Arbitration Clause*, *in* 9 IMPROVING THE EFFICIENCY OF ARBITRATION AGREEMENTS AND AWARDS: 40 YEARS OF APPLICATION OF THE NEW YORK CONVENTION 197, 201 (Albert Jan Van den Berg ed., ICCA Congress Series, 1999).

137 BERNARDINI, *supra* note 136, at 202; see, e.g., LCIA Arbitration Rules, art. 23(1) (2020); ICC Arbitration Rules, art. 6(9) (2021); UNCITRAL Arbitration Rules (2021), art. 23(1); SIAC Arbitration Rules (2016) art. 28(2). This solution, though, may not be able to sidestep mandatory rules of the arbitral seat imposing specific form requirements for the validity of the arbitration agreement. BERNARDINI, *supra* note 136.

138 France No. 49, Société d'études et représentations navales et industrielles – Soerni (France) et al. v. Air Sea Broker Limited – ASB (Switzerland), Cour de Cassation [Supreme Court], First Civil Chamber, 956, July 8, 2009, 35 Y.B. Comm. Arb. 356, at [4] (A. J. Van den Berg, ICCA & Kluwer Law International 2010).

good faith in business."[139] In contrast to the Supreme Court of the United Kingdom, the Cour d' appel de Paris endorsed such reasoning. It seems, indeed, that if the arbitral tribunal is not convinced that a party is not a true party to the arbitration agreement, good faith may be utilized to justify the solution adopted.[140]

Third, one additional parameter that decisively influences the interpretive outcome is international public policy. The tribunal in *ICC Case No. 6474/1992* reasoned that it would be a violation of the international public policy if the defendant state was allowed "'*to conclude an arbitration agreement without revealing its incapacity or lack of authority and then later to invoke such lack of authority in order not to respect the agreement*'"[141] (emphasis in original). An interpretation based on the international principle of good faith and *estoppel* would prohibit the party from acting inconsistently.[142]

Fourth, just like national judges imply in the contract rules derived from community standards, which ensure "faithfulness to the common purpose of the parties in the face of contractual incompleteness,"[143] the principle of good faith may give leeway to arbitrators to resort to international trade usages in case of contractual silence.[144] As Derains illustrated, "[t]he interpretation of contracts is one of the areas in which international commercial arbitrators are most inclined to disengage from national laws."[145] That is further corroborated by Article 28 (4) of the UNCITRAL Model Law. It stipulates that "[i]n all cases, the arbitral tribunal shall decide in accordance with the terms of the contract and shall take into account the *usages of the trade* applicable to the transaction" (emphasis added).

Finally, Mayer supports that in cases where the applicable national law gives a solution to the dispute that does not satisfy the international nature of the dispute, it would be absurd to give effect to such domestic law provisions.[146] Such cases would concern domestic rules applicable to the contract, which "fix the rate of interest at a certain percentage, regardless of the place of payment and of the currency in which the debt was expressed."[147] This may lead to the solution that "the law is sometimes disregarded."[148] The counterargument is that parties empower the arbitrator to act only within the limits of the chosen law. This argument is fraught

139 ICC Case No. 9987, Second Partial Award, Jan. 19, 2004, 2 Int'l J. Arab. Arb. 370, 393 (2010).

140 ICC Case No. 9987, *supra* note 139, at 403.

141 ICC Case No. 6474 of 1992, Partial Award on Jurisdiction and Admissibility, 25 Y.B. Comm. Arb. 11, [109] (Albert Jan Van den Berg ed., ICCA & Kluwer Law International 2000).

142 ICC Case No. 6474 of 1992, *supra* note 141, at [12].

143 Bertolini, *supra* note 89, at 599; see, e.g., U.C.C. §2–103(b) (describing a practice-based good faith: "Good faith in the case of a merchant means honesty in fact and the observance of reasonable commercial standards of fair dealing in the trade.")

144 Karton, *supra* note 16, at 32; see also Translex Principle No. I.2.2. on implying international trade usages into the contract.

145 Karton, *supra* note 16, at 5 (quoting ICC Case No. 2291 of 1975 [1976] JDI 989, obs. Yves Derains).

146 Mayer, *supra* note 43, paras. 15–52.

147 Mayer, *supra* note 43, paras. 15–52.

148 Mayer, *supra* note 43, paras. 15–54.

with the fallacy that the parties' reasonable expectations are only reflected in the strict application of the rules chosen by them. However, it befalls the arbitrator to assess whether the parties' expectations are fulfilled by such strict application or whether they seek a more practical and fair interpretation of the contract.[149]

6.5 Conclusion

This chapter provided a detailed account of different concretizations of the interpretive good faith. Having analyzed the contours of good faith in the interpretation process, it is stressed that three main parameters determine the effect of a good faith interpretation: The parties' intentions, the law applicable to the contract or the arbitration agreement and the unique position of the arbitrator to be "above the law, since he is the one who renders it applicable."[150] While adjudicating the merits of the dispute, arbitrators are not, in principle, authorized to do justice detached from the parties' contractual will.[151] However, the interpretive principle of good faith may be used to supplement or even correct the contractual framework in case unreasonable conduct or absurd legal results do not comport with business common sense.[152] It should not be deduced that party autonomy is inevitably restricted, but only that a good faith interpretation 'cures' the incompleteness or ineffectiveness of the intent. Ultimately, the transnational angle of the interpretive good faith may not only be justified in the absence of national law but also when the contract or arbitration agreement is subject to domestic law. The uniformity and harmonization propelled by international instruments and international public policy call *inter alia* for certain autonomy in interpretation, without this suggesting that a one-size-fits-all conceptualization of good faith should be the norm.

149 Mayer, *supra* note 43, paras. 15–38; *accord* Marc Blessing, Introduction to Arbitration – Swiss and International Perspectives, para. 597 (Helbing & Lichtenhahn 1999).

150 Mayer, *supra* note 43, paras. 15–27.

151 Karton, *supra* note 16, at 40.

152 Karton, *supra* note 16.

7 Interpretive Good Faith in Determination of the Law Applicable to the Merits

7.1 Evolution of Methodology

7.1.1 Abandonment of Conflict-of-Laws Approach

Finding the applicable law is fundamental for the prescription of "the ambit of argument as to liability and rights of the parties in a given situation."[1] For a long time, there was a misconception that the arbitrator enjoyed the same status as a national judge. The arbitrators applied the arbitration seat's conflict-of-laws rules in order to determine the applicable law to the merits of the dispute.[2] They did so both in case of parties' failure to designate a specific law (where the arbitrator had to examine what the conflict-of-laws rule of the seat of the arbitration designates as applicable law by virtue of some connecting factor) and the case where the parties had designated a particular law to govern their dispute (in which case the adjudicator had to make sure that certain conditions in the conflict-of-laws rules should be complied with).[3] A firm proponent of that view was Mann, who advanced the idea that international arbitration must be conducted within a national jurisdiction, therefore the applicable law should follow the application of the conflict of laws of the *forum* as the place of arbitration.[4]

Pamboukis eloquently explained that the arbitrator should not be perceived as an organ of the place of arbitration.[5] The reason is that the arbitrator does not

1 Julian D. M. Lew et al., *Comparative International Commercial Arbitration*, paras. 18–21 (Kluwer Law International 2003).

2 Pierre Mayer, *Reflections on the International Arbitrator's Duty to Apply the Law*, *in* 16 Arbitration Insights: Twenty Years of the Annual Lecture of the School of International Arbitration, Sponsored by Freshfields Bruckhaus Deringer, paras. 15–19 (Julian David Mathew Lew & Loukas A. Mistelis eds., 2007).

3 Mayer, *Reflections on the International Arbitrator's Duty to Apply the Law supra* note 2, paras. 15–18.

4 Charalambos P. Pamboukis, Lex Mercatoria as Applicable Law in International Contractual Obligations (Sakkoulas 1996) [ΧΑΡΑΛΑΜΠΟΣ Π. ΠΑΜΠΟΥΚΗΣ, Η LEX MERCATORIA ΩΣ ΕΦΑΡΜΟΣΤΕΟ ΔΙΚΑΙΟ ΣΤΙΣ ΔΙΕΘΝΕΙΣ ΣΥΜΒΑΤΙΚΕΣ ΕΝΟΧΕΣ (ΣΑΚΚΟΥΛΑΣ 1996)], para. 123.

5 Pamboukis, Lex Mercatoria as Applicable Law in International Contractual Obligations, *supra* note 4.

DOI: 10.4324/9781003527596-9

have a *forum*.[6] The argument that their *forum* is the place of arbitration has no merit since the arbitrator does not decide a dispute from the perspective of a specific legal system.[7] The influence of this approach is hailed in the 1961 European Convention on International Commercial Arbitration, which was the first instrument that set the arbitrator free of their obligation to apply the arbitration seat's conflict-of-laws rule.[8] Despite the liberation from territorialism, Article 28 of the UNCITRAL Model Law is – to some extent – conservative since it provides that in the absence of a chosen law, the tribunal should apply the law suggested by the conflict-of-laws rules and which the tribunal considers applicable. On the contrary, Article 187 of the Swiss Private International Law (PIL) Act stipulates in relation to arbitrations seated in Switzerland that, absent parties' explicit choice of law, the tribunal shall apply the law that has the closest connection to the case. However, as Mayer advocates, this rule of proximity is not binding on the arbitrator as there is no sanction in relation to the violation of Article 187, nor does it constitute an annulment ground by virtue of Article 190 of the PIL Act.[9]

7.1.2 The Convergence Method

The convergence method, which has regularly been used in practice and has been applauded for its predictability, suggests that if the arbitrator ascertains that the conflict-of-laws rules of the respective countries of the parties converge and direct to the same applicable law, that particular law would be applicable to the substance.[10] In case the parties' countries are member states of the European Union, the convergence of the parties' conflict-of-laws systems will usually be reflected in the conflict-of-laws

6 PAMBOUKIS, LEX MERCATORIA AS APPLICABLE LAW IN INTERNATIONAL CONTRACTUAL OBLIGATIONS, *supra* note 4, para. 122. The arbitrator is deprived of any sovereign power in the making of the decision, which is not enforceable *per se*, as opposed to the case of a national judge. PIERRE MAYER, *The Laws or Rules of Law Applicable to the Merits of a Dispute and the Freedom of the Arbitrator*, *in* IS ARBITRATION ONLY AS GOOD AS THE ARBITRATOR? STATUS, POWERS AND ROLE OF THE ARBITRATOR 47, para. 10 (Yves Derains & Laurent Levy eds., ICC Dossier VIII 2011).

7 PAMBOUKIS, LEX MERCATORIA AS APPLICABLE LAW IN INTERNATIONAL CONTRACTUAL OBLIGATIONS, *supra* note 4, para. 123. Further, the application of a substantive law based on conflict-of-laws rules may lead to a result that the parties never intended. LEW ET AL., *supra* note 1, paras. 17–54.

8 PAMBOUKIS, LEX MERCATORIA AS APPLICABLE LAW IN INTERNATIONAL CONTRACTUAL OBLIGATIONS, *supra* note 4, para. 124; see European Convention on International Commercial Arbitration, Geneva, Apr. 21, 1961, United Nations, Treaty Series, vol. 484, p. 349, art. VII (1) ("The parties shall be free to determine, by agreement, the law to be applied by the arbitrators to the substance of the dispute. Failing any indication by the parties as to the applicable law, the arbitrators shall apply the proper law under the rule of conflict that the arbitrators deem applicable. In both cases the arbitrators shall take account of the terms of the contract and trade usages").

9 MAYER, *The Laws or Rules of Law Applicable to the Merits of a Dispute and the Freedom of the Arbitrator*, *supra* note 6, para. 12.

10 MAYER, *The Laws or Rules of Law Applicable to the Merits of a Dispute and the Freedom of the Arbitrator*, *supra* note 6, para. 19. The advantages of this approach are arguably a lot. Arbitrary results are avoided, and the equality of the parties is effectively enforced. MAYER, *The Laws or Rules of Law Applicable to the Merits of a Dispute and the Freedom of the Arbitrator*, *supra* note 6.

rules of Rome I Regulation.[11] Another proposed solution is the application of the common content of the substantive rules of the parties' respective countries.[12]

7.1.3 The Direct Method

The application of the direct method (*voie directe*) is now recognized as the prevailing modern trend[13] by many national legislations on international arbitration. In the absence of a choice of law, the arbitrator is free to determine directly the applicable substantive law that they deem appropriate, and without reference to any conflict-of-laws rules.[14] A significant number of modern laws adopt this method, including French law[15] and Dutch law.[16] The freedom of the arbitrator to choose the substantive law is also encouraged by arbitral institutions. The 2021 ICC Arbitration Rule 21(1) stipulates that "[i]n the absence of any such agreement [regarding the applicable rules of law], the arbitral tribunal shall apply the rules of law which it determines to be appropriate" (alteration to the original). A similar wording is also endorsed in the revised LCIA Rules.[17]

The objective of the foregoing methodologies is *in toto* to ascertain the applicable law to the contract which in turn determines the scope and boundaries of substantive good faith. This process leads to the application of some national law in case the parties have remained silent as to the choice of law. However, the tribunal is also vested with a limited power to apply transnational law, even if the parties have designated a national law to govern their dispute.[18]

7.2 Good Faith in the Assessment of Applicable Law

7.2.1 Scope

The traditional methods of identifying the proper substantive law would be handicapped if no explanation was provided regarding the interpretive role of good faith in guiding the determination of the law applicable to the substance. For example,

11 Mayer, *The Laws or Rules of Law Applicable to the Merits of a Dispute and the Freedom of the Arbitrator*, *supra* note 6, para. 19.

12 Mayer, *Reflections on the International Arbitrator's Duty to Apply the Law*, *supra* note 2, paras. 15–21.

13 There is an argument that other methods used to determine the applicable law, such as the application of conflict-of-laws rules, which have the closest connection to the dispute, may not be regarded as suitable for international arbitration because they advance the state's interests incorporated in its conflict-of-laws rules. Lew et al., *supra* note 1, paras. 17–57.

14 Mayer, *Reflections on the International Arbitrator's Duty to Apply the Law*, *supra* note 2, paras. 15–22.

15 C.P.C., art. 1496: "The arbitrator determines the dispute according to rules of law that the parties have chosen; in default of such a choice, in accordance with rules he deems appropriate."

16 See Rv, art. 1054 (2) reading that the arbitral tribunal must make an award pursuant to the chosen rules of law, failing which it befalls the tribunal to decide on the appropriate rules.

17 LCIA Arbitration Rules, art. 22(3) (2020): "If and to the extent that the Arbitral Tribunal decides that the parties have made no such choice, the Arbitral Tribunal shall apply the law(s) or rules of law which it considers appropriate."

18 See, *e.g.*, ICC Arbitration Rules (2021), art. 21(2) ("The arbitral tribunal shall take account of the provisions of the contract, if any, between the parties and of *any relevant trade usages*") (emphasis added).

to what extent is the arbitrator allowed to decide to apply a law different from the one designated by the parties based on a reasonable interpretation of the contract? Under what circumstances can the arbitrator supplement the applicable law by resorting to trade usages? These questions wrestle with the essence of arbitration as a creature of party autonomy and pave the way for ceaseless debates among scholars as to the foundation of the intervening role of good faith. The antithesis between the principle of sanctity of contracts and the regulatory notion of good faith reflects the tension between the wording of the contract and the parties' fair and reasonable expectations. Solely the axiological antinomy between party autonomy and arbitrator's freedom will be explored. The case of absence of choice of law will not be addressed because good faith cannot be used to generate an intent for, and instead of, the parties. Good faith cannot construct the intent of the parties, nor can any recourse to good faith determine in itself what law should be applicable in case of absence of choice. Even if it could (*quod non*), there would be no basis legitimizing the arbitrator to do so. Pamboukis is supportive of this argument on the grounds that the arbitrator cannot interfere with the foundation of their authority, as well as on the basis that such an approach is inflicted with legal uncertainty due to the violation of the parties' legitimate expectations and subjective judgment of the tribunal.[19] Accordingly, recourse to good faith is rendered redundant since the arbitrator, in case of absence of choice, can readily use the instruments of *voie directe*, *voie indirecte* or even the law that is closely connected to the dispute in order to determine the applicable law.

7.2.2 Foundation

The contractual foundation of the conferral of the arbitrator's power is universally accepted to be the arbitration clause, namely the parties' consent to constitute an arbitral tribunal vested with the power to resolve their dispute in a binding manner. It follows that, the power of the tribunal to interpret the arbitration clause is rooted in party autonomy, yet the arbitral tribunal's discretion is decisive. The prevalence of party autonomy must not be absolute because the tribunal "has the power to ascertain the basis for its decision on its own motion."[20] However, the antagonism between party autonomy and the exercise of the arbitral tribunal's discretion does not mean that these are irreconcilable since specific safeguards of due process are in place *i.e.,* the obligation of the tribunal not to exceed its powers that only the parties conferred upon it.[21] Strictly adhering to the parties' will with respect to the choice of law without acknowledging the arbitrator's discretion to correct the legal

19 PAMBOUKIS, LEX MERCATORIA AS APPLICABLE LAW IN INTERNATIONAL CONTRACTUAL OBLIGATIONS, *supra* note 4, para. 135.

20 GIUDITTA CORDERO-MOSS, *Iura Novit Curia*, *in* HANDBOOK OF EVIDENCE IN INTERNATIONAL COMMERCIAL ARBITRATION: KEY CONCEPTS AND ISSUES 111, 113 (Franco Ferrari & Friedrich Jakob Rosenfeld eds., 2022).

21 CORDERO-MOSS, *supra* note 20.

consequences of its application cannot be supported by modern legal scholarship.[22] The argument that such a practice would potentially circumvent the parties' wishes should be equated with not being able to see the forest for the trees. In this respect, little attention has been drawn to the systemic role of good faith. As the word 'systemic' implies, a good faith interpretation entails a balancing exercise between consensualism and regulatory interventionism.

Derains rigorously explained that both the parties and the arbitrator determine the applicable law. When the parties have chosen an applicable law, the arbitrator must apply it along with any mandatory provisions therein.[23] When one party invokes mandatory provisions of a law other than the one applicable to the merits, the arbitrator must justify *why* the said mandatory provisions should not be applied.[24] Mayer meticulously explained why a hostile attitude towards the application of mandatory rules is fraught with fallacy. First, even if the parties exclude a mandatory rule, the arbitrator may not be bound by that stipulation since "arbitrators should pay heed to the future of their award."[25] The country where enforcement is sought might refuse enforcement of the award on the grounds that the mandatory rule is not complied with.[26] Besides, Article 42 of ICC Rules provides that "the arbitral tribunal shall . . . make every effort to make sure that the award is enforceable at law." Second, Mayer also elucidated that the arbitrator is free to depart from *pacta sunt servanda* in the event that more powerful considerations must be prioritized, such as a contract pursuing illicit purposes, and which may be torpedoed by the *ex hypothesi* conflict of the parties as to the applicability of the

22 Daniel Hochstrasser, *Choice of Law and "Foreign" Mandatory Rules in International Arbitration*, 11(1) J. Int. Arb. 57, 64 (1994) (discussing the situation in Switzerland regarding the binding effect of foreign mandatory law). Even in private international law, scholars eloquently advocate the need to adapt the function of the conflict-of-laws rule (*Anpassung*) insofar as such function and the ensuing direction to the applicable substantive law led to inequitable solutions. That is based on that (a) the predictability and fairness of a rule should be distinguished from the fairness of the solution adopted by the adjudicator *ex post* – and which cannot be perceived *ex ante* – and that (b) importance should be attached to the legitimate expectations of the parties, as a result of the substantive fairness principle penetrating the entirety of the system of private international law. In the field of international commercial arbitration, such legitimate expectations urge the arbitrator to render a valid decision in line with the place of arbitration as well as an enforceable decision in line with the place where such a decision is assumed to be enforced. An illustrative example in private international law is the *Ponnoucannamalle case*, where French law did not recognize the rights of an adopted child of Indian nationality to the inherited property because of the existence of a natural child; as a result, the adopted child was excluded from the estate in France in contrast to Indian law suggesting otherwise. Such adaptation requiring coordination between these two laws would seem desirable nowadays by virtue of Article 8 of the ECHR. Charis P. Pamboukis, Private International Law [Χαρησ Π. Παμπουκησ, Ιδιωτικο Διεθνεσ Δικαιο], paras. 193, 196, 199 and 420 (Nomiki Vivliothiki 2020).

23 Hochstrasser, *supra* note 22.

24 Hochstrasser, *supra* note 22, at 69.

25 Pierre Mayer, *Mandatory Rules of Law in International Arbitration*, 2(4) Arb. Int'l 274, 284 (1986).

26 Mayer, *Mandatory Rules of Law in International Arbitration*, *supra* note 25.

mandatory rule.[27] In this case, the arbitrator is free to uphold the argument of one or the other party without being bound by any conflict-of-laws method.[28] Mayer specifically cited arbitral awards, which considered the applicability of mandatory rules that were not originally chosen by the parties.[29]

Even if the parties explicitly desire to exclude the application of mandatory rules, such as rules of the contract's place of performance, Derains advocated that the arbitrator must resort to the 'truly international public policy' theory.[30] For the purpose of upholding the parties' will, the arbitrator has to assess whether the exclusion is contrary to the truly international public policy.[31] The cradle of this argument is that the arbitrator has to respect the intentions of the parties in interpreting their contractual commitments unless their intentions bypass mandatory laws in contravention of international public policy.[32] Ultimately, an interpretive principle of good faith should not be mobilized in such a manner that the arbitrator ends up a marionette to the parties' will, nor as if the arbitrator were supposed to substitute their choice of law for the parties' will. Instead, an interpretation in good faith mirrors the idea that the intentions of the parties should be upheld only to the extent that "the parties' trust in the ability of an arbitral tribunal to reach an equitable and practicable dispute resolution"[33] is not sabotaged. In Hochstrasser's words, "only intentions that do not violate the internationally recognized principle of good faith and fair dealing deserve protection."[34] What this analysis illustrates is that good faith is employed as a method of balancing respect to the parties' intentions and the cardinal duty of the arbitrator to resolve the dispute fairly.

7.3 The Two-Prong Test for Application of the Principle in Law Determination

7.3.1 Legitimate Expectations

There is a strong correlation between party autonomy and arbitral discretion. The discretion of arbitrators is pertinent not only when the parties' intent is not robust enough but also when a clear intent undermines the effectiveness and integrity of the system of international commercial arbitration. The question that is accordingly pegged is what kind of test an arbitrator should apply for the purpose of meeting

27 Mayer, *Mandatory Rules of Law in International Arbitration*, *supra* note 25 ("Arbitrators should use their *freedom* in the best way possible") (emphasis added).

28 Mayer, *Mandatory Rules of Law in International Arbitration*, *supra* note 25.

29 Mayer, *Mandatory Rules of Law in International Arbitration*, *supra* note 25, at 286 (discussing *ICC Case No. 4132 of 1983* where, although the governing law in a dispute between an Italian and Korean party was Korean law, the tribunal had to examine whether European competition law was contravened by virtue of its public policy nature).

30 Hochstrasser, *supra* note 22, at 69.

31 Hochstrasser, *supra* note 22.

32 Hochstrasser, *supra* note 22.

33 Hochstrasser, *supra* note 22, at 86.

34 Hochstrasser, *supra* note 22.

the requirements of good faith interpretation in the determination of the proper law. Blessing is supportive of "the test of the fair and reasonable expectations of the parties."[35] He emphasizes that "the contract itself and . . . the reasonable contract interpretation will have to be the essential source of guidance."[36] Derains highlighted that "[a]n examination of the arbitral jurisprudence reveals a body of solutions, all having as common denominator the desire of the arbitrators to meet the *legitimate expectations of the parties* for which they act"[37] (emphasis added). He discovered that arbitrators sometimes applied a mandatory law in addition to the one governing the contract since that interfering law was in consonance with the legitimate expectations of the parties.[38] This is especially so in case the legitimate expectations of the parties that their award be enforced are in stark contrast with the original contractual wording to choose a specific law to govern their contract, the sole application of which eventually leads to a violation of transnational public policy.

Beyond the conventional methods of determining the applicable law to the contract, the contribution of good faith as an interpretive tool is to 'regulate' and further calibrate the choice of law by resorting to the parties' legitimate expectations. Were it not for good faith in the ascertainment of the proper law, the legal reasoning of the arbitrator would have been devoid of their accountability to the parties' legitimate expectations for a valid and enforceable award. To this end, the close connection of good faith with the legitimate expectations of the parties is, in fact, endorsed in the scholarship.[39]

35 George A. Bermann, International Arbitration and Private International Law (The Hague Academy of International Law 2017), at 175 n.447.

36 Bermann, International Arbitration and Private International Law, *supra* note 35.

37 Yves Derains, *Possible Conflict of Laws Rules and the Rules Applicable to the Substance of the Dispute*, *in* 2 UNCITRAL's Project for a Model Law on International Commercial Arbitration, para. 49 (Pieter Sanders ed., ICCA Congress Series, 1984).

38 Derains, *supra* note 37, para. 47.

39 The legitimate expectations of the parties should be seen as an inherent consequence of the principle of good faith. For instance, "a legitimate situation of trust generated by a previous behaviour with conclusive meaning must not be frustrated by a subsequent behaviour with an opposite significance without breaching the obligation to act in good faith." Duarte G. Henriques, *Pathological Arbitration Clauses, Good Faith and the Protection of Legitimate Expectations*, 31(2) Arb Int'l 349, 356 (William W. Park ed., OUP 2015). Thus, and this is important, the legitimate expectations must not be envisioned as frustrating the clear intentions of the parties. Instead, they provide the legitimizing perimeter of their existence. Such expectations are detected in the arbitration agreement and are shaped by the discretion of the arbitrator, taking into account the entire relationship. From the standpoint of private international law, it has been argued that the legitimate expectations of the parties 'regulate' the law indicated by the conflict-of-laws system of the *forum* when the behavior of the parties, which is grounded on a different law other than previously stated, is sufficiently validated and the parties legitimately believe in the legal status of their rights acquired, despite the opposite unjust solution arrived based on the conflict-of-law rule of the *forum*, and which is temporally and spatially remote to the contested situation. Lycette Corbion, Le déni de justice en droit international privé, paras. 359–65 (Presses universitaires d'Aix-Marseille 2004).

7.3.2 Public Policy

An interpretation in good faith requires an assessment of whether an arbitrary selection or invocation of a specific law – or part of it – complies with public policy grounds, on the basis of which an award may be annulled or resisted thereafter, mainly because the very principle of good faith forming part of public policy might be transgressed.[40] Indeed, the special role that good faith plays in an arbitrator's legal reasoning is also associated with the annulment risk. It is argued that the arbitrator considers the award as a "self-standing piece of work that has to be perfect and correct by reference to [arbitrators'] own standards and criteria, even if this should expose it to the risk of nullification"[41] (alteration to the original). However, it is unrealistic to claim that arbitrators do not want to see their awards be enforced or at least do not weigh in their decision-making a potential violation of public policy. In fact, they might be compelled to do so. Article 42 of ICC Rules provides that the tribunal "shall make every effort to make sure that the award is enforceable at law." As a result, provided that good faith normally forms a pillar of public policy, it will accordingly influence the arbitrator's reasoning with respect to the validity of the chosen substantive law. An example of such contradiction to the public policy doctrine may be the application of a law allowing for punitive damages, which cannot be permitted by the public policy of the place of arbitration or the country of enforcement. The result would be that the arbitral tribunal may disregard such permitting law to the previous extent. Even though compliance with good faith may be sought – depending on the case – at different levels of public policy, including state public policy, international public policy and transnational public policy,[42] it can be inferred that a public-policy-related good faith should be

40 See, *e.g.*, Peru No. 2019-1, D.P. Trade SA v. Metalyck SAC, Corte Superior de Justicia, Lima, Case No. 352-2017, Mar. 5, 2018, 44 Y.B. Comm. Arb.1, at [42] (Stephan W. Schill ed., ICCA & Kluwer Law International 2019) ("[T]he . . . award must not contain declarations that violate fundamental principles of the . . . legal system of the State where recognition is sought. This includes the principles of non-abuse of rights, good faith, the binding force of contracts and the prohibition of discrimination . . . as well as the prohibition of activities contrary to good morals"); *accord* Hochstrasser, *supra* note 22, at 61; see also GCC 1:33 (Greece) on the notion of international public policy that includes fair dealing too.

41 Mayer, *Reflections on the International Arbitrator's Duty to Apply the Law*, *supra* note 2, para. 15.13.

42 Mayer explains that state public policy is a component of a national legal system. Contrariwise, international public policy is a limited public policy segment by virtue of which the application of a foreign law can be resisted by a state court and which derives from public international law. Transnational public policy is distinct from national law or international law in that it is rather associated with *lex mercatoria* and a set of principles that are considered "inviolable by the community of men, or by a majority of States having enacted legislation or entered into treaties in order to protect them." Pierre Mayer, *Effect of International Public Policy in International Arbitration*, *in* 15 Pervasive Problems in International Arbitration, paras. 2.2, 2.12–.21 (Julian D. M. Lew & Loukas A. Mistelis eds., 2006). However, the categories of public policy are not easily distinguishable. The international *ordre public* of a state being an EU member may be extended to cover European Union principles, too. See ECJ, Case C-126/97, 1 June 1999, Eco Swiss China Ltd v. Benetton International NV, E.C.R. I-3055; *accord* George A. Bermann, *Mandatory Rules of Law in International*

viewed not only as a legitimacy rule that justifies the solution that the respective arbitrator applies *in concreto*, but also a methodological rule that prevents from methodological anarchy.[43]

7.4 The Tension of Legitimate Expectations and Foreign Mandatory Rules

A tension is likely to arise between the legitimate expectations to apply a specific law and a third country's mandatory rules of law. There is the possibility that the parties' legitimate expectations are not necessarily incongruent with mandatory rules outside the *lex contractus*, in which case the arbitrator applies such mandatory rules.[44] On the other hand, there is the possibility that the legitimate expectations of the parties to apply a specific law conflict with other mandatory rules allegedly applicable. How should the arbitrator reconcile such discrepancies? The tribunal in *ICC Case No. 1512* found that the bank guarantee expressly provided for Indian law to be applicable, yet the question arose whether the Pakistani emergency decrees that prevented the payment to an Indian party were instead applicable.[45] As the legitimate expectations of the parties were embedded in their unambiguous intent to apply Indian law and not Pakistani mandatory law, the arbitrator determined that Indian law was the proper law.[46] There was a

> deep incompatibility between the Pakistani decrees prohibiting any payment to an Indian party and the legitimate expectations of the parties to a guarantee validly concluded in order to secure payment to an Indian party which led the arbitrator to give total pre-eminence to the proper law.[47]

The legitimate expectations of the parties must be the starting point in ascertaining the proper law and whether any mandatory rules, including those of a third country, are pertinent. Even if an international arbitrator may *sua sponte* invoke the mandatory rules of the governing law, the legitimate expectations of the parties have a special bearing on whether the arbitrator can also resort to the mandatory rules of a third country. This is also corroborated by the fact that the arbitrator, as opposed to a national judge, does not feel bound by any rules of law of any jurisdiction and is more prone to applying mandatory rules of a country, in addition

---

Arbitration, *in* CONFLICT OF LAWS IN INTERNATIONAL ARBITRATION 325, 328 (Franco Ferrari & Stefan Kröll eds., 2010).

43 See PAMBOUKIS, LEX MERCATORIA AS APPLICABLE LAW IN INTERNATIONAL CONTRACTUAL OBLIGATIONS, *supra* note 4, para. 140.

44 DERAINS, *supra* note 37, para. 43 (discussing that the tribunal in *ICC Case No. 1704* found that "[i]t is, therefore, because the intervention of mandatory Indian Law is not necessarily incompatible with the legitimate expectation of the parties that the arbitrator accepts to apply it").

45 ICC Case No. 1512 of 1971, 1 Y.B. Comm. Arb. 128 (1976) (Pieter Sanders ed., ICCA & Kluwer Law International 1976).

46 DERAINS, *supra* note 37, para. 32.

47 DERAINS, *supra* note 37, para. 43.

to the ones of the governing law.[48] The contribution of good faith in this case is attributed to the arbitrator's general sense of appropriateness in the application of such mandatory rules.[49] Importantly, good faith as a reasoning rule is embedded in the legitimate expectations of the parties given that the arbitrator cannot always be in a position to consider in advance while ascertaining the appropriateness of a law, all foreign mandatory rules involved in order to ensure the effectiveness – thus the enforceability – of their decision-making.[50]

7.5 Good Faith as a Balancing Rule

A critic may well argue that good faith is merely redundant in this exercise. However, it must be acknowledged that its employment is connected to giving pre-eminence to the parties' legitimate expectations, especially when these are unequivocal. It must not be overlooked, though, that a good faith interpretation requires both adherence to parties' legitimate expectations and public policy values that are so fundamental and universal that they cannot be derogated from.[51] Even if the arbitrator feels bound by the express will of the parties to exclude a mandatory rule of law,[52] there are certain rules of law that cannot be opted out. For example, the tactical contractual exclusion of the *pari passu* principle among creditors, therefore, the safeguards of equality of treatment, non-discrimination and good faith. Further, the protection of the weaker party and elimination of asymmetrical and opportunistic treatment of a party is grounded too on notions of good faith; thus, it cannot be waived.[53]

48 BERMANN, *Mandatory Rules of Law in International Arbitration*, *supra* note 42, at 333.

49 BERMANN, *Mandatory Rules of Law in International Arbitration*, *supra* note 42, at 333.

50 DERAINS, *supra* note 37, para. 43. Derains handily explains that the effectiveness of the award, which depends on the question of what the place of enforcement would be, cannot be adequately predicted by the arbitrator by virtue of the international spread of goods and the fact that such prediction depends on who the losing party will be, which is a question that subsequently depends on the approval or rejection of the law that is supposed to be directly applicable. DERAINS, *supra* note 37. As such, it is possible that the public policy of the country where enforcement is sought may not be sufficiently foreseen. Derains suggests that the best criterion to consider whether foreign mandatory rules – other than mandatory rules of the law governing the contract – are applicable is the legitimate expectations of the parties. DERAINS, *supra* note 37.

51 BERMANN, *Mandatory Rules of Law in International Arbitration*, *supra* note 42, at 339. Bermann emphasizes that a distinction between mandatory rules of law and public policy should be justified on the basis that public policy encompasses mandatory rules, too, in the sense that a rule of public policy can both trump the application of the law chosen by the parties and prevent the parties from sidestepping a mandatory rule of law. BERMANN, *Mandatory Rules of Law in International Arbitration*, *supra* note 42, at 328.

52 Mayer, *Mandatory Rules of Law in International Arbitration*, *supra* note 25, at 283.

53 BERMANN, *Mandatory Rules of Law in International Arbitration*, *supra* note 42, at 326; see, *e.g.*, Regulation (EC) No 593/2008 of the European Parliament and of the Council of 17 June 2008, on the law applicable to contractual obligations (Rome I Regulation) O. J. (L 177/13), art. 21 on the international public policy as a limit to the application of a certain law; see also GCC 1:33 (preventing the application of a foreign law that transgresses the international public policy of the state which includes, *inter alia*, art. 178 on agreements opposing the notion of fair dealing).

7.6 Implications of the Interpretive Principle of Good Faith

Most arbitral awards fail to adequately explain first what the implications of a good faith interpretation are and second how the process of interpretation is involved in the determination of the applicable law. Importantly, there are quite a few benefits of clarifying the role of interpretive good faith in the determination of the applicable law. It can insulate the arbitral award from litigious efforts to annul the award on the grounds of excess of power or public policy. It may also better inform the judgment of the arbitrator as to the legitimacy of the solution that the arbitrator should adopt *in concreto*. In case the parties have clearly demonstrated their intent to have a specific law govern their contract, the arbitrator has no authority whatsoever to substitute her choice for the parties' choice. Nonetheless, the arbitrator is granted the power by the parties to supplement or correct their intent under limited circumstances. One should not be narrow-minded to disengage interpretation from its effects. The impression that interpretation and construction are totally distinct functions is unrealistic.[54] On the one hand, interpretation may be recognized as an invaluable method in case of failure of language[55] and help the arbitrator determine the intent of the parties or fix the communicative meaning of the words used.[56] On the other hand, construction describes the next phase of interpretation; it is a more holistic method of interpretation since it ascribes certain legal effects to the words used and effectively invites the arbitrator to understand the entire contractual framework through the lens of policy-related doctrines, such as good faith, reasonableness and commercial sense.[57]

7.6.1 Suppletive Effect

Some arbitral awards have applied a-national rules deriving from trade usages. Such a-national rules have been applied by virtue of the applicable arbitration rules, such as UNCITRAL Rule 33(3) stipulating that irrespective of whether the parties have designated a specific law to govern their dispute, the arbitral tribunal shall, in all cases, decide in accordance with the contract and trade usages applicable to the transaction.[58] Such nuances of a-national rules should not be envisaged as replacing the applicable domestic law but as supplementing it.[59] They escort the applicable law. What is not obvious, though, is that an interpretation in good faith, which requires the understanding of the whole contract in a commercially

54 Catherine Mitchell, Interpretation of Contracts 107 (2nd ed., Taylor & Francis 2018).

55 Mitchell, *supra* note 54, at 106.

56 Mitchell, *supra* note 54.

57 Mitchell, *supra* note 54, at 107 (citing David Charny, Hypothetical Bargains: The Normative Structure of Contract Interpretation, 89 Mich. L. R. 1815, 1816 (1991)).

58 See also NAI Arbitration Rules (2010), art. 47 ("In all cases the arbitral tribunal shall take into account any applicable trade usages"); BAC Arbitration Rules (2015), art. 69 (4) ("In all cases, the Arbitral Tribunal shall render its award in accordance with the valid terms of the parties' agreement and take into account the relevant industry practices and trade usages").

59 Derains, *supra* note 37, para. 37.

reasonable fashion, necessitates the previously mentioned supplementary effect. Functionally, it would not be pragmatic to treat the principle of good faith as not providing the power to the arbitrator to create the law.[60] Interpretation *per se* as a method cannot effectively be separated from the process of creating the law.[61] For example, in case of antagonism between a contractual term and a trade usage, the arbitrator has the discretion to give precedence to the trade usage over the term of the contract.[62] That is particularly true from a common law perspective where "common law judges make use of practice-based good faith to supplement the contract with rules derived from community standards."[63]

The supplementation by virtue of good faith is justified on the basis that the parties "tacitly accept the normative expectations commonly accepted in their relevant contractual community."[64] The U.C.C. § 2–103(1) imports trade usages into the contract as a matter of good faith, which "means honesty in fact and the observance of reasonable commercial standards of fair dealing in the trade." This should not, however, lead to the arbitrary assumption that the suppletive effect of the interpretive principle of good faith operates generally in competition with the parties' intent. Thus, even if the parties have alluded to an express choice of law, it is still likely that the arbitrator will be entitled to fill in any gaps in the selection of the applicable law by resorting to supplementary rules, provided that such rules are not against the parties' intentions.[65] This solution cannot render the contract void either entirely or in part.[66] The tribunal in *CRCICA Case No. 120/1998* applied trade usages along with the law of the respondent according to UNCITRAL Rule 33.[67] It went on that this solution resonated with the "implicit, common intention of the parties."[68]

60 See Lisa Beisteiner, *The Arbitration Agreement and Arbitrability, The (Perceived) Power of the Arbitrator to Revise a Contract – The Austrian Perspective*, *in* 2014 Austrian Yearbook on International Arbitration 77, 121 (Christian Klausegger et al. eds., 2014) ("Some 30 years ago a skeptical *Jan Paulsson* wondered whether contract adaptation by an arbitrator would be a notion of the future, a *'big idea'* for later generations of arbitrators . . . . Under Austrian law, as will be the case under many other legal systems, *arbiter substituit* – arbitrators do make contracts") (citations omitted) (emphasis in original).

61 Beisteiner, *supra* note 40, at 80 ("*The distinction between interpreting and creating the law is a fiction*") (emphasis added) (quoting Alan Boyle & Christine Chinkin, The Making of International Law 268 (OUP 2007)).

62 Joshua Karton, *The Arbitral Role in Contractual Interpretation*, 6(1) J. Int. Disput. Settl. 4, 32 (Thomas Schultz ed., OUP 2015).

63 Daniele Bertolini, *Toward a Framework to Define the Outer Boundaries of Good Faith in Contractual Performance*, 58 Alberta L. Rev. 599 (2021).

64 Bertolini, *supra* note 63.

65 Pamboukis, lex mercatoria as applicable law in international contractual obligations, *supra* note 4, para. 133.

66 Pamboukis, lex mercatoria as applicable law in international contractual obligations, *supra* note 4.

67 An African furniture company (seller) v. An Asian company (buyer), Partial Award, CRCICA Case No. 120/1998, June 23, 2000, *in* Arbitral Awards of the Cairo Regional Centre for International Commercial Arbitration II 25, 29 (Mohie-Eldin & Alam-Eldin eds., 2003).

68 An African furniture company (seller), *supra* note 67.

Nonetheless, it is worth noting that there is no consensus reached as to what extent a good faith interpretation will require supplementation by reference to trade usages "only to the extent this is admissible under the applicable domestic law,"[69] as an ICC study supports, or to the extent that "very little depends on the question of the applicable law,"[70] as Böckstiegel proposes. At any rate, supplementing the applicable domestic law with transnational rules derived from trade usages reflects pragmatism. Such a solution must be accepted by virtue of the incompleteness of domestic laws and their insufficiency in exceptional cases to give solutions to unexpected situations in the rapidly changing cosmos of international business.[71] Even Section 46 of the English Arbitration Act 1996 does not preclude the application of trade usages to the extent parties have so agreed or the applicable law allows such an application or finally by reference to implied terms.[72]

7.6.2 Corrective Effect

Waincymer reasons that if the parties have chosen a national law that is perceived to be invalid by the tribunal, the tribunal, under its broad duties with respect to public policy, as well as good faith, has the right to adopt a differing law[73] and disregard the law originally selected. A neat example is a bad faith purpose, such as the selection of an inappropriate law by the parties in order to avoid certain tax provisions.[74] That would be the case of "a circuitous set of contracts thought to be designed to route a commercial transaction through a tax haven."[75] In such limited instances, and after giving the parties a full opportunity to make their respective representations, the arbitrator may feel bound to intervene.[76] More illustrative is

69 *Developing Neutral Legal Standards for International Contracts: A-national Rules as the Applicable Law in International Commercial Contracts with Particular Reference to the ICC Model Contracts*, International Chamber of Commerce Policy and Business Practices, study conducted by the Task Force chaired by Fabio Bortolotti and Franco Silvano Toni di Cigoli (Nov. 4, 2015), at 24, *available at* https://iccwbo.org/news-publications/policies-reports/developing-neutral-legal-standards-international-contracts/ (last visited Aug. 23, 2023).

70 Karton, *supra* note 62, at 6–7 (quoting Karl-Heinz Böckstiegel, Arbitration and State Enterprises: A Survey of the National and International State of Law and Practice 27 (Kluwer 1984)).

71 Stewart R. Shackleton, *The Applicable Law in International Arbitration Under the New English Arbitration Act 1996*, 13(4) Arb. Int'l 375, 387 (William W. Park ed., OUP 1997).

72 Shackleton, *supra* note 71, at 388.

73 Jeffrey Maurice Waincymer, Procedure and Evidence in International Arbitration 1089 (Kluwer Law International 2012).

74 Waincymer, *supra* note 73; *accord* Franz T. Schwarz & Christian W. Konrad, The Vienna Rules: A Commentary on International Arbitration in Austria, paras. 24–27 (Kluwer Law International 2009) ("[T]he parties' freedom to apply a law of their choosing may indeed be limited by good faith considerations and public policy. Consequently, a choice of law for the purpose of tax evasion could be found invalid") (citations omitted). The analogue of such abusive change of law in private international law is reflected in *fraus legis* and *forum shopping*. See generally Pamboukis, Private International Law, *supra* note 22, paras. 378–85.

75 Waincymer, *supra* note 73, at 1090.

76 Waincymer, *supra* note 73.

Lörcher's example, where the parties made a choice of a certain legal system to govern their dispute by waiving its internal mandatory rules, opting for another law's mandatory rules and later invoking the former's internal mandatory rules.[77] Strictly speaking, it is not the law per se that is corrected but the parties' *abusive intent* or the *extent* of the application of the selected law, especially where the strict application of a chosen law obstructs the effectiveness of the arbitral decision by violating the public policy of the country of enforcement.

Mayer explained that a party may raise the objection that the law chosen contravenes either another country's public policy or does not comply with transnational public policy requirements.[78] As Born championed, relevant to that rationale is the duty of the arbitrator to apply the applicable law by virtue of their "adjudicative mandate comparable to that of a judge,"[79] which may even result in that "this mandate may be directly contrary to the parties' agreement."[80] Rogers emphasized that the application of a substantive law echoes "[a] commitment to determining an appropriate, law-bound outcome of a dispute [that] necessitates the *sine qua non* of the adjudicator – some degree of objectivity or impartiality necessary for rational analytic discernment of the law and application to the facts."[81] Such solutions in most laws are embedded in the principle of good faith and its status within a particular system *i.e.*, a public policy rule prohibiting unreasonableness and arbitrariness of conduct. In essence, the principle of good faith permeates the arbitrator's determinative task and regulates not only the proper choice of law *stricto sensu*, but it also regulates and effectively fine-tunes the arbitrator's legal reasoning with respect to *why* a particular law should eventually be preferred. However, under no circumstances should the generic assumption be formed that good faith authorizes the arbitrator to override the intention of the parties and effectively create new rights and obligations for the parties by virtue of some irrelevant law.

7.7 Controversial Cases Justifying Correction of Applicable Law – The Effectiveness Argument

Apparently, the corrective effect of the interpretive good faith is a twilight issue since there is a grave risk that the arbitrator may violate their jurisdictional mission to adhere to the will of the parties. Fouchard, Gaillard and Goldman believed that the arbitrator's intervention may be justified on the basis of the incompleteness

77 Hochstrasser, *supra* note 22, at 70 (citing GINO LÖRCHER, Wie zwingend sind in der internationalen Handelsschiedsgerichtsbarkeit zwingende Normen einer "dritten" Rechtsordnung? in 27 ENCLOSURE 17 ad., 6 (Betriebsberater 1993).

78 MAYER, *Reflections on the International Arbitrator's Duty to Apply the Law*, *supra* note 2, paras. 15.25–26. Pamboukis argues that the arbitrator should apply the mandatory rules of the arbitral seat and of the country or countries of enforcement since such a duty derives from their mandate and the legitimate expectations of the parties to obtain a valid and enforceable award. PAMBOUKIS, PRIVATE INTERNATIONAL LAW, *supra* note 22, paras. 455, 469; see also Rome I Regulation, art. 9.3 (on overriding mandatory provisions).

79 CATHERINE A. ROGERS, ETHICS IN INTERNATIONAL ARBITRATION, para. 9.44 (OUP 2014).

80 ROGERS, *supra* note 79, para. 9.45.

81 ROGERS, *supra* note 79, para. 9.50.

theory, pursuant to which the chosen law does not give answers to the issues arising from the dispute.[82] The traditional arbitration practice speaks for itself. Lord Asquith, in the 1951 case of *Petroleum Development Ltd. v. The Sheikh of Abu Dhabi,* reasoned that English law to the extent that it mirrored universal legal principles should apply because the chosen law of Abu Dhabi that governed the parties' contract was not yet sufficiently codified; thus, it was excluded as applicable law.[83] The tribunal in the subsequent *Aramco case* followed a similar argument that the applicable Saudi Arabian law was inadequate to deal with complex petroleum contracts, therefore, it applied transnational rules instead.[84] A similar rationale is portrayed in the ICSID award of the *SPP* case. The tribunal applied public international law to the specific issue of "the starting-point for the accrual of interest . . . on the basis that Egyptian law was allegedly insufficiently developed to adequately address that subject."[85]

Even though the solutions adopted in these heavily criticized awards do not follow from good faith and despite the unsatisfactory proposition that a legal system may not be sophisticated enough to find a solution to a specific issue of dispute,[86] the theoretical framework of the principle of good faith might well serve the purpose of liberating tribunals from constraints of intentions that do not uphold the effectiveness of the applicable law, Party autonomy is *ostensibly* restricted, yet the end result is that the arbitrator's intervention enhances the objective of party autonomy, that being "the parties will do all they can to fully and effectively perform their obligations under the contract . . . [and] nothing to sabotage or render impossible performance of the contract."[87] (alteration to original). In those rare cases, the underlying rationale of corrective good faith is the effectiveness principle resting on: (a) the *appropriateness* of the applicable law, as evinced by a teleological balancing of that law against the nature of the dispute;[88] having regard to (b) the *legitimate and reasonable expectations of the parties*, which reflect the rational expectations of the average person at the time of the commencement of the proceedings,[89] and which are targeted to the enforceability of the award. It shall be deduced, therefore, that the arbitrator is, in principle, confined by the common intentions of the parties. However, such intentions are not conclusive but only decisive given that there is scope for deviation if solutions derived from good

82 Emmanuel Gaillard & John Savage, Fouchard Gaillard Goldman on International Commercial Arbitration 820 (Kluwer Law International 1999), para. 1512.

83 Gaillard & Savage, *supra* note 82.

84 Gaillard & Savage, *supra* note 82.

85 Gaillard & Savage, *supra* note 82. See Southern Pacific Properties (Middle East) Limited v. Arab Republic of Egypt, ICSID Case No. ARB/84/3, Award, paras. 234–35, May 20, 1992.

86 Gaillard & Savage, *supra* note 82.

87 Lew et al., *supra* note 1, paras. 18–83.

88 See Pamboukis, lex mercatoria as applicable law in international contractual obligations, *supra* note 4, para. 137.

89 Pamboukis, lex mercatoria as applicable law in international contractual obligations, *supra* note 4, para. 138.

faith fulfill the jurisdictional mission of the arbitral tribunal.[90] Arbitral tribunals are best suited to know the law.[91] In fact, it is the sacred principle of *iura novit arbiter* innate to the arbitration agreement that obliges the arbitrator to "amend and to replace wrongly invoked law"[92] when she has legitimate doubts about its application.[93]

7.8 Misapplication of Interpretive Good Faith and Consequences

A pressing question can be whether an erroneous application of the substantive law must constitute a ground for annulment or refusal of enforcement of the award. A thorough analysis of this problem exceeds the scope of this monograph, which only focuses on the tribunal's perspective and does not extend to domestic courts' review. Nonetheless, it would have been an omission had this chapter failed to touch upon the implications of arbitrators' interpretive task. Normally, if the arbitrator applies the chosen law in an incompetent manner or decides on some basis other than the applicable law itself, the award cannot be challenged under NYC Article V or most national laws in conformity with the UNCITRAL Model Law.[94] Importantly, a tribunal's untenable interpretation of the proper law may not be subject to a challenge.[95] It is equally maintained that, even if the parties have explicitly chosen a specific law to govern their dispute, the fact that the tribunal disregarded such a law, as a consequence of its own good faith interpretation of the contract, may not be regarded as a tribunal's excess of power, effectively it may not constitute a ground of annulment.[96]

Only to the extent that such good faith interpretation is no less than an *ultra vires* act on the part of the arbitrator shall it be sanctioned. This approach resonates with actual practice, too. A setting aside procedure was brought before the

90 PAMBOUKIS, LEX MERCATORIA AS APPLICABLE LAW IN INTERNATIONAL CONTRACTUAL OBLIGATIONS, *supra* note 4, para. 145.

91 Christian Collantes, *Give Me the Facts and I'll Give You the Law: What are the Limits of the Iura Novit Arbiter Principle in International Arbitration?* KLUWER ARBITRATION BLOG, Jan. 10, 2019, *available at* http://arbitrationblog.kluwerarbitration.com/2019/01/10/give-me-the-facts-and-ill-give-you-the-law-what-are-the-limits-of-the-iura-novit-arbiter-principle-in-international-arbitration/#:~:text=The%20discussion%20about%20whether%20and,not%20invoked%20by%20 (last visited Oct. 27, 2022).

92 Collantes, *supra* note 91.

93 Collantes, *supra* note 91.

94 Karton, *supra* note 62, at 29.

95 MANUEL ARROYO, *Commentary on Chapter 12 PILS, Article 190 [Finality, Challenge: Principle]*, *in* ARBITRATION IN SWITZERLAND: THE PRACTITIONER'S GUIDE 266, para. 196 (Manuel Arroyo ed., 2nd ed., 2018) (supporting that, provided the contract is governed by Swiss law, an untenable interpretation of certain articles thereof and its legal consequences, for instance, the seller's liability, cannot form a ground for any challenge).

96 GIUDITTA CORDERO-MOSS, *Iura Novit Curia*, *in* HANDBOOK OF EVIDENCE IN INTERNATIONAL COMMERCIAL ARBITRATION: KEY CONCEPTS AND ISSUES 111, 124 (Franco Ferrari & Friedrich Jakob Rosenfeld eds., 2022).

Austrian Supreme Court by the plaintiff to annul certain parts of the award on the basis that the arbitrators exceeded their power by not applying German law, which was the law originally selected by the parties, and that an arbitrary interpretation of the agreement constituted a violation of procedural public policy.[97] The Austrian Supreme Court reasoned that it could not uphold the claim of the tribunal's excess of competence.[98] It further held that "[a] 'simple' wrong application of the law designated by the parties is not relevant . . . unless it amounts to an arbitrary application of the law which leads to an untenable violation of the Austrian legal order (*ordre public*)."[99] Based on the foregoing, it would be prudent to subscribe to the view that, unless there is an egregious error in terms of an arbitrary interpretation and a blatant disregard of a law, the arbitrator's interpretive task to determine the law is originally insulated.[100] Essentially, it is not about *what* the substantive law should be (which is an exercise directly related to the *jura novit curia* doctrine) but *how* the substantive law is applied and, specifically, whether the parties were given the opportunity to make submissions on that law.[101]

7.9 Conclusion

This chapter sought to explain the role of good faith interpretation in the process of determining the proper law. It was expounded that the foundation of the interpretive good faith must be the dialectic symbiosis of party autonomy and arbitrator's discretion, while the mechanisms of good faith are only relevant when the parties have explicitly chosen a specific law. By contrast, interpretive good faith cannot replace the parties' intentions when the parties have remained silent. The arbitrators must not be short-sighted to disregard the unequivocal application of the substantive law that the parties have chosen. However, the arbitrator is vested with the power to supplement the law and, under limited circumstances, to correct an ill-conceived or arbitrary choice of law. That though requires the protection of the parties' legitimate expectations, especially where a bad faith choice of law entails a wrongdoing or the engineering of the application of law in such a way that duress or other illegal conduct is present.[102] In any case, a choice of law should

97 Markus Schifferl & Venus Valentina Wong, *The Award and the Courts, Decisions of the Austrian Supreme Court on Arbitration*, *in* Austrian Yearbook on International arbitration 2019 371, 388–90 (Christian Klausegger et al. eds., 2019).

98 Schifferl & Wong, *supra* note 97.

99 Schifferl & Wong, *supra* note 97, at 391.

100 Karton, *supra* note 62, at 29.

101 Laurent Lévy, *Jura Novit Curia? The Arbitrator's Discretion in the Application of the Governing Law*, Kluwer Arbitration Blog, Mar. 20, 2009, *available at* https://arbitrationblog.kluwerarbitration.com/2009/03/20/jura-novit-curia-the-arbitrators-discretion-in-the-application-of-the-governing-law/ (last visited Apr. 17, 2023).

102 Yock Lin Tan, *Good Faith Choice of a Law to Govern a Contract*, sjls 307, 310–14, 327 (2014) (advocating that a choice of law in private international law should be made in good faith and further exploring whether it is in good faith to rely on an express choice of law if that reliance may result in injustice for the non-relying contractor by virtue of evasion of law or *fraus legis*).

also take into consideration a public-policy-related doctrine of good faith for the purpose of facilitating the effective enforcement of the award. The significance of constantly observing the interpretive good faith, even in the context of a choice of law, is reflected in the efforts of challenging the award on some basis of arbitrary application of the chosen law.

Part III

Procedural Function of Good Faith

8 Good Faith as a Standard of Procedural Fairness

8.1 Meaning and Scope of Procedural Good Faith

The rule of good faith, which provides for a behavioral standard, applies not only to the substance of the dispute but also to the procedural conduct of the parties before courts and tribunals,[1] especially in the taking of evidence, conduct of the hearing, time limits, examination of witnesses as well as constitution and challenge of arbitrators. For instance, the *CAM Award No. 115/2016* portrays the respondent's dilatory tactics in raising an arbitration exception in court litigation and thereafter striving to deprive the arbitration process of having a binding effect.[2] The respondent did so by insisting on the provision of the arbitration agreement – which it had drafted itself – that any arbitral award under the agreement "shall not be regarded as final and binding on the parties."[3] The tribunal ruled that such procedural conduct would be against the principle of good faith, estoppel and consistent conduct, enshrined in UNIDROIT Principles, Article 1.8, pursuant to which a party cannot act inconsistently with an understanding it has caused to the other, and based on which the latter has relied to its detriment.[4] It is evident, therefore, that resorting to good faith helps arbitrators identify procedural irregularities. Most importantly, it instills confidence in the proceedings in the sense that it formulates the bedrock of certain standards of procedural conduct.

8.1.1 Distinction from Substantive Function of Good Faith

The difference between substantive and procedural functions is deeply associated with their respective legitimacy foundation. The substantive good faith is ingrained in the applicable substantive law of the contract, whereas the procedural good faith

1 Klaus Peter Berger, *Cost Sanctions for Delaying Tactics in International Arbitration, in* Finances In International Arbitration: Liber Amicorum Patricia Shaughnessy, para. 2.05 (Sherlin Tung et al. eds., 2019).

2 CAM Case No. 115, Feb. 11, 2016 (Stefano Azzali & Benedetta Coppo, A contribution by the ITA Board of Reporters).

3 CAM Case No. 115, *supra* note 2.

4 CAM Case No. 115, *supra* note 2.

DOI: 10.4324/9781003527596-11

is primarily entrenched in the arbitration agreement, the applicable institutional rules and the law of the seat. It becomes apparent that the content of procedural good faith is diversified, taking also into account the ample discretion the arbitral tribunal is vested with. Failing the parties to designate the applicable substantive or procedural law, the arbitral tribunal enjoys wide discretion in determining it. However, the discretion regarding the rules of procedure and the ensuing standard of procedural good faith is wider than the applicable substantive law. Support for that proposition, albeit not flawless, is also related to the fictive nature of the arbitral seat. Smit, Mavromati and Waincymer rightly confirmed that the discretion of the arbitral tribunal under the institutional rules and national laws in respect to procedural matters is *wider* than the discretion in relation to the applicable law to the merits.[5] However, conferring such a broad discretion may open the floodgates of "arbitrators' personal moral values or self-interested desire to uphold party autonomy, thus raising fears of inconsistency."[6] The direct effect of such a phenomenon is the arbitrator's arbitrary exercise of powers as a result of their wide discretion, which may lead to the annulment of the award.

8.1.2 Procedural Good Faith and Fairness

Fundamental notions for the mission of the arbitral process, such as

> party autonomy and the arbitral tribunal's discretion [can] both [be] restricted under certain circumstances to ensure due process, in particular with regard to the parties' *right to equal treatment* and *right to be heard*, as well as the participants' general *good faith* obligation.[7]
>
> (alteration to the original) (emphasis in the original)

The parties' intentions as well as the competent tribunal's discretion, should not be allowed to be unbridled as that would contravene the very purpose of procedural good faith, that is, fairness. On this basis, the extent to which the behavioral standard of good faith in the proceedings can be equated with procedural fairness is a moot point. It is buttressed that, whereas estoppel can be explained by reference to the mechanism of good faith in the execution of contracts, the mechanisms of good faith and *estoppel* are, in fact, distinct, since *estoppel* is closer to the notion of fairness.[8] Pinsolle argues in favor of the autonomy of

5 Saar A. Pauker, *Substance and Procedure in International Arbitration*, 36(1) Arb. Int'l. 14 n.65 (William W. Park ed., OUP 2020); see also UNCITRAL Rules 2021, art. 17(1) ("[T]he arbitral tribunal may conduct the arbitration in such manner as it considers appropriate").

6 Andrew Barraclough & Jeff Waincymer, *Mandatory Rules of Law in International Commercial Arbitration*, 6 Melb. J. Int. Law 205–44 (2005), *available at* http://classic.austlii.edu.au/au/journals/MelbJIL/2005/9.html.

7 Nadia Smahi, *Due Process Under the Swiss Rules of International Arbitration,* 38 ASA Bull. 930, 932 (Matthias Scherer ed., 2020).

8 Philippe Pinsolle, *Note – Cour de cassation (1re Ch. civ.), July 6, 2005*, 2005 Revue de l'Arbitrage, 994, paras. 12–15 (Comité French for Arbitration 2005).

estoppel because of the different sanctions imposed in case of violation of good faith in the execution of the arbitration agreement *vis-à-vis* the rule of *estoppel.*[9] He maintains that the appropriate penalty for not performing the arbitration agreement in good faith should not be the inadmissibility of the claim but that the claim should be denied on the merits,[10] as the inadmissibility is a consequence of the application of the rule of *estoppel.*[11] To support his analysis, he relied on the case of Abrahim Golshani, a US citizen of Iranian origin, who brought a claim of roughly USD 1.7 billion before the Iran-US tribunal against the Republic of Iran for alleged expropriation of his interests in an Iranian development company and other entities.[12] The arbitral tribunal rejected Golshani's claim and ordered him to pay the Government of Iran USD 50,000 in legal fees and expenses.[13] Golshani turned to the Court of Appeal and invoked, *inter alia*, the absence of an arbitration agreement.[14] The Court of Appeal rejected his request as inadmissible. On 6 July 2005, the Court of Cassation confirmed the ruling of the Court of Appeal for the inadmissibility of the plea was grounded on the *estoppel* rule, which was resorted to by virtue of the contradictory conduct of Golshani of arbitrating for nine years without contesting the existence of the arbitration agreement and then seeking to reap the benefits of its alleged absence.[15]

Pinsolle suggests it is not good faith in the arbitration agreement that constitutes the foundation of the inadmissibility of the plea but *estoppel* because it would not be possible to justify the prohibition to raise later on at the annulment stage a claim on the invalidity of the arbitration agreement if that invalidity was raised within reasonable time,[16] unless one wants to perceive arbitrating in good faith with procedural fairness in the annulment proceedings.[17] In spite of the astuteness of this observation, the consequences of this approach overlook the primordial affinity of good faith and fairness. It is true that both these closely interrelated concepts counterpoise legal rules leading to inappropriate results.[18] They enjoy the same grandiosity, as the one is the destiny of the other.

As a result, it would be meaningless to maintain that procedural fairness is not a reflection of parties' good faith expectations as crystallized in their arbitration agreement but only a direct consequence of *estoppel.* Put another way, good faith would be an empty shell if the good faith expectations of the parties, as depicted in the arbitration agreement, were disconnected from fairness throughout the proceedings, including the annulment stage, thus undermining the enforceability of

9 Pinsolle, *supra* note 8.
10 Pinsolle, *supra* note 8, para. 15.
11 Pinsolle, *supra* note 8.
12 Pinsolle, *supra* note 8, para. 4.
13 Pinsolle, *supra* note 8.
14 Pinsolle, *supra* note 8.
15 Pinsolle, *supra* note 8, para. 6.
16 Pinsolle, *supra* note 8, para. 15.
17 Pinsolle, *supra* note 8.
18 William W. Park, *Neutrality, Predictability and Economic Co-operation*, 12 (4) J. Int. Arbitr. 99, 106–7 (Kluwer Law International 1995).

the award. This analysis shows that fairness is not actually distinct from good faith. It infuses the application of good faith with certain norms, such as those of due process, prohibition of abuse of process and *estoppel*. Accordingly, it should not be envisaged that the execution of the arbitration agreement in good faith is independent of the parties' expectations for fair and consistent procedural conduct and for an enforceable award. To be more specific, arbitrating in good faith is not confined to just invoking a nullity of an arbitration agreement in good faith (supposedly within reasonable time). And that is also because the arbitration agreement has not come to an end until the arbitral award is annulled.

8.1.3 Relative Standard of Procedural Conduct

The duty of procedural good faith is highly relative, as opposed to substantive good faith. The procedural good faith concerns both the conduct of the parties and the conduct of arbitrators. It might also concern the conduct of other stakeholders, such as counsel and arbitral institutions. For example, a reticent tribunal might suffer from the phenomenon of due process paranoia.[19] It might be partial, too. On the other hand, the parties may employ guerilla tactics, such as intimidating the tribunal or engaging in aggressive correspondence or even bribery.[20] It is evident, therefore, that a different standard of procedural conduct attaches to each and every one of the arbitral participants. According to Section 33(1) of the English Arbitration Act 1996, the tribunal must:

> (a) act fairly and impartially as between the parties, giving each party a reasonable opportunity of putting his case and dealing with that of his opponent, and (b) adopt procedures suitable to the circumstances of the particular case, avoiding unnecessary delay or expense, so as to provide a fair means for the resolution of the matters falling to be determined.

In essence, the standard of conduct attached to arbitrators is centered more on notions of impartiality and fairness *vis-à-vis* the one attached to the parties that are more centered on notions of cooperation during the proceedings.[21] That must be accepted by virtue of the consensualism upon which the entire system of international arbitration is built. Due to the leadership role bestowed upon the arbitrator to control the procedure in a manner that ensures efficiency as well as to guide the

19 Referring to the situation where the tribunal succumbs to any unreasonable requests of the parties, because it anticipates that the award will be challenged.

20 Gary B. Born, International Commercial Arbitration 2292 (3rd ed., Kluwer Law International 2021).

21 See, *e.g.*, 2021 JAMS Arbitration Rule 16(2)(f)(iii) ("The Parties should meet and confer in good faith prior to presenting any issues for the Arbitrator's decision") and Rule 17(a) ("The Parties shall cooperate in good faith in the voluntary and informal exchange of all non-privileged documents and other information (including electronically stored information ('ESI')) relevant to the dispute or claim immediately after commencement of the Arbitration").

parties' freedom to conduct their own proceedings as they want,[22] the arbitrator's procedural duty of good faith is of a different nature. Arbitrators must not only be fair and balanced but they must "be seen by both parties to accept the challenge of equal action in good faith to both parties."[23] In short, it can be asserted that a duty of good faith applies to all agents and stages of the arbitration proceedings,[24] yet differently.

8.2 Sources of Procedural Good Faith

There are mainly three distinct locations where the procedural good faith resides. First, the arbitrator will typically start from the arbitration agreement to identify whether a specific standard of good faith is explicitly incorporated. However, it must be accepted that a duty of good faith is inherent in the arbitration agreement. The tribunal in *ICC Case No. 6149/1990* held that "[a]ll arbitration agreements must be implemented by the parties in good faith. A provision in an arbitration agreement must never be abused as a tool to delay the proceedings. On the contrary, arbitration proceedings require the bona fide cooperation of both parties."[25] Indeed, many arbitration clauses are crafted in a way that references good faith as protecting against undue influence, trickery or any effort to sabotage cooperation and bring the proceedings to a halt.

Second, a duty of good faith may also be rooted in the applicable procedural law of the arbitration, which is normally the *lex loci arbitri* or curial law. That would be the national law of the seat of the arbitration. Each time, the respective jurisdiction will have its own *lex loci arbitri* that will determine the conduct of the proceedings. For instance, Australia's International Arbitration Act 1974 stipulates in Article 34(1) that "[t]he parties shall cooperate in good faith with the Commission in order to enable the Commission to carry out its functions, and shall give their most serious consideration to its recommendations."[26] In the same vein, the French Arbitration Law provides in Article 1464(c) that "[b]oth parties and arbitrators shall act diligently and in good faith in the conduct of the proceedings."[27]

Third, the institutional or *ad hoc* rules applicable to the procedure may form the basis of the parties' procedural duty of good faith. For example, the CAM Arbitration Rules contain a provision that "the arbitrators, the experts, the parties and their counsel shall act in good faith along any phase of the proceedings" and "[t]he

22 Derek Sharp, *The Arbitrator's Duty of Good Faith*, 66(3) Int'l J. of Arb. Med. & Disp. 226, 228 (Kluwer Law International 2000).
23 Sharp, *supra* note 22.
24 Duarte Gorjão Henriques, *The Role of Good Faith in Arbitration: Are Arbitrators and Arbitral Institutions Bound to Act in Good Faith?* 33 ASA Bull. 514, 532 (2015).
25 ICC Case No. 6149 of 1990, 20 Y.B. Comm. Arb. 41, [21] (A. J. Van den Berg ed., 1995).
26 *International Arbitration Act 1974* (Cth) No. 136 (Austl.).
27 Décret n° 2011-48 du 13 janvier 2011 portant réforme de l'arbitrage [Decree no. 2011-48 of Jan. 13, 2011 reforming arbitration law] Journal Officiel de la République Française [J.O.] [Official Gazette of France] Jan. 14, 2011.

Arbitral Tribunal may sanction any breach of its decisions and any unlawful conduct that is contrary to good faith."[28] The Swiss Arbitration Rules similarly provide that all participants in the proceedings shall behave in accordance with good faith.[29] Soft law instruments, such as the IBA Rules, have similar provisions directing parties to comply with a duty of good faith in the taking of evidence.[30]

Fourth, it is principally for the arbitrator to sense what is right and determine the parties' standard of good faith. Their own perception of good faith will be essentially influenced by their ethical standards, commercial awareness, and prior experience.[31]

8.3 Content of Procedural Good Faith

The arbitral theory and practice fail to pay proper attention to good faith as a systemic procedural standard, the transgression of which results in certain consequences for the parties. There is, therefore, a gap in the literature to the extent that the procedural function of good faith is understood in a very generic and fragmented fashion, and in most cases, its role is undermined as a merely superfluous norm. Veeder had succinctly identified the special role of good faith in arbitral proceedings. He had emphasized the need for "practical guidance on good faith for the legal representatives of parties,"[32] especially in contentious procedural matters, such as "document production, the preparation of factual witness statements and the commissioning of independent expert reports."[33] The need to systemize its application is all the more imperative by virtue of the endemic feature of international arbitration to "generate procedural rules and practices, and to a lesser extent substantive rules, that serve as precedent for future arbitrations and beyond."[34] True, the generation of procedural rules in international arbitration confirms the need to infuse proceedings with integrity, legitimacy and a "minimal degree of impartiality, autonomous from the parties' control and directions, [which] is essential for arbitrators to perform the adjudicatory function by which the parties ultimately agreed to have their dispute resolved."[35] The following contours of good faith form the essence of what contributes to the legitimacy of the system of international arbitration, which in turn urges parties to comply with arbitral decision-making voluntarily.[36]

28 CAM Arbitration Rules, art. 9(1) and (3) (2023).
29 Swiss Arbitration Rules, art. 16(1) (2021).
30 IBA Rules in the Taking of Evidence in International Arbitration, Preamble (3); art. 9(8) (2020).
31 Sharp, *supra* note 22, at 229.
32 V.V. Veeder, *The 2001 Goff Lecture – The Lawyer's Duty to Arbitrate in Good Faith*, 18 Arb. Int'l 431, 441 (William W. Park ed., 2002).
33 Veeder, *supra* note 33.
34 Catherine A. Rogers, Ethics in International Arbitration, para. 9.55 (OUP 2014).
35 Rogers, *supra* note 34, para. 9.21.
36 Rogers, *supra* note 34, para. 9.65.

8.3.1 Certainty

Procedural certainty should be construed broadly to encompass, on the one hand, a lack of any kind of inconsistency or ambiguity and, on the other, the notion of predictability. Inconsistent conduct leading to uncertainty is raising a delayed objection. According to SCC Arbitration Rules, "[a] party who . . . fails to object without delay to any failure to comply with the arbitration agreement, the Arbitration Rules or other rules applicable to the proceedings, shall be deemed to have waived the right to object to such failure."[37] Such a rule ensures procedural certainty by not allowing a party to be idle and then raise an objection, while it could have raised that objection much earlier in the proceedings.[38]

Arbitral case law reveals that any such inconsistent conduct is assimilated to bad faith conduct, which can be passive or silent, too. The tribunal in *ICC Case No. 16570* reasoned that a good faith respondent could have replied to the claimant much earlier and informed them that any dispute under their agreement should have been resolved through arbitration instead of letting time elapse, not informing the counterparty of its error and then relying on a statute of limitations.[39] The tribunal held that the respondent was not in a position to raise the statute of limitations, and effectively, the claimant's claim should not be time-barred.[40]

Predictability, on the other hand, should be understood as a manifestation of procedural good faith as it counterweighs the unwelcome effects of unbounded flexibility in the proceedings. Flexibility is not a panacea. Park highlighted that the law would be deprived of its mission, absent the predictability of treating similar cases in a similar fashion.[41] He went on that, without a shared perspective on procedural rules and issues, "litigants lack common assumptions about what fairness means. The absence of standards fixed in advance, while perhaps making arbitration less cumbersome in some instances, can generate feelings of inequality."[42] In particular, the need for predictability resulting from the faithfulness to customary rules of procedure, especially with respect to procedural debates on matters that appear to diverge between common and civil law traditions, such as the discovery process, significantly contributes to what the parties regard as procedural fairness.[43]

37 SCC Arbitration Rules, art. 36 (2023).

38 Jakob Ragnwaldh et al., A Guide to the SCC Arbitration Rules 117 (Wolters Kluwer 2019).

39 ICC Case No. 16570, ICC Disp. Res. Bull. No. 1, para. 187 (2015).

40 ICC Case No. 16570, *supra* note 39; see also *France Quick v. MDL*, where the French Court of Cassation confirmed that a company cannot assert a violation of an international public policy on the basis of the absence of the chairman of the company in the proceedings at the same time the chairman initiated arbitration against the counterparty by using the company's name. It indicatively held that "MDL breached the principle of estoppel in contradicting itself at the expense of France Quick, and thus, the requirement of procedural good faith was breached." Bertrand Derains & Yves Derains, *Société Marocaine des Loisirs MDL v. France Quick AS, Cour de Cassation, 09–14280, July 8, 2010*, A contribution by the ITA Board of Reporters, Kluwer Law International.

41 William W. Park, Arbitration of International Business Disputes: Studies in Law and Practice 638 (2nd ed., OUP 2012).

42 Park, *supra* note 42, at 639.

43 Park, *supra* note 42, at 79.

However, no existing arbitral rule enforces a standard of predictability in the conduct of the parties. That would not be feasible because of the diversity of the legal traditions involved and the confidential nature of the proceedings that fails to deliver a public record of types of predictable conduct. This is also because the arbitrator does not have a legal obligation *per se* to follow arbitral precedent, albeit desirable for the purpose of consistency.[44] As such, it must be concluded that it would be impossible to identify a duty of normal and regular conduct. Only proactiveness should be encouraged to the extent it prevents mischief and unwelcome surprises for the parties. Take, for example, the problematic article ICC Rule 23, which prescribes that the document of Terms of Reference should contain "a summary of the parties' respective claims"[45] early in the proceedings. Given that this Article has been criticized by practitioners on the grounds that it might be too early to prepare such a summary at that point in time, a parties' good faith conduct of proactively employing the Terms of Reference as a living instrument that depicts the positions of the parties as the case unfolds, with the possibility of supplementing or amending such positions in the course of the pleadings, would make it more difficult for one to hide or obfuscate critical details of the case for the reason that all arguments of the parties would be explicitly stated next to each other.[46] This route would further conduce to efficiency as the volume of the pleadings would be significantly reduced.[47]

8.3.2 Integrity

Procedural integrity is embedded in the principle of abuse of process and the need to abstain from any interference with the administration of justice. It is part and parcel of due process.[48] Late Gaillard rightly pointed out that "[w]hile common law systems do not recognize any general principle of abuse of right, English courts have long upheld their inherent jurisdiction to sanction a party's exercise of its procedural rights in an abusive manner."[49] It is widely accepted that the principle of abuse of process is universal,[50] and it is enshrined in and applied by all legal

44 Gabrielle Kaufmann-Kohler, *Arbitral Precedent: Dream, Necessity or Excuse? The 2006 Freshfields Lecture*, 23 Arbitr. Int. 357, 374 (2007).

45 ICC Arbitration Rules, art. 23(1)(c) (2020).

46 Irene Welser & Samuel Mimnagh, *The Arbitrator and the Arbitration Procedure, An Arbitrator's Imperative – How to Avoid Disappointing the Parties, Preventing Surprises and Enabling Efficient and Progressive Arbitral Proceedings*, in Austrian Yearbook on International Arbitration 2021 127, 147–48 (Christian Klausegger et al. eds., 2021).

47 Welser & Mimnagh, *supra* note 46.

48 Cremades has described due process as a principle constituted of two fundamental notions, "access to justice and reasonableness of the proceedings." Bernardo M. Cremades, *The Use and Abuse of "Due Process" in International Arbitration*, 9 Arbitraje 661, 668 (2016).

49 Emmanuel Gaillard, *Abuse of Process in International Arbitration*, ICSID Review 1, 17 (2017).

50 See *Hunter v. Chief Constable*, where the House of Lords reasoned that an abuse of process "concerns the inherent power which any court of justice must possess to prevent misuse of its procedure in a way which, although not inconsistent with the literal application of its procedural rules, would

systems, even though there is some kind of skepticism about its normative foundation given that no institutional rule or arbitration law expressly provides for its application.[51] In principle, courts find an abuse of process when a "procedural right is exercised for a purpose other than that for which the right was granted"[52] or in the case where pursuing the claim occurs to be unreasonable.[53] The lack of propriety of the conduct or undue influence undermines the integrity of the proceedings and effectively transgresses procedural good faith. Such a violation may follow from a tribunal finding that a party failed to preserve the documents reasonably, the so-called spoliation of evidence.[54] Citing exhibits in the briefs that were not previously produced is another example. A more reprehensible conduct is forging or falsifying the documents that a party was requested to disclose.[55] A further procedural irregularity can be the multiplication of the proceedings by initiating arbitration in different *fora* and before different tribunals.[56] In that case, an opportunistic party, especially where construction arbitrations are concerned and which involve a great number of claims, would think about testing the waters by submitting only a portion of its claims to one arbitral tribunal, and once it realized that the newly constituted tribunal did not best serve its interests, it would then reserve the rest of its claims for a second more sympathetic tribunal.[57] Maximizing the chances of securing a favorable arbitral award by manipulating the process in that manner should be objectionable.[58] It fragments the adjudication of the dispute and incurs exorbitant costs for the parties.[59]

During cross-examination of witnesses, good faith as a procedural standard may be transgressed in a myriad of ways. Those might include misleading the witness regarding the context of the document that the witness is questioned about, mischaracterizing the witness's responses to certain questions, interrupting the witness or preventing them from completing their answer or reviewing evidence, pressuring the witness to speculate about matters not included in their witness statement, attributing contentions to the witness that are contradicted by documents that the

nevertheless be manifestly unfair to a party to litigation before it, or would otherwise bring the administration of justice into disrepute among right-thinking people." Hunter v. Chief Constable of the West Midlands [1982] AC 529 (HL) 536.

51 Ahmed Mohsen El Far, Abuse of Rights in International Arbitration (Mar. 1, 2018) (Ph.D. dissertation, Queen Mary University of London), para. 737, *available at* https://qmro.qmul.ac.uk/xmlui/bitstream/handle/123456789/44689/Elfar_A_PhD_final_04092018.pdf?sequence=1&isAllowed=y (last visited Sept. 6, 2022) (Author's consent to citation is obtained).

52 El Far, *supra* note 51, para. 219.

53 El Far, *supra* note 51 (citing among others Jameel v. Dow Jones and Co. Inc. [2005] EWCA Civ 75, [2005] QB 946).

54 Frédéric G. Sourgens et al., Evidence in International Investment Arbitration, para. 8.42 (OUP 2018).

55 Sourgens et al., *supra* note 55, para. 8.49.

56 Gaillard, *supra* note 49.

57 Gaillard, *supra* note 49.

58 Gaillard, *supra* note 49, at 6–7.

59 Gaillard, *supra* note 49.

questioning party has in possession but has not allowed the tribunal to see, as well as other forms of disrespecting or treating them unfairly during the examination.[60]

Abuse of process is indeed so pervasive in international arbitration that an eminent practitioner has pronounced that even if "the conditions for *[r]es judicata* are not met, I would suggest that a tribunal nevertheless should consider whether it should not allow the second claim from proceeding, on grounds of abuse of process or abuse of rights"[61] (emphasis in original). Further, even if the conduct of one party may not be necessarily incongruent with a literal application of the procedural rules, there is always the risk of procedural misuse.[62] Indeed, even if the procedural right seems to be *a fortiori* legitimate, it might be exercised unreasonably and in a way that it frustrates its very purpose.[63] The so-called 'guerilla tactics' offer an illustrative example. The term describes the phenomenon where a procedural rule or law is abused in such a way that the purpose of its existence is eventually compromised.[64] For example, while it may be *prima facie* legitimate for a party to make extensive submissions and time extension requests, procedural misconduct is evident where such efforts are nothing more than a litigation strategy to bring the procedure to a halt, produce unnecessary costs and defeat the opposing party in a mischievous way.[65] It must be stressed that not all guerilla tactics are sanctioned. A characteristic example is one party's objection to the other party's few-minutes delay in its electronic submission due to technical glitches. However, the employment of guerilla tactics may lead the arbitrators to draw adverse inferences, impose cost sanctions and security for costs or may even result in the challenge of the award.

Several procedural misconducts in international arbitration seem to be increasingly propagated by the imprudent use of AI tools. Following the outbreak of the COVID-19 pandemic and the adaptation of all stakeholders to the inevitable invasion of technology in the administration of arbitral justice, a 2021 international arbitration survey revealed that "AI tools and algorithms for predictive justice . . . raise ethical considerations and doubts as to how much such tools can or should interfere with the adjudicative function"[66] (alteration to original). Notwithstanding the advantages of virtual hearing rooms and other IT tools, such as those employed in e-discovery, the risk that "some IT tools may lead to claims of due

60 These observations are drawn from the author's professional engagement in cases and reflect personal insights.

61 Audley Sheppard, *Res Judicata and Estoppel*, *in* Parallel State and Arbitral Procedures in International Arbitration 219, 234 (ICC Dossier III, 2005).

62 Sheppard, *supra* note 61, para. 235.

63 El Far, *supra* note 51, para. 506.

64 El Far, *supra* note 51, para. 496.

65 El Far, *supra* note 51, para. 495.

66 Queen Mary University of London and White & Case LLP, *2021 International Arbitration Survey: Adapting Arbitration to a Changing World*, 2021, 22, *available at* https://arbitration.qmul.ac.uk/media/arbitration/docs/LON0320037-QMUL-International-Arbitration-Survey-2021_19_WEB.pdf (last visited May 8, 2023).

process violations"[67] must be taken seriously into consideration. Overall, it must be highlighted that procedural integrity is so fundamental for the system of international commercial arbitration that "[e]ven a good and correct [substantive] result does not compensate for a bad and unfair procedure"[68] (alteration to the original). Assuming the parties have agreed to arbitrate in good faith and stay away from tactical maneuvers, any effort to harass the other party or obstruct the proceedings would defeat the parties' expectations.[69] To this effect, the NYC provides for the grounds of resisting the enforcement of the award as a consequence of a breach of the procedural good faith[70] unless the competent tribunal is able to remediate such types of conduct much earlier in the proceedings *i.e.*, by characterizing through a procedural order the various forms of conduct that it will not sustain.

8.3.3 Equality

If reasonableness of procedural conduct is the first leg of what is meant by due process, the second must be the right of the parties to put up an argument, submit evidence and contradict the opposing party.[71] In other words, the second leg of due process is constituted of "hearing, contradiction and equality."[72] Equality arises as a fundamental byproduct of due process and effectively good faith, both in terms of protecting parties' legitimate expectations and as a fundamental public policy rule. It denotes the understanding that both parties must have the same opportunity while presenting their case.[73] In this regard, it is correctly advanced that,

> both parties [must be evaluated based on] the same yardstick . . . so that the parties can have the same rights, opportunities and burdens in order to defend their respective interests, and one of the parties is not denied what the other has been granted in like conditions.[74]
>
> (alteration to the original) (citation omitted)

Yet, one should not infer "that all the parties be accorded the same treatment, whatever the circumstances."[75] Equality is not absolute. Instead, it implies that "no one may be arbitrarily subjected to a treatment other than that accorded to others: only

67 Queen Mary University of London and White & Case LLP, *supra* note 66.
68 Fabricio Fortese & Lotta Hemmi, *Procedural Fairness and Efficiency in International Arbitration*, 3 GroJIL 110, 116 (2015).
69 El Far, *supra* note 51, para. 478.
70 See, *e.g.,* NYC art. V1(b), which stipulates that enforcement of the award may be resisted if one party was not given appropriate notice of the arbitrator's appointment or the arbitral proceedings or was otherwise unable to present its case.
71 Roque J. Caivano, *The Conduct of the Proceedings*, *in* Arbitration in Argentina 109, 114–15 (Fabricio Fortese ed., 2020).
72 Caivano, *supra* note 71, at 115.
73 Caivano, *supra* note 71, at 143.
74 Caivano, *supra* note 71, at 143–44.
75 Caivano, *supra* note 71, at 144.

identical situations should be accorded the same treatment."[76] Mayer analyzed the concept of procedural equality in the context of cross-examination. He explained that if one party must cross-examine five witnesses, whereas the other only has to cross-examine one witness, it would be improper to require the same allocation of time because equality is a concept more complex than the division of time by two.[77] Another instance where procedural equality becomes pertinent is third-party funding. Litigation funding may contribute to leveling the playing field for unequally positioned parties and ensuring access to justice, even for the weaker parties who do not have the financial means to advance their case in arbitration against the stronger ones and who would otherwise be pressured to settle their case from the beginning.[78]

In particular, it might be argued that a procedural duty of good faith would likely be breached in case of non-disclosure of a third-party funder.[79] Yet, it is unlikely that non-disclosure will lead to that effect because that would mean by analogy that the non-disclosure of insurance coverage for the claim (which constitutes a common practice in litigation) would also have to be considered in that case as an action in bad faith.[80] On the other hand, procedural good faith does have a role in balancing the right of a financially weak party to access justice against disclosure of the funding arrangement and the need for transparency, especially where conflicts of interest regarding, for example, the relationship between arbitrator and funder are at stake. Equal treatment does not lead to a strict mathematical equation. Instead, it is a fine exercise of balancing.

8.3.4 Efficiency

It is well-established that procedural efficiency constitutes one of the core advantages of international commercial arbitration. It offers the opportunity of "relatively quick and inexpensive resolution of contractual disputes by avoiding the expense and delay of extended court proceedings,"[81] even if international arbitration sometimes becomes disturbingly expensive and costly, especially when cases of billions of dollars with complicated factual and legal issues are at issue.[82]

A procedural duty of good faith to conduct the proceedings in an efficient manner is a *conditio sine qua non* for meeting the reasonable expectations of the parties

76 Caivano, *supra* note 71.

77 Sciences Po Mayer Brown Arbitration Lecture, *Pierre Mayer: Must Justice Be a Goal for the Arbitrator?* YouTube, Oct. 30, 2020, *available at* https://youtu.be/OlUFkR_m32Q (last visited Apr. 8, 2022).

78 Tamir Livschitz, *Third Party Funding in Arbitration*, *in* Arbitration in Switzerland: The Practitioner's Guide, para. 23 (Manuel Arroyo ed., 2nd ed., 2018).

79 Livschitz, *supra* note 78, para. 50.

80 Livschitz, *supra* note 78.

81 Born (3rd ed.), *supra* note 20, at 84 (quoting Diapulse Corp. of Am. v. Carba, Ltd, 626 F.2d 1108, 1110, 2d Cir. 1980).

82 Born (3rd ed.), *supra* note 20, at 85.

and ensuring the legitimacy of international arbitration. The LCIA Rules provide that "at all times the parties shall do everything necessary in good faith for the fair, efficient and expeditious conduct of the arbitration."[83] The SCC Arbitration Rules similarly stipulate that "the Arbitral Tribunal and the parties shall act in an efficient and expeditious manner."[84] The HKIAC Arbitration Rules dictate that "[t]he arbitral tribunal and the parties shall do everything necessary to ensure the fair and efficient conduct of the arbitration."[85] Moreover, the close connection between good faith and procedural efficiency has actually been endorsed in arbitral case law. The tribunal in *ICC Case No. 17538/VRO/AGF* clarified that "[b]oth Parties . . . contributed to the procedural efficiency of these proceedings by behaving in good faith."[86]

Efforts have been made in recent years to make arbitration rules more time-efficient and cost-effective. For instance, provisions were added through the 2012 ICC amendment with respect to case management conferences and emergency procedures, while a streamlined arbitration procedure based on reduced fees was introduced through the 2017 ICC amendment.[87] In that vein, JAMS adopted in 2011 its Efficiency Guidelines for the Pre-Hearing Phase of International Arbitrations in order to ensure cost-effectiveness.[88] These include *inter alia* the need to limit document requests to what is directly pertinent to the case, the need to set meaningful limitations when one party requests broad pre-hearing disclosure and the other party wishes a narrow one and finally, the need to deny document requests or set specific requirements when the cost of e-discovery ends up being disproportionate to the amount or nature of the dispute.[89] Further, the Prague Rules on the Efficient Conduct of the Proceedings in International Arbitration published in 2018 herald a duty of procedural good faith for the parties in the sense that the parties should cooperate and assist the tribunal "in conducting the proceedings in a cost-efficient and expeditious manner,"[90] failing which the tribunal may take that into account "when deciding on the allocation of costs in an award."[91]

However, the framework for arbitral efficiency remains fragile, according to recent empirical surveys. Interviewees have complained that arbitration is becoming more expensive and slower, while it is still being inflicted with ineffective

83 LCIA Arbitration Rules, art. 14.2 (2014).
84 SCC Arbitration Rules, art. 2(1) (2017).
85 HKIAC Arbitration Rules, art. 13.5 (2018).
86 ICC Case No. 17538/VRO/AGF, Feb. 25, 2013, para. 269 (Arbitrator Intelligence Materials, Kluwer Law International).
87 Born (3rd ed.), *supra* note 20, at 200.
88 Born (3rd ed.), *supra* note 20, at 223.
89 JAMS Efficiency Guidelines for the Pre-Hearing Phase of International Arbitrations (Executive Summary), Effective Feb. 1, 2011, *available at* www.jamsadr.com/files/uploads/documents/jams-international-efficiency-guidelines-arbitration-executive-summary.pdf.
90 Rules on the Efficient Conduct of Proceedings in International Arbitration (Prague Rules), 2018, art. 11; See also art. 8.2.
91 Rules on the Efficient Conduct of Proceedings in International Arbitration (Prague Rules), *supra* note 90.

sanctions in case of dilatory tactics.[92] Arguably, such dilatory tactics may pertain to periodical requests to amend the procedural timetable or push back deadlines for submission.

In that regard, expeditiousness forms another procedural principle informing the rule of procedural good faith and fortifying the idea that "justice delayed is justice denied."[93] Any shortcomings resulting from inefficient conduct can potentially be regulated by: (a) simplifying arbitrations instead of complicating them,[94] (b) encouraging parties to agree on how to conduct the proceedings,[95] (c) resorting to functional soft law instruments designed to bolster honesty and integrity between the parties in the course of the proceedings[96] and finally, (d) by strengthening the framework of sanctions.[97]

8.4 Uniform Standard of Procedural Good Faith in Transnational Disputes

8.4.1 Criticism

During the proceedings, parties from common and civil law traditions are inherently entitled to have different expectations in relation to the commencement and presentation of the dispute.[98] While the American legal system takes a liberal approach to document discovery, discovery in civil law jurisdictions is rarely allowed as it is perceived to negate parties' expectations with respect to confidentiality and privacy.[99] The presentation of evidence at the hearing significantly varies

92 Queen Mary University of London and PricewaterhouseCoopers LLP, 2015 *International Arbitration Survey: Improvements and Innovations in International Arbitration*, 2015, at 7, *available at* https://arbitration.qmul.ac.uk/media/arbitration/docs/2015_International_Arbitration_Survey.pdf (last visited Sept. 5, 2022).

93 Filip J.M. De Ly, *Paradigmatic Changes – Uniformity, Diversity, Due Process and Good Administration of Justice: The Next Thirty Years*, *in* 37 The Evolution and Future of International Arbitration, para. 2.39 (Stavros L. Brekoulakis et al. eds., Kluwer Law International 2016).

94 Fabricio Fortese & Lotta Hemmi, *Procedural Fairness and Efficiency in International Arbitration*, 3 GroJIL 110, 117 (2015).

95 Fortese & Hemmi, *supra* note 94, at 118.

96 Fortese & Hemmi, *supra* note 94.

97 Varesis supports that the inherent power of the arbitrators to impose sanctions emanates from their mandate to run the proceedings smoothly and efficiently as well as from the dogma of arbitrating in good faith. Further, the imposition of such sanctions finds its limits to criminal or other public law components outside the perimeter of the arbitrator's mandate. Faidon Varesis, Private International Law and Arbitral Jurisdiction 207 (Routledge 2023) (citing Reliastar Life Insurance v. EMC National Life Co, 564 F3d 81, 2d Cir. 2009).

98 Siegfried H. Elsing & John M. Townsend, *Bridging the Common Law Civil Law Divide in Arbitration*, 18 Arb. Int'l 1, 1 (2002).

99 Javier Rubinstein, *International Commercial Arbitration: Reflections at the Crossroads of the Common Law and Civil Law Traditions Perspective*, 5 Chic. J. Int. Law 303–4 (2004); see also Rolf Trittmann & Boris Kasolowsky, *Taking Evidence in Arbitration Proceedings between Common Law and Civil Law Traditions – The Development of a European Hybrid Standard for Arbitration Proceedings*, 31 UNSWLJ 330, 336 (2008) (quoting Claude Reymond, Civil Law and Common Law

between common and civil law systems. A civil lawyer will present the documents ahead of the hearing without attaching importance to the practice of using a witness to authenticate or explain the document submitted, whereas a common law practitioner will resort to a live witness submitting their testimony to explain the respective document.[100] Considerable disparity exists with regard to the weight attached to witness testimony. It has been rightly pointed out that, "[t]he common law tends to be skeptical that the sun has risen unless a witness can be found to testify under oath that he saw it do so. The civil law believes that the best evidence comes from documents."[101] Further, cross-examination is generally not permitted in civil law jurisdictions, which reserve for the court the power to ask questions to the witness, not the opposing party's counsel, which is the leading practice in a common law tradition.[102]

Townsend and Rubinstein express concern that it is unlikely that the divide between common and civil law will be bridged in the foreseeable future and that a universal set of procedural rules will ever govern arbitral proceedings.[103] This view is due to the fact that the procedure each time will be largely influenced by the applicable arbitration law at the seat of arbitration, along with the arbitrator's training.[104] Accordingly, an endeavor to solidify a uniform standard of procedural conduct on the grounds of a common understanding of procedural good faith may be too difficult to bear fruit.

8.4.2 Support

Notwithstanding the seemingly insurmountable obstacles toward the formulation of a universal procedural standard of good faith, international arbitration is a cosmos entirely different from any domestic legal adjudication, be it of common or civil law. To a certain degree, this idea is riveted on the delocalization theory. In his prophetic article back in 1983, Paulsson advocated for the normalcy of an arbitral process free from domestic law peculiarities.[105] Kaufmann-Kohler defended the emergence of a new procedural *lex mercatoria*, which "rise[s] to the level of

Procedures: Which is the More Inquisitorial? A Civil Lawyer's Response, 5 ARB. INT'L 357, 360–61 (1989)) ("We react to the notion of discovery, be it English or, worse, American style, as an invasion of privacy by the court, which is only acceptable in criminal cases, where the public interest in involved").

100 Elsing & Townsend, *supra* note 98, at 3.

101 Elsing & Townsend, *supra* note 98, at 4.

102 Rubinstein, *supra* note 99, at 308.

103 Rubinstein, *supra* note 99, at 310; *accord* Elsing & Townsend, *supra* note 98, at 7.

104 Trittmann & Kasolowsky, *supra* note 99, at 332 ("Arbitration proceedings are mostly conducted by lawyers . . . . As such, they are generally educated primarily in one particular legal tradition, have experience practising in that jurisdiction and are therefore most familiar with a particular approach to the taking of evidence that they consider to be fair and just.")

105 Jan Paulsson, *Delocalisation of International Commercial Arbitration: When and Why It Matters*, 32 INT'L & COMP. L. Q. 53, 57 (1983).

a standard arbitration procedure"[106] and "has the invaluable merit of merging different procedural cultures."[107] Other scholars speak of *lex proceduralia* as a due process law constituted of "a set of norms that floats above national jurisdiction and various systems of soft law."[108] This procedural merger or, more precisely, the relative detachment of procedural rules from the influence of domestic rules is largely dictated by the IBA Rules of evidence, the UNCITRAL Arbitration Rules, institutional arbitration rules and *ad hoc* rules adopted by arbitrators.[109] However, it is not intended herein to propose a complete detachment of procedural rules from the law of the seat, because any globalization effort would be handicapped absent the very national arbitration laws upon which the freedom of arbitrators and parties is established.[110] It only shows the need for *relative autonomy*. The convergence of common and civil law rules in transnational arbitration should be examined under the progressive development of a *universal* procedural standard of good faith. The latter is still embedded in national legislation to the extent that it is pertinent as a matter of applicable arbitration law yet relatively autonomous to the extent that "arbitration laws are increasingly harmonized."[111] Further, the technological advancements associated with the increasing use of online arbitration confirm the fictive nature of the seat of arbitration.[112]

This revolution is also torpedoed by the standardization of institutional arbitration rules and the demand for less yet better regulation. Indeed, an explicit reference to such good faith obligations does exist within certain arbitration rules,[113] while the most admirable effort of establishing a uniform duty of good faith in arbitral proceedings is the adoption of the IBA Rules on the Taking of Evidence. Preamble 3 stipulates that "[t]he taking of evidence shall be conducted on the principles that each Party *shall* act in good faith" (emphasis added). Its content is not merely aspirational, as one would carelessly assume since Article 9.8 of the IBA Rules further provides that the tribunal may take into account the failure of the party to act in good faith "in its assignment of the costs of the arbitration." The 2021 Commentary on the revised 2020 IBA Rules highlights that

> the revi[sed] paragraph 3 of the Preamble . . . now includes a requirement that each Party shall act "in good faith" in the taking of evidence pursuant to the IBA Rules. At the discretion of the arbitral tribunal, violation of the good

106 Gabrielle Kaufmann-Kohler, *Globalization of Arbitral Procedure*, 36 Vanderbilt Law Rev. 1313, 1323 (2021).
107 Kaufmann-Kohler, *supra* note 106.
108 Fortese & Hemmi, *supra* note 94, at 115 (citing Matti Kurkela & Santtu Turunen, Due Process in International Arbitration 8, OUP 2010).
109 See Kaufmann-Kohler, *Globalization of Arbitral Procedure*, *supra* note 106, at 1324–25 (discussing the instruments of the procedural merger).
110 Kaufmann-Kohler, *Globalization of Arbitral Procedure*, *supra* note 106, at 1333.
111 Kaufmann-Kohler, *Globalization of Arbitral Procedure*, *supra* note 106, at 1320.
112 Kaufmann-Kohler, *Globalization of Arbitral Procedure*, *supra* note 106, at 1318.
113 See, *e.g.*, LCIA Arbitration Rules, art. 14.2, 32.2 (2020); Swiss Arbitration Rules, art.16 (2021); CEPANI Arbitration Rules, art. 18.1 (2013).

faith requirement can result in the consequences set forth in Articles 9.6, 9.7 and 9.8.[114]

(alteration to the original)

8.5 Plausibility of a Uniform Rule of Good Faith

The novelty of this chapter is to delineate the situations where a rigorous – though uniform – standard of procedural good faith may prove invaluable in regulating certain procedural issues that are not otherwise regulated. It also aims to iron out procedural disagreements between civil and common law traditions. Various concerns prevent the systemization of procedural good faith. These include: (a) the lack of a universal all-embracing definition of procedural good faith, (b) the lack of adequate guidance by arbitration rules as to how good faith is applied, (c) the lack of awareness regarding the consequences of the breach of a uniform rule, (d) the doubt whether a uniform procedural duty of good faith is more or less than what is required by the applicable arbitration rules and finally, (e) whether the introduction of a regulatory concept of procedural good faith in the era of digitalization of arbitration offers added value.

8.5.1 Lack of Universal Definition

The absence of a common definition of procedural good faith might lead to further uncertainty. The reason is that it is becoming more and more difficult on the international plane to draw a line between unfair procedural conduct and what is outside that perimeter.[115] That uncertainty may further be enhanced by the different expectations of the parties coming from civil and common law jurisdictions. Nonetheless, a rigid definition or an exhaustive list of types of good faith conduct is not (and should not be) desirable since there is the risk that "parties may become more confident engaging in conduct that they feel they can demonstrate falls outside of the definition."[116]

The universality of the rule must be affirmed for the reason that the gap between civil and common law traditions is gradually being bridged. The more the gap is eliminated, the more uniform the application of the rule. English case law recognized an implied duty of good faith for the purpose of "not do[ing] anything to

114 IBA Task Force for the Revision of the IBA Rules on the Taking of Evidence in International Arbitration/Consolidated Amendments, *Commentary on the Revised Text of the 2020 IBA Rules on the Taking of Evidence in International Arbitration*, Jan. 2021, at 4, *available at* www.ibanet.org/MediaHandler?id=4F797338-693E-47C7-A92A-1509790ECC9D (last visited July 12, 2022) [hereinafter *Commentary on the Revised IBA Rules*].

115 Roman Mikhailovich Khodykin et al., *Commentary on the IBA Rules on Evidence, Preamble*, *in* A Guide to the IBA Rules on the Taking of Evidence in International Arbitration, para. 2.54 (2019).

116 Khodykin et al., *supra* note 115, para. 2.55.

frustrate the purpose of the contract"[117] (alteration to the original). In *Yam Seng*, Justice Leggatt was careful in highlighting the importance of good faith in English law, specifically with regard to long-term contracts. The judge saw good faith as honesty in the sense that it is dishonest to deceive by making a statement that the other party is going to rely on[118] or try to be silent in that regard.[119] Good faith might also refer to "fidelity to the parties' bargain."[120] Other epithets that describe what good faith is not include, in the judges' words, " 'improper', 'commercially unacceptable' or 'unconscionable'"[121] conduct. Though that decision was criticized by subsequent courts, the *Tahnoon* case confirms that good faith entails an "obligation to act reasonably and with fair dealing having regard to the interests of the parties . . . and to the provisions, aims and purposes of the contract, objectively ascertained."[122] Such types of good faith conduct are not foreign at all to civil law practitioners. Considerable differences still exist between common and civil law jurisdictions, yet convergence is possible since what would be reprehensible conduct as a breach of good faith in a common law system is similarly unacceptable in civil law traditions and typically in international arbitration.[123]

Despite the legal system's inherent differences, the universality of the procedural rule of good faith is not any more a chimera but has the potential of being firmly established. It would be helpful toward a harmonization effort if tribunals clarified from the beginning what types of conduct would qualify as a breach of the standard of good faith.[124] At any rate, a wide interpretation of such a descriptive catalog of attitudes must be preferred, since there is a significant risk that the parties will perceive a restrictive list as exhaustive and try to bring in the process the meaning of a good faith conduct that best serves their own interests.[125]

8.5.2 Lack of Adequate Guidance in Arbitral Rules

Admittedly, there is poor guidance on how the procedural good faith applies in the context of arbitral rules. The LCIA Rules provide that "each of the parties shall act at all times in good faith, respecting the spirit of the Arbitration Agreement, and shall make every reasonable effort to ensure that any award is legally recognised and enforceable at the arbitral seat."[126] Yet, the said rules fail to describe what

117 Hamsard 3147 Ltd (t/a Mini Mode Childrenswear) v. Boots UK Ltd [2013] EWHC 3251 (Pat) [86].
118 Yam Seng Pte Limited v. International Trade Corporation [2013] EWHC 111 (QB) [141]. Another instance, according to Justice Leggatt, can be "deliberately avoiding giving an answer, or giving an answer which is evasive, in response to a request for information." *Yam Seng*, *supra* note 118.
119 *Yam Seng*, *supra* note 118.
120 *Yam Seng*, *supra* note 118, at [139].
121 *Yam Seng*, *supra* note 118, at [138].
122 Sheikh Tahnoon Bin Saeed Bin Shakhboot Al Nehayan v. Ioannis Kent (AKA John Kent) [2018] EWHC 333 (Comm) [175].
123 See Khodykin et al., *supra* note 115, para. 2.58.
124 Khodykin et al., *supra* note 115, para. 2.68.
125 Khodykin et al., *supra* note 115.
126 LCIA Arbitration Rules, art. 32.2 (2020).

a procedural good faith conduct is constituted of. One would assume that a uniform procedural rule of good faith cannot be less obscure. Nonetheless, a uniform application of the rule can be consistent with two core objectives of international arbitration: neutrality and even-handedness. The most profound example of such a uniform rule of good faith is the IBA Rules on the Taking of Evidence. To the extent that the parties have agreed to such rules, or the arbitrators deem it appropriate, a uniform application of a duty of good faith hinges on the increasing compromise between diverging legal traditions and the balancing thereof that the arbitrators are required to exercise to maintain equality and fairness across different legal rules.[127]

The uniform rule of procedural good faith consists of individual standards, either positive or negative. Examples of such positive standards include the duty of transparency, including the duty that a party must disclose any prior or present relationship between the party-appointed expert and the party itself.[128] Further, a duty of cooperation, which is based on Article 2, provides that "the Arbitral Tribunal shall consult the Parties at the earliest appropriate time in the proceedings and invite them to consult each other *with a view to agreeing* on an efficient, economical and fair process for the taking of evidence."[129] (emphasis added). A hasty interpretation that the level of cooperation between the parties is voluntary should not be admissible, since it opens the floodgates for a non-cooperative attitude and sabotages the fair and efficient conduct of the proceedings.[130] Arbitral case law indeed confirms the obligation of "the bona fide cooperation of both parties,"[131] which is primarily entrenched in the arbitration agreement.[132] To that effect, a duty of cooperation reflects the obligation of a requested party to produce all requested documents that are in its possession to the requesting party.[133] Another special manifestation of procedural good faith that ensures the fairness of the proceedings must be the affirmative duty to reasonably give notice "in advance of any Evidentiary Hearing or any fact or merits determination [about] the evidence on which the other Parties rely"[134] (alteration to the original). A violation of such duty may result in

127 Stephen L. Drymer & Valérie Gobeil, *Document Production in International Arbitration: Communicating Between Ships in the Night*, *in* 18 Legitimacy: Myths, Realities, Challenges 205, 209 (A. J. Van den Berg ed., 2015); see also IBA Rules on the Taking of Evidence in International Arbitration (2020), art. 9(4)(e) ("The Arbitral Tribunal may take into account . . . the need to maintain fairness and equality as between the Parties, particularly if they are subject to different legal or ethical rules") [hereinafter IBA Rules].

128 IBA Rules, art. 5(2)(a); *accord* Khodykin et al., *supra* note 115, at 25 n.54. Martinez-Fraga supported that transparency "does provide for some uniformity and universality concerning the affirmative exercise of good faith" (citing Pedro J Martinez-Fraga, King or Arbitrator: Exploring the Inherent Authority of Arbitrators to Impose Sanction within the Framework of the 2010 IBA Rules on the Taking of Evidence in International Arbitration (2011) 12 Spain Arbitration Review 57).

129 IBA Rules, art. 2(1).

130 *Contra* Khodykin et al., *supra* note 115, para. 2.72.

131 Born (3rd ed.), *supra* note 20, at 995 n.1714 (quoting ICC Case No. 6149, XX Y.B. Comm. Arb. 41, 48, 1995).

132 Born (3rd ed.), *supra* note 20.

133 IBA Rules, art. 3(4).

134 IBA Rules, Preamble 3.

the challenge of the award on the basis that a party was unable to present its case,[135] even though the question of what a reasonable period means will be assessed *ad hoc*.[136] Another concrete manifestation of such duty of arbitrating in good faith is the expectation to abide by the Tribunal's procedural direction to resort to mediation for efficiency purposes — first and before arbitration — especially if there is a clear reference to mediation as a condition precedent to arbitration."[137]

Contrariwise, the negative standards of good faith portray a number of procedural issues that are directly inflicted with bad faith conduct. It must be accepted that these standards are in consonance with the *raison d'être* of the IBA Rules, namely fairness and efficiency, and are derived largely from the incessant observance of these principles. Those include the duty not to deliberately withhold documents that are well known to exist or not to surprise the opposing party by failing to identify all expert witnesses.[138] Other prohibited conduct would be raising objections to the production of documents unreasonably,[139] submitting fraudulent testimony or manipulating the witness.[140] Another example is not to delay or increase the costs of arbitration by making document requests that are intentionally onerous, and which an under-resourced party is not in a position to process, or not to produce a high volume of documents that are substantively unrelated to the dispute,[141] and which sometimes have the same effects as fishing expeditions.

8.5.3 Consequences of Breaching the Rule

A clear illustration of the obligatory nature of procedural good faith is Article 9.8 of the IBA Rules of Evidence. The Article stipulates that:

> If the Arbitral Tribunal determines that a Party has failed to conduct itself in good faith in the taking of evidence, the Arbitral Tribunal may, in addition to any other measures available under these Rules, take such failure into account in its assignment of the costs of the arbitration, including costs arising out of or in connection with the taking of evidence.

First, the language mentioned previously expressly grants the power to a tribunal to impose cost sanctions on the party breaching the duty of good faith.[142] Monetary

135 NYC, art. V1(b).
136 Khodykin et al., *supra* note 115, para. 2.105.
137 Maxwell Conversations: Good Faith in International Arbitration, YouTube, Mar. 8, 2022.
138 Khodykin et al., *supra* note 115, para. 2.71.
139 Khodykin et al., *supra* note 115.
140 Khodykin et al., *supra* note 115, para. 2.76.
141 Khodykin et al., *supra* note 115, para. 2.75.
142 Certain awards have indeed endorsed such an approach, although not in the context of the IBA Rules. See, *e.g.*, the *Cessna v. Gulf Jet* case, where the competent ICC tribunal held that the respondent was continuously indifferent to the deadlines introduced by the tribunal and later withdrew from participation, which both led to an increase in costs and effectively to undermining the arbitral process. The respondent's failure to comply with the arbitration agreement

sanctions may be ordered when a party deliberately obstructs the proceedings by not producing critical documents that have been ordered.[143] Any other irrational request or baseless application, such as insisting on a specific hearing that makes no sense, may entail the dismissal of the request along with cost sanctions.[144] In addition, the refusal of a party to make an advance payment of expenses may prompt the tribunal to allow the other party's recovery of such advance payment from the recalcitrant party based on an interim award.[145]

Second, the wording "in addition to any other measures available under these Rules" indicates that the assignment of costs is not the only available sanction that a tribunal may levy upon the defaulting party. For instance, the tribunal may review the procedural timetable in response to bad faith conduct and "make appropriate adjustments that will mitigate the consequences of that conduct,"[146] pursuant to the fairness of the procedure required by Preamble 1.[147]

Third, Article 9.6 of the IBA Rules proffers that a failure to comply with a procedural order with respect to document production may lead the tribunal to infer that the content of the document is adverse to the non-producing party' interests. Article 9.7 is similarly vocal concerning the adverse inferences drawn by the tribunal in case a party does not make a proper objection in due time or fails to make a testimony available, notwithstanding a production order by the tribunal. Adverse inferences could streamline the reasoning of the tribunal in this direction.[148]

Other arbitration rules, such as the CAM Rules, expressly grant the power to the tribunal to sanction the conduct of the parties if that is contrary to good faith. However, it would be unacceptable to characterize all kinds of consequences as a breach of a duty of good faith. For example, the tribunal's power to uphold an anti-suit injunction against parties' endeavors to litigate the dispute before national courts does not reflect an application of good faith but the negative effect of opting for arbitration.[149]

Fourth, a conduct that violates procedural good faith may, under certain circumstances, constitute a ground for setting aside the award. Such a ground is the violation of public policy found in UNCITRAL Model Law Article 34(2)(b)(ii). Just like good faith forms part of substantive public policy, it is a critical component of procedural public policy, too. A specific manifestation in that regard is a party abusing the process or succumbing to arbitrariness. The Supreme Court of Singapore

in good faith urged the tribunal to uphold the claimant's reasonableness of costs. ICC Case No. 18769/VRO/AGF, Final Award, Jan. 17, 2014, para. 232, *available at* https://jusmundi.com/en/document/decision/en-cessna-finance-corporation-v-gulf-jet-llc-khalid-mohammad-saeed-al-mulla-hussein-mohamed-salem-al-meeza-final-award-friday-17th-january-2014.

143 Maxwell Conversations, *supra* note 137.

144 Maxwell Conversations, *supra* note 137.

145 Maxwell Conversations, *supra* note 137.

146 Khodykin et al., *supra* note 115, para. 2.91.

147 Khodykin et al., *supra* note 115.

148 Maxwell Conversations, *supra* note 137.

149 Maxwell Conversations, *supra* note 137.

reasoned that certain guerilla tactics, to the extent they result in "a breach of the agreed arbitral procedure,"[150] may qualify as grounds to set aside the award on the basis of a breach of public policy.[151] However, not all kinds of conduct should hastily be classified as a breach of good faith because that would "expand the categories of conduct on the basis of which an arbitral award may be set aside."[152] A trivial procedural misconduct should not be conflated *per se* with a violation of public policy as the latter requires a significant departure from fair trial, such as awards predicated on document fraud.[153] Another ground is enshrined in Article 34(2)(ii) on violation of due process and fair defense of one's case. In the evolving landscape of post-pandemic virtual hearings, a witness' accountability may be contested by virtue of third parties' presence in the same room with the witness during their cross-examination on the grounds that a third person may attempt to influence the witness's responses to opposing counsel's questions. Further, the phenomenon of Zoombombing may constitute another tactic aimed at sabotaging the confidentiality of the proceedings, which may result in the setting aside of the award due to violations of due process. However, breaching procedural good faith is rather rare in practice, since the threshold of such conduct is quite high to qualify as an annulment ground. Further, a national court has significant discretion as to whether to annul the award or resist enforcement, as the word "may" of UNCITRAL Model Law Art. 34(2) and NYC Art. V(1) and (2) suggests.

Aside from arbitral proceedings *per se*, the procedural good faith also extends to the enforcement stage, thus acting in certain cases as a balancing rule between the duty to enforce the award and allegations of public policy violation. The Supreme Court of Spain granted the enforcement of a German award obtained notwithstanding the contentions of a party that litispendence was at issue and there existed a violation of public policy in accordance with NYC Art. V(2)(b) as a result of pending court proceedings in Spain.[154] The Supreme Court, by examining the temporal sequence of the proceedings, ruled that the preventive effect of the Spanish proceedings upon the German arbitral proceedings would paralyze the enforcement of all awards and that "would mean promoting and allowing procedural fraud, and protecting conducts that violate good faith and the obligations and agreements freely entered into by the parties."[155] Likewise, the High Court of India upheld the enforcement of an LCIA award despite the contentions that public policy and due process

150 Michael Hwang & Rachel Ong, China Machine New Energy Corporation v. Jaguar Energy Guatemala LLC and another [2018] SGHC 101, Supreme Court of Singapore, High Court, Originating Summons No. 185 of 2016, Apr. 26, 2018, para. 213(b) (A contribution by the ITA Board of Reporters; Kluwer Law International).

151 Hwang & Ong, *supra* note 150.

152 Hwang & Ong, *supra* note 150.

153 Stefan M. Kröll, *Recognition and Enforcement of Awards, § 1061 – Foreign Awards, in* Arbitration in Germany: The Model Law in Practice 443, paras. 147, 150 (Kröll et al eds., 2015).

154 Spain No. 43, Angel (Germany) v. Bernardo Alfageme, S.A. (Spain), Tribunal Supremo [Supreme Court], Civil Chamber, First Section, Mar. 20, 2001, in 31 Y.B. Comm. Arb. 821, 821 (Van den Berg ed., ICCA & Kluwer Law International 2006).

155 Spain No. 43, *supra* note 154, at 821.

violations hindered its enforcement.[156] It reiterated the Swiss Supreme Court decision *4A_374/2014* that, at the enforcement stage, good faith requires that one should not raise setting aside grounds if they did not raise such grounds in due time earlier in the arbitral proceedings.[157] In common law jurisdictions, a failure to raise an objection at the annulment stage before the supervisory court would prevent a party from raising it later before the enforcing court in order to resist enforcement. That is so true from the perspective of Hong Kong courts since *estoppel* or waiver is perceived as a manifestation of good faith, the breach of which permits the enforcing court to eventually enforce the award.[158] Not only that, but national courts may take any such breach into account when allowing for recovery of legal costs in case a party unsuccessfully challenges an award.[159] It is said that such consequence derives from a duty to enforce the award by virtue of parties' arbitration agreement to resolve any dispute arising from the contract in a final and binding manner.[160]

Ultimately, a breach of procedural good faith may result in the non-enforcement of the award. That is so true when it comes to resisting enforcement on the grounds of public policy. Despite the indeterminacy of public policy and the differences among states as to its reach, what is meant by procedural good faith in terms of fair and appropriate conduct is reflected in the commonality of procedural public policy rules among states. As the International Law Association (ILA) emphasized, international public policy reflects the "fundamental principles, pertaining to justice or morality, that the State wishes to protect,"[161] thus encapsulating the notion of abuse of rights, that parties should be placed on equal footing, the prohibition of fraud or corruption[162] or even the prohibition of one-sided conduct, all of which constitute the essence of transnational public policy as the emerging order of *boni mores*.[163]

156 India No. 54, Cruz City 1 Mauritius Holdings v. Unitech Limited, High Court of Delhi, New Delhi, Apr. 11, 2017, in 42 ICCA Y.B. Comm. Arb. 407, 407 (Van den Berg ed., ICCA & Kluwer Law International 2017).

157 India No. 54, *supra* note 156, at [49].

158 Alex Ye, *The Good Faith Principle in the Context of the Enforcement of New York Convention Awards: An Analysis of Hong Kong's Position in Light of the Apparently Conflicting Court Decisions*, 36(3) J. Int. Arbitr. 361, 382–84 (Maxi Scherer ed., Kluwer Law International 2019).

159 Maxwell Conversations, *supra* note 137.

160 Maxwell Conversations, *supra* note 137.

161 *ILA Resolution on Public Policy as a Bar to Enforcement of International Arbitral Awards, Resolution 2/2002*, 70th Conference of International Law Association in Delhi, India, Apr. 2–6, 2002, *available at* www.ila-hq.org/en_GB/documents/conference-resolution-english-new-delhi-2002-1 (last visited Oct. 19, 2023). Substantive international public policy may also become relevant when, *inter alia*, contractual duress is at stake or penalty clauses in the contract are not admissible in the country of enforcement.

162 Monique Sasson, *Public Policy in International Commercial Arbitration*, 39(3) J. Int. Arbitr. 411, 413 (Maxi Scherer ed., Kluwer Law International 2022).

163 Pierre Lalive, *Transnational (or Truly International) Public Policy and International Arbitration*, *in* 3 Comparative Arbitration Practice and Public Policy in Arbitration, para. 186(6) (Pieter Sanders ed., ICCA Congress Series, 1987).

8.5.4 The Added Value in Relation to Existing Arbitral Rules

The inclusion of good faith in the LCIA Rules, as well as other sets of rules, confirms the valid assumption that the exclusion of a duty of good faith by the parties would not correspond to pragmatism. The 2021 Swiss Arbitration Rules provide that "[a]ll participants in the arbitral proceedings shall act in good faith."[164] The same unconditional obligation is also envisaged in the CIAM-CIAR Rules of 2024, which stipulate: "All those participating in the arbitration proceedings shall act in accordance with the principles of confidentiality and good faith in the conduct of the proceedings."[165] The 2013 CEPANI Arbitration Rules 18(1) and 23(1) provide for a duty of good faith in the proceedings. The most challenging question, therefore, is whether a uniform duty of good faith, as discussed previously, adds anything more to the provisos of a number of institutional rules. Does it entail a higher or lower standard of conduct for the parties? One may submit that a uniform rule does nothing more than simply reflect what experienced arbitrators typically do in practice. In the words of a well-versed scholar:

> [A]s with all general principles, ad hoc solution by parties and arbitrators in particular cases must still be found and the 'good faith' rule does no more and not more and not less than what is already reflected in the practice as applied by experienced international arbitrators.[166]

Nonetheless, glossing over the issue of procedural good faith underestimates two of its capabilities. First, its application in the context of the IBA Rules – which explicitly provide for sanctions and thereby attach to good faith additional compulsive strength – confirms that procedural good faith in the transnational environment can be elevated to a self-standing rule, giving rise to concrete obligations for the parties. That means, in principle, that "the parties' conduct in proceedings with regard to fairness and good faith is more strictly scrutinized and sanctioned"[167] in light of the tribunal's objective to minimize cost and time. That additional enforcement strength draws upon the fact that "the manifestations or corollaries of the principle of good faith are generally understood in the same fashion in several – if not all – jurisdictions."[168] As Henriques put it, what would qualify as frustration of legitimate expectations or inconsistent conduct on the one side of the Pyrenees would be the same as on the other side of the Andes.[169]

164 Swiss Arbitration Rules, art. 16(1) (2021).
165 CIAM-CIAR Rules, art. 28(3) (2024).
166 KHODYKIN ET AL., *supra* note 115, para. 2.48 (quoting Georg von Segesser, The IBA Rules on the Taking of Evidence in International Arbitration, 28 ASA BULL. 735, 740 (2010)).
167 KHODYKIN ET AL., *supra* note 115, n.46 (quoting Detlev Kuhner, The Revised IBA Rules on the Taking of Evidence in International Arbitration, J. Int'l Arb. 667 (2010)).
168 Henriques, *supra* note 24, at 530.
169 Henriques, *supra* note 24, at 531.

Second, a uniform application of procedural good faith does not merely mirror a compromise between cultures. Nor does it impose *per se* a harder rule upon the parties in terms of requiring a higher standard of conduct. On the contrary, it instills flexibility in the proceedings. That flexibility translates to the power of the arbitrator to balance truth-seeking objectives against legitimacy and efficiency concerns. For instance, the witness examination and document production provisions in the IBA Rules provide for more truth-seeking options than the corresponding ones in civil procedural laws.[170] That means that good faith conduct is premised on one party's demand for more balance when the other party presents an incomplete evidential picture.[171]

On the other hand, what is procedurally characterized as a good faith conduct is limited by party consent and fundamental adjudicatory principles, since an 'absolute' truth-seeking purpose is – or should be – limited by efficiency concerns. In other words, the arbitrator has ample discretion to apply the good faith rule by balancing the "necessary fact-finding"[172] against what "the other party may conceive as a burdensome fishing expedition."[173] By way of an example, to what extent should a party's last-minute, though meritorious, challenge of an arbitrator be considered good faith conduct if the real purpose of such disqualification attempt is to delay the proceedings and bring them to a dead end? No answer is definite. Instead, it depends on the set of competing values: fairness on the one hand and legitimacy on the other. Ultimately, the cross-cultural background of a uniform instrument, such as the IBA Rules, is a fertile ground for enforcing a flexible yet balanced demand for observance of good faith. The constant competition between accuracy and legitimacy forges the content of good faith, and ultimately reflects an optimal balancing of common law and civil law that the system of cross-border arbitration often requires.[174]

8.5.5 A Regulatory Conceptualization of Good Faith in the AI World

To what extent good faith can be elevated to a uniform standard of regulating procedural conduct in the era of AI-assisted arbitration, virtual hearings and metaverse disputes may be rather a wishful thinking. Yet, several arbitration rules have recognized the revolutionary change of the landscape by including the option of videoconferencing in relation to witness examination[175] or allowing the tribunal to decide

170 MARIEKE VAN HOOIJDONK & YVES HERINCKX, *The Impact of IBA Guidelines and Rules on the Search for the Truth in Arbitration*, *in* DO ARBITRAL AWARDS REVEAL THE TRUTH? 93, para. 38 (Luc Demeyere ed., 2019).

171 JEFFREY MAURICE WAINCYMER, PROCEDURE AND EVIDENCE IN INTERNATIONAL ARBITRATION 839 (Kluwer Law International 2012).

172 HOOIJDONK & HERINCKX, *supra* note 170, para. 37.

173 HOOIJDONK & HERINCKX, *supra* note 170.

174 See, *e.g.*, *Commentary on the Revised IBA Rules*, *supra* note 114, at 9 ("A Continental European party may . . . find that these Rules are useful in seeking to restrict an overly broad request from a common law party, while a common lawyer may be able to use the . . . Rules . . . to obtain documents from a Continental European party").

175 CRCICA Arbitration Rules, art. 28(4).

whether the hearing is to be conducted physically or remotely.[176] National arbitration laws have also been robust in affirming this reality and protecting the parties' rights and interests accordingly.[177] In the same vein, courts have resisted actions to set aside an arbitral award because of virtual hearings.[178] The role of procedural good faith in that regard would not be minor. It should be seen as preserving the integrity of the arbitral proceedings by extending the parties' obligations to the duty to cooperate and be ready to coordinate for the trouble-free use of technology-assisted arbitration, to be compliant with – and attentive to – all cyber security and confidentiality in place, and not take advantage of the technological features associated with the conduct of the proceedings *i.e.,* by assisting a witness testifying remotely or by inappropriately insisting on a physical hearing or objecting to the online hearing most likely on the grounds of violation of due process and fair and equal representation.[179]

On the plane of on-chain dispute resolution and virtual reality disputes (including the so-called metaverse arbitration), where the somewhat slow and expensive *modus operandi* of arbitrations of our century would be progressively replaced by parties' autonomy to opt for fast, inexpensive and flexible resolution through technologically advanced platforms, such as Kleros (kleros.io), Jur (jur.io) or Aragon (aragon.org) and despite the many benefits incurred, the risk is evident that the drawbacks might outweigh the benefits. Anonymous decision-making, lack of requirement to give reasons for decisions or lack of obligation to disclosure are among the most problematic features of such decentralized platforms.[180] Due process, therefore, might be severely undermined, partly because of the unbridled party autonomy to use the products of technology, even at the cost of parties' own interests.[181] In that cosmos, a uniform understanding – and application – of a regulatory notion of good faith, as enshrined in the mandatory provisos of several jurisdictions and as codified in uniform instruments,[182] could be seen as the gatekeeper of fairness. At the same time, it would warrant that the parties cannot depart from due process axioms, such as that none should be allowed to be their own judge.[183]

8.6 Arbitrator's Procedural Duty of Good Faith

A key participant in the arbitral process, the arbitrator could not ever be absolved of an overarching duty of good faith, which effectively regulates their services

176 ICC Arbitration Rules (2021), art. 26(1); LCIA Arbitration Rules (2020), art. 19(2).

177 See, *e.g.,* Austrian Arbitration Act 2013, Section 595(2).

178 Mohamed Hafez, Remote Hearings and the Use of Technology in Arbitration, Global Arbitration Review, Apr. 21, 2023 (highlighting that the Egyptian Court of Cassation on 27 Oct. 2020 upheld the judgment not to set aside the award on the grounds that virtual hearings were compatible with Egyptian law).

179 Hafez, *supra* note 178.

180 Elizabeth Chan & Emily Hay, *Something Borrowed, Something Blue: The Best of Both Worlds in Metaverse-related Disputes*, 15(2) Contemp. Asia Arb. J. 205, 234 (2022).

181 Chan & Hay, *supra* note 180, at 235.

182 See, *e.g.,* IBA, Guidelines on Conflicts of Interest in International Arbitration (International Bar Association 2024).

183 Chan & Hay, *supra* note 180, at 235.

and circumscribes their mission. The present section answers three main questions: (a) what the sources of arbitrator's procedural duty of good faith are, (b) whether arbitrators determine their good faith conduct solely by themselves or they are subject to judicial intervention and lastly, (c) what the content of such procedural duty is.

8.6.1 Sources

The proposition must be ascribed to the tension between the consent-based theory and the adjudicatory paradigm.[184] According to the consent-based theory, the powers and duties of the arbitrator are always determined by the very agreement of the parties. This school of thought proffers that the legitimacy of the decision-making power of the arbitrator is measured by their mission to satisfy the interests of the parties, as enshrined in the contract; thus, any association with the domestic function performed by the judge is ill-conceived.[185] On the contrary, the adjudicatory archetype of arbitration reflects the theorem that arbitrators essentially replace judges.[186] The proponents of this view explain that the enforcement of the arbitration agreement and the legitimacy of the arbitral process are subject to state action.[187] Arbitration agreements are subject to due process restrictions often invoked in the enforcement of arbitral awards.[188] The practical implication of such collision is the inevitable question of where the arbitrator's duty of good faith should be grounded. Should it be determined by reference to the consensual framework of the parties' agreement, including any modifications thereof and any set of arbitral rules explicitly adopted? Should it be instead detected in a specific *forum*, such as the *lex loci arbitri* or the place of enforcement? A third hybrid theory seems to integrate the results of the diverging rationales by reaffirming that

> an arbitrator's jurisdiction is in part a function of the agreement of the parties but also a function of the willingness of national legal systems to recognize the validity of such agreements and to provide practical utility to the process through guaranteeing enforceability of awards.[189]

8.6.2 Arbitrators as Self-Regulators: Party Autonomy vs Arbitral Discretion

All evidence collected favors the arbitrator's ample procedural discretion and the absence of judicial interference as founding pillars of the system of international

184 ROGERS, *supra* note 34, para. 9.11.
185 ROGERS, *supra* note 34.
186 ROGERS, *supra* note 34, para. 9.04. Lord Mustill in the *Succula* case argued that an "arbitrator . . . becomes a judicial officer, with exactly equal duties towards both parties. It is unnecessary to discuss whether the relationship is contractual in nature." Succula Ltd and Pomona Shipping Co. Ltd v. Harland and Wolff Ltd, 2 Lloyd's Rep. 381, 388 (1980).
187 ROGERS, *supra* note 34, para. 9.07.
188 ROGERS, *supra* note 34.
189 WAINCYMER, *supra* note 171, at 50.

arbitration.[190] Born elucidates that NYC, the UNCITRAL Model Law and national arbitration legislations establish the binding force of these principles.[191] The rationale is that judicial intervention has to be held to the bare minimum so that arbitral proceedings are not deprived of their expediency, flexibility and finality. The approach of the English common law system confirms the correctness of this view. It is thus left to the arbitrator's good sense to decide how to conduct the proceedings, and the courts should abstain from correcting the arbitrator's procedural directions on the basis of an error of fact or law or wrong exercise of discretion under Section 68 of the English Arbitration Act 1996.[192] In other words, there is considerable arbitral freedom with regard to the perimeter of arbitrators' good faith conduct. That means that it befalls the arbitrator to observe their duty of good faith in the sense that they must justify their procedural decisions. This conclusion is bolstered by the procedural judgment rule. Berger and Jensen, to whom the term is attributed, argue that such a rule protects arbitrators' procedural decisions from court interference in the sense that "a court will not second-guess an arbitrator's exercise of his procedural judgment, if his decision is grounded in a *bona fide* assessment of the case and is reasonable under the circumstances"[193] (emphasis in original). The effect of the rule is not that courts are *ipso facto* precluded from reviewing the award in case a bad exercise of discretion amounts to a manifest disregard of parties' due process rights, but that "it is first and foremost for the arbitrators to determine what is 'reasonable'"[194] under the circumstances.

Even though the arbitrator's procedural standard of good faith would largely be determined by the parties' private agreement, the applicable institutional rules and arbitration legislations and be regulated via a *minimum* court interference, the arbitrator's broad procedural discretion would allow them to arrive at a reasoned justification for any controversial procedural decision they make.[195] That explains why the content and extent of the standard of good faith that the arbitrator has to meet will be influenced by the arbitrator's ample discretion in the proceedings. For example, it is submitted that the arbitrator's duty of "confidentiality may be one area where the personal integrity and ethical *discretion* of individual arbitrators provides the most important protection"[196] (emphasis added). Further, the duty of the arbitrator to propose the settlement of the dispute before the adjudicatory outcome is delivered

190 Born (3rd ed.), *supra* note 20, at 3503.

191 Born (3rd ed.), *supra* note 20.

192 Karyl Nairn et al., *National Report for England and Wales (2021 through 2022), in* ICCA International Handbook on Commercial Arbitration IV.2(f) (Lise Bosman ed., Supp. No. 120, 2022).

193 Klaus Peter Berger & J. Ole Jensen, *Due Process Paranoia and the Procedural Judgment Rule: A Safe Harbor for Procedural Management Decisions by International Arbitrators*, 14 Rev. Bras. Arb. 73, 87 (2017).

194 Berger & Jensen, *supra* note 193.

195 Waincymer, *supra* note 171, at 52.

196 Waincymer, *supra* note 171, at 104 (quoting Catherine Rogers, *The Ethics of International Arbitrators, in* The Leading Arbitrators' Guide to International Arbitration 646–47 (Lawrence W. Newman & Richard D. Hill eds., 2008).

is either affirmed or denied depending on the arbitrator's discretion, given that the majority of statutes do not make such a duty obligatory.[197] However, one should be careful not to undermine the overriding nature of good faith, since any broad procedural discretion granted to the arbitrator does not eventually absolve them of their commitment to the good faith exercise of such discretion.

8.6.3 Content of Arbitrator's Duty of Good Faith

Good faith operates as a limit to the arbitrator's procedural discretion. A series of more specific duties may be regarded as stemming from an overarching duty of good faith, the latter being attached to arbitrators as well. Such duties may include the duty of the arbitrator to cooperate with the parties and the institution, because the consent to arbitration was provided in good faith and was intended by the parties to be sustained in good faith.[198] Another manifestation of good faith must be a duty to confidentiality. The arbitrator must refrain from using any information they gained access to for personal interests *i.e.,* insider trading.[199] The types of different duties arising from good faith should not be seen as *numerus clausus*. However, it is reasoned that three organizing duties of good faith must be recognized: (1) a minimum standard of due process, (2) a duty of vigilance in honoring the reasonable expectations of the parties and (3) a duty of efficiency. It must be pointed out from the outset that not all possible duties stem from good faith. The systemization of such duties is of paramount importance, since an underlying violation may lead to the removal of the arbitrator, the annulment of the award, a contract or tort claim against the arbitrator or even a severe impact upon future appointment.[200]

8.6.3.1 Minimum Standard of Due Process

The requirement of due process is a more specific manifestation of the overarching duty of good faith and is also reflected in that the parties' reasonable and fair expectations can be integrated into the "contractual obligations owed by arbitrators, at least where directed towards the protection of the parties and where otherwise consistent with the arbitration agreement."[201] As a minimum standard of due process, it should be distinguished from the respective standard required in national jurisdictions in that in arbitration; the said standard is cemented on the free will (voluntariness) of the parties and the need for more flexibility and speed in arbitral procedural rules.[202] A less stringent standard, therefore, is adopted.

197 WAINCYMER, *supra* note 171, at 93.
198 WAINCYMER, *supra* note 171, at 119.
199 WAINCYMER, *supra* note 171, at 91 n.123.
200 WAINCYMER, *supra* note 171, at 75.
201 WAINCYMER, *supra* note 171, at 90–91 (citing GARY B. BORN, INTERNATIONAL COMMERCIAL ARBITRATION 1622–23 (Kluwer Law International 2009).
202 Caivano, *supra* note 71, at 114. The minimum standard of due process also corresponds to the idea that the parties' right to fair trial is balanced against their freedom to determine the arbitration

However, this minimum standard can be said to counterbalance the significant freedom that the arbitrator enjoys in making procedural decisions and managing the case.[203] Broad procedural discretion, though desirable, is subject to certain limits. As Fortier highlighted, freedom entails responsibility and discretion entails obligation.[204]

Two pillars of a minimum standard of due process attached to arbitrators must be recognized: the duty of equal treatment of the parties and the duty of impartiality and independence. The obligation to treat the parties equally and provide each one the opportunity to present their case fully is a fundamental requirement of natural justice. Article 18 of the UNCITRAL Model Law stipulates that "[t]he parties shall be treated with equality and each party shall be given a full opportunity of presenting his case." Article 23(2) of the SCC Arbitration Rules provides: "[T]he Arbitral Tribunal shall conduct the arbitration in an impartial, efficient and expeditious manner, giving each party an equal and reasonable opportunity to present its case." However, the concept of treating the parties equally is fraught with some misunderstanding. First, a rigid understanding of equality requiring the arbitrator to pose the same number of questions to both parties' witnesses or granting both parties' the same number of requests for an extension of time is not commensurate with what true equality bespeaks.[205] Second, treating the parties equally does not necessarily mean that the parties will be treated fairly. Equality without properly offering the parties the opportunity to develop their case fully or without the safeguards of the arbitrator's impartiality undermines the minimum standard of due process.

The duty of impartiality, on the other hand, should not be perceived separately from the duty of equality. Equality shall not be interpreted restrictively but liberally in order to encompass all elements of fairness, including the arbitrator's impartial judgment. Article 11(1) of the ICC Rules enshrines the continuing duty of impartiality: "Every arbitrator must be and remain impartial and independent

---

procedure, without suggesting that the fundamental human rights principles, as accommodated in Article 14 of the ICCPR, Article 6 of the ECHR and Article 10 of the UDHR, should be compromised. On the contrary, their manifestation in commercial arbitration provides the system of international arbitration with its legitimacy foundation and assists the arbitrator in addressing puzzling or borderline cases of procedural unfairness. Petra Butler, *Human Rights in International Arbitration*, *in* 1 Cambridge Compendium of International Commercial and Investment Arbitration 161, 184 (Stefan Kroll et al. eds., 2023).

203 See Oliver J. Armas & Thomas N. Pieper, *The Impact of U.S. Litigation*, *in* International Commercial Arbitration in New York, para. 2.18 (James H. Carter & John Fellas eds., 2nd ed. OUP 2016).

204 L. Yves Fortier, *The Minimum Requirements of Due Process, in Taking Measures against Dilatory Tactics: Arbitral Discretion in International Commercial Arbitration: "A Few Plain Rules and a Few Strong Instincts," in* Improving the Efficiency of Arbitration Agreements and Awards: 40 Years of Application of the New York Convention 396, 403 (A.J. Van den Berg ed., ICCA Congress Series No. 9 1999).

205 Waincymer, *supra* note 171, at 82.

of the parties involved in the arbitration." That is accompanied by a corollary duty of disclosure:

> The prospective arbitrator shall disclose . . . any facts or circumstances which might . . . call into question the arbitrator's independence in the eyes of the parties, as well as any circumstances that could give rise to reasonable doubts as to the arbitrator's impartiality.[206]

A number of rules from other arbitral institutions contain similar language.[207]

Recourse to the twofold minimum standard of due process proves to be invaluable in borderline cases. Should an arbitrator raise *ex officio* a non-obvious argument that was not raised before by one of the parties and has an outcome-determinative impact upon the course of the case? Fellas pondered on whether a good faith arbitrator can raise the issue of a time-barred claim where, under the applicable New York law, the statute of limitations can be waived if not invoked by the respondent and provided that the respondent has failed to raise such a limitation defense.[208] Is the arbitrator permitted to raise the issue, provided she is diligent and non-biased? Similarly, if the parties have overlooked a contractual provision that has some material relevance to the case, a diligent arbitrator would like to ask the parties how they would interpret that provision, especially if the arbitrator's legal education and the applicable law to the dispute are anchored in the *iura novit curia* principle.[209] However, there is wide consensus that the arbitrator must not indirectly formulate a claim for the parties by bringing forward a result-determinative reasoning because this practice would assist one of the parties in winning their case, thus transgressing the duty of equality and even-handedness.[210]

Ultimately, good faith in the form of a minimum due process requirement must always be adhered to, even if no sound basis for challenging the award exists. Albeit contested, that means that the arbitrator must not be allowed to assist one party and hurt the other, despite the absence of any irregularity that could possibly form the ground for annulment of the award.[211] In that vein,

> [i]t is important not only that an award is enforceable, but also that the parties have confidence in the process, feel that they were treated fairly even when the perceived unfair treatment does not rise to the level of a ground to challenge an award.[212]

206 ICC Arbitration Rules, art. 11(2) (2021).

207 See, *e.g.*, SCC Arbitration Rules, art. 18(2), 19(1) (2020); LCIA Arbitration Rules, art. 5(4)–(5) and 10(1) (2020).

208 John Fellas, *Arbitrators' Questions: Can They Cross a Line?* 262 N.Y. Law J. No. 61 (Sept. 25, 2019), *available at* https://files.hugheshubbard.com/files/NYLJ-Sept-25-John-Fellas.pdf (last visited Sept. 7, 2022).

209 Bernard Hanotiau, *The Arbitrator's Duty to Render Justice: Constraints and Prerogatives*, *in* International Arbitration: When East Meets West – Liber Amicorum Michael Moser 77, 82 (Neil Kaplan et al. eds., 2020).

210 Hanotiau, *supra* note 209.

211 Fellas, *supra* note 208.

212 Fellas, *supra* note 208.

As such, a subtle third prong of the arbitrator's duty for minimum due process may be envisaged. That would echo the maxim that "justice should not only be done, but should manifestly and undoubtedly be seen to be done."[213] A disruptive attendance of the hearing by the arbitrator, where they fail to respond to questions, go offline, travel from one place to another, cannot hear what parties or counsel say, and without being able to be totally focused on the hearing, would constitute a ground for resisting enforcement by virtue of public policy violations, taking into account the reasonable third person's perception of fairness.[214]

8.6.3.2 Duty of Vigilance in Honoring Parties' Reasonable Expectations

In principle, the arbitrator's procedural freedom to tailor-make the proceedings as they deem fit should not be in tension with party autonomy. Article 19(2) of the UNCITRAL Model Law prescribes that if the parties fail to freely agree on what procedure the tribunal will follow in the conduct of the proceedings, "the arbitral tribunal may, subject to the provisions of this Law, conduct the arbitration in such manner as it considers appropriate." The Explanatory Note by the UNCITRAL Secretariat, as amended in 2006, emphasizes the 'supplementary' nature of such discretion.[215] Fortier had rightly described the point of the alleged tension between party autonomy and arbitral discretion as dialectical, in contrast to 'either/or.'[216] An overarching duty of good faith would, therefore, dictate that the arbitrators should be vigilant in honoring parties' reasonable expectations[217] by making sure at all times that they do not exercise such discretion outside the ambit of their mandate.

Even so, there are circumstances – albeit limited – where the intention of the parties as enshrined in their procedural agreement is unreasonable or contravenes mandatory procedural rules. A tension arises, therefore, between party autonomy and arbitral freedom. Such a conflict involves, on the one hand, the parties' freedom

213 R v. Sussex Justices, ex parte McCarthy [1924] 1 K.B. 256, 259 (Eng.).

214 Song Lihua v. Lee Chen Hon (Que Wenbin), Reasons for Decision of the Court of First Instance of the High Court of Hong Kong [2023] HKCFI 2540, Oct. 5, 2023, paras. 49, 61.

215 UNCITRAL Model Law on International Commercial Arbitration 1985, Part Two, Explanatory Note by the UNCITRAL Secretariat on the 1985 Model Law on International Commercial Arbitration as Amended in 2006, United Nations, Vienna 2008, para. 35, *available at* https://uncitral.un.org/sites/uncitral.un.org/files/media-documents/uncitral/en/19-09955_e_ebook.pdf (last visited Sept. 8, 2022).

216 Fortier, *supra* note 204, at 402.

217 It is difficult to determine the *time* of the reasonable expectations of the parties. Marghitola supports that it might be the case that the reasonable expectations of the parties with respect to the extent of document production are determined *ex post i.e.*, at the beginning of the procedure, and not *ex ante i.e.,* at the moment of the conclusion of the contract. It might be problematic to tie the time of such expectations to the beginning of the procedure since, from that moment onwards, the parties may employ tactical conduct in their effort to win the case. Reto Marghitola, Document Production in International Arbitration 132 (Kluwer Law International 2015).

over the procedure and the duty of the arbitrator to resolve the dispute on the other. Effectively, a question emerges whether the arbitrator's overarching duty of good faith requires that they should flex their muscles to override the parties' procedural direction. An example would be the case where the parties agreed that only one of them was entitled to present their case or include witnesses to testify or enjoy representation by counsel.[218] Other examples include the high number of expert witnesses and the lengthy, hence, overwhelming, proceedings.[219] A more interesting example is the case where the parties unreasonably agreed that extremely tight deadlines apply despite the mandatory procedural rule that each party must have sufficient time to present their case.[220] The power of the arbitrator to proceed by correcting the procedural agreement of the parties and invalidating the part which is purported to be unreasonable or unfair also arises from the arbitrator's duty to be vigilant in honoring the legitimate expectations of the parties.

True, the parties are not regarded as the sole masters of the arbitral process and arbitrators may deviate from the parties' procedural agreements.[221] That is proven in hindsight by the fact that a deviation from the party agreement is not always sanctioned.[222] Courts have rejected contrary arguments centered on potential non-enforcement of the award based on the fact that, even though the tribunal exceeded the time frame agreed to by the parties for rendering its decision, the causal link between the final result of the award and the deviation from the agreement was not materialized.[223] Born and Carter are supportive of the exceptional adjudicatory power of the arbitrators to sidestep the parties' agreement in order to proceed as they deem fit and in the interest of expediency and fairness.[224] Sometimes, the parties may have their own reasons for displaying such attitudes, yet the arbitrators, too, can have their own legitimate and reasonable expectations arising under the arbitrator contract,[225] allowing them to override the will of the parties. But even if the parties' intention is not clear or is absent in relation to a specific matter *i.e.*, in conducting the arbitration physically or online, the arbitrator's authority should not be undermined.

218 WAINCYMER, *supra* note 171, at 121.

219 DIEGO P. FERNÁNDEZ ARROYO, *Arbitrator's Procedural Powers: The Last Frontier of Party Autonomy?*, *in* LIMITS TO PARTY AUTONOMY IN INTERNATIONAL COMMERCIAL ARBITRATION 218 (Franco Ferrari ed., JURIS 2016).

220 WAINCYMER, *supra* note 171, at 121.

221 FRANCO FERRARI & FRIEDRICH ROSENFELD, *Limitations to Party Autonomy*, *in* 1 CAMBRIDGE COMPENDIUM OF INTERNATIONAL COMMERCIAL AND INVESTMENT ARBITRATION 72–73 (Stefan Kroll et al. eds., 2023).

222 FERRARI & ROSENFELD, *supra* note 221.

223 FERRARI & ROSENFELD, *supra* note 221 (discussing Bavarian Court of Appeals, decision, Sept. 23, 2004, (2009) BeckRS 21310).

224 FERRARI & ROSENFELD, *supra* note 221, at 71.

225 FERNÁNDEZ ARROYO, *Arbitrator's Procedural Powers: The Last Frontier of Party Autonomy?*, *supra* note 218, at 217.

It is for them to resort to the legitimate expectations of the parties and "conduct the arbitration in such manner as it considers appropriate."[226]

8.6.3.3 Duty of Efficiency

It is trite to say that timeliness and speed in arbitration are of the essence. A constellation of arbitration statutes and institutional rules provide for the duty of the arbitrator to be efficient. Section 33(1)(b) of the English Arbitration Act 1996 dictates that the tribunal must "adopt procedures suitable to the circumstances of the particular case, avoiding unnecessary delay or expense, so as to provide a fair means for the resolution of the matters falling to be determined." Article 14(1)(ii) of the 2020 LCIA Rules stipulates that the tribunal's duties must always include "a duty to adopt procedures suitable to the circumstances of the arbitration, avoiding unnecessary delay and expense, so as to provide a fair, efficient and expeditious means for the final resolution of the parties' dispute." The 2021 ICC Rules adopt similar language in Article 22(1): "The arbitral tribunal and the parties shall make every effort to conduct the arbitration in an expeditious and cost-effective manner, having regard to the complexity and value of the dispute." A duty of efficiency in the 2016 SIAC Rules is cemented in Article 19(1): "The Tribunal shall conduct the arbitration in such manner as it considers appropriate, after consulting with the parties, to ensure the fair, expeditious, economical and final resolution of the dispute."

Efficiency must not be hastily identified with speed and cost reduction. A careful consideration of the previous laws and rules suggests that the nature of the duty of efficiency must be described as the arbitrator's obligation to render "a good award without wasting time or money."[227] Smit emphasizes that if justice is equated with the accuracy of an outcome, efficiency must correspond to the time and cost of achieving that outcome.[228] Thus, there is diligence in its essence and an element of propriety to the effect that any expeditiousness employed should not undermine the quality of the proceedings or the award. By way of example, the arbitrator might have conducted the proceedings quite fast, yet this very fact does not mean that they complied with their duty of efficiency if the award rendered is eventually unenforceable due to certain deficiencies resulting from such haste.[229] Yet, the perfect strike of balance between getting things right and expeditiousness is somewhat elusive, especially in international arbitration. The parties, counsel and arbitrators usually reside in different countries or even parts of the world, and that means that a huge amount of work is inevitable given that the law applicable to the dispute might be foreign to the counsel or critical documents have to be translated into

226 See UNCITRAL Model Law, art. 19(2).

227 NADIA DARWAZEH, *Is Efficiency an Arbitrator's Duty or Simply a Character Trait?*, *in* THE POWERS AND DUTIES OF AN ARBITRATOR: LIBER AMICORUM PIERRE A. KARRER 57–58 (Patricia Louise Shaughnessy & Sherlin Tung eds., 2017).

228 ROBERT H. SMIT, TOWARDS GREATER EFFICIENCY IN DOCUMENT PRODUCTION BEFORE ARBITRAL TRIBUNALS – A NORTH AMERICAN VIEWPOINT, 93–94 (ICC Bull., Special Supplement, 2006).

229 DARWAZEH, *supra* note 227, at 61.

another language.[230] Fortier aptly stated that "[w]hat may be considered unduly dilatory in one case may, though it causes additional delays and expense, be entirely appropriate, even necessary, in another."[231] To that effect, an arbitrator acting in good faith is required to adopt a reasonable attitude in balancing speed against quality. Acting in good faith would not *per se* result in that the arbitrators must not unreasonably succumb to every request or application for further submissions, but that they are principally committed to offering the parties quality of service and, of course, a reasonable opportunity of presenting their case.[232]

Likewise, the duty of the arbitrator to use their best efforts in achieving efficiency in the proceedings[233] would be quite meaningless, absent a purposeful recourse to an overarching duty of good faith. The counterargument would be that a fixed normative content of what good faith dictates is rather illusory. One should readily acknowledge, however, that the particularities of each case and the effect of the arbitrator's decision-making upon the parties' rights to a full and fair hearing exert a deterministic influence over the specification of such duty.[234]

8.7 Conclusion

This chapter argued that the content of procedural good faith draws upon the procedural principles of certainty and predictability, equality between the parties, integrity in the administration of justice, and efficiency. The calibration of a uniform standard of procedural good faith – albeit elusive – is the holy grail of trans-nationalization of the arbitral procedure. It is grounded on uniform international rules employed in international arbitration and harmonizes the application of good faith across the spectrum of disparate legal systems. It also enhances the integrity of the system in the sense that the parties' good faith conduct is more strictly observed and sanctioned by tribunals. A self-standing rule of good faith resulting from such uniform application constitutes solid evidence that the different expectations of the parties rather converge than diverge. It must be ascertained that a uniform standard of procedural good faith does not add anything more to what is already provided in existing arbitral rules. Instead, the arbitrator's arsenal is strengthened as the arbitrator is better positioned to balance truth-seeking procedural tools against procedural legitimacy. In the upcoming era of full immersion into virtual arbitrations, the understanding and conceptualization of a regulatory notion of procedural good faith is inevitable. This chapter finally explains that the arbitrator's duty of good faith is grounded on three more specific duties *i.e.*, a duty to minimum due process, a duty of vigilance in respecting parties' reasonable

230 Fortier, *supra* note 204, at 406.
231 Fortier, *supra* note 204.
232 Darwazeh, *supra* note 227.
233 Darwazeh, *supra* note 227, at 63 (citing Pierre Karrer, *Responsibility of Arbitrators and Arbitral Institutions, in* The Leading Arbitrator Guide (Lawrence W. Newman & Richard D. Hill eds., 3rd ed., 2014).
234 Fortier, *supra* note 204, at 407.

expectations and a duty of expediency. The first imbues good faith with the obligation to be impartial, equal and to be seen as fulfilling their mission. The second balances party autonomy against arbitral discretion. The third balances speed against quality. Ultimately, these three duties have a regulatory function since they operate as a limit to the broad discretion that arbitrators are sometimes supposed to be vested with. This chapter also conveys that, although the arbitrator's duty of good faith is hard to decode, the sources of procedural good faith, including the ethical and cultural background and prior experience of the arbitrator, all inform the application of good faith.[235]

235 Sharp, *supra* note 22, at 229.

9 Conclusion

9.1 Recognition and Nature of Good Faith

The repertory of the various operations of good faith reveals that the principle has a certain depth, notwithstanding the unjustified criticism that its content is abstract. Substantial differences do exist between continental and common law worlds. The former codifies the principle and attaches a contextual meaning to it. In terms of English law, there has been scarcely a need to resort to the principle of good faith, mainly because of the adoption of piecemeal solutions. The previous argument supports the practice of common law courts to employ the specific rules of undue influence, duress, estoppel, mistake and misrepresentation to police any kind of unfairness in the performance of the contract.[1] Nevertheless, it is well maintained that the introduction of the principle in common law may protect the interests of the parties and ensure consistency.[2]

In the field of international commercial arbitration, the enforcement of good faith is deemed critical. The UNIDROIT Principles and national arbitration laws require compliance with good faith from all parties involved.[3] It is pertinently stressed that good faith ensures the effectiveness of the arbitration system, contains the backwash of the adversarial system due to the parties' obstructionist conduct and guards against arbitrator biases.[4] Without recognizing the binding nature of good faith, injustice will persevere.[5] Although the scope of good faith is heavily influenced by the applicable national law, one should not be short-sighted to believe that the status of the international arbitrator as well as their background and thinking process, are irrelevant. This is especially so in cross-border transactions, where the application of transnational law is deemed critical.

1 William Tetley, *Good Faith in Contract: Particularly in the Contracts of Arbitration and Chartering*, 35 J. Mar. L. & Com. 561, 571 (2004).
2 Tetley, *supra* note 1, at 584.
3 Tetley, *supra* note 1, at 599.
4 Tetley, *supra* note 1, at 601.
5 Tetley, *supra* note 1.

DOI: 10.4324/9781003527596-12

9.2 Substantive and Procedural Standard of Good Faith

It has been demonstrated that the substantive function of good faith informs arbitrators about the possibility of deducing normative standards from a 'vague' principle. That is the standard of minimum loyalty toward the fulfillment of the purpose of the contract. The standard of honesty suggests that one is not permitted to lie, withhold critical information or take advantage of a misinformed decision, especially where reliance by the aggrieved party is justified by prior action or representation. The general standard of reasonableness implies a limitation to the legitimate ways that the parties can exercise their rights. It encompasses a duty of diligence. Certain overarching negative standards have also been specified. These include the standard of not acting capriciously, arbitrarily or maliciously. Further, any inconsistent or unconscionable conduct should be impermissible. Good faith as an open-ended rule would have been deprived of its added value had the list of such types of conduct been narrowly construed.

On the other hand, an increased duty of good faith is not readily fathomed in pre-contractual negotiation as far as arbitral practice is concerned. However, the harsh common law position progressively recedes to the benefit of a duty of honesty and credibility, as recent case law demonstrates (see Section 3.2.4.2). In case of contract termination, good faith may be employed to invalidate the termination and give rise to damages. A standard of reasonableness and good faith is also adopted in the determination of damages. Relatedly, the innocent party has a duty not to increase or aggravate the damages incurred, whereas the exceptional awarding of punitive damages may be seen as a consequence of a breach of a standard of good faith.

In contrast, the procedural function of good faith behooves that parties adhere to certain standards of procedural conduct. The principle of procedural certainty would be transgressed if a party raised an objection that could have been effectively raised earlier in the proceedings. Other types of violation would be the falsification of evidence, multiplication of proceedings, misleading or treating the witness unfairly during cross-examination or utilizing guerilla tactics to obstruct the proceedings. In addition, treating the parties unequally is prohibited as a profound manifestation of procedural equality. Granting a request for extensive e-discovery that is disproportionate to the amount of the dispute may undermine procedural efficiency. A duty to cooperate is also required for the (cost)efficient taking of evidence.

A procedural standard of good faith applies to arbitrators, too. Arbitrators should always be impartial and give an equal chance to both parties in order to present their case fully. Further, they should be vigilant when it comes to the fulfillment of parties' expectations in the sense that they are entitled to override unreasonable procedural arrangements. In this regard, their discretion is decisive, yet they should not exercise it in a manner inconsistent with and out of the perimeter of their mandate. Finally, they shall conduct the proceedings efficiently, not in the sense of speediness but of diligence.

9.3 Demystifying Interpretive Good Faith

Whereas the subjective interpretation requires the discovery of the real intent of the parties, the objective interpretation focuses more on legal criteria. It is a question of law and rather hinges upon the understanding of a reasonable third person. As such, the functionality of good faith in interpretation directs to a reasonable solution in case the real intent cannot be revealed. Where the natural consensus between the parties cannot be achieved, the interpretive good faith helps arbitrators arrive at the normative or implied consensus dictated by a rational understanding of the contract. In so doing, what matters is the reasonable expectations of a third party in the same circumstances and what that party could have understood in good faith.

Even if good faith is unfit for discovering the subjective will of the parties because of the risk of degenerating the parties' intent, resorting to good faith may be appropriate in certain cases. That is the case of a discrepancy between the literal intent and the subsequent conduct. Another illustration is the case where a literal consideration of the wrong term used must be abandoned for the sake of the parties' true intentions.

In general, specific applications of good faith encompass the *effet utile* and *favor validitatis* principles, pursuant to which the contract and arbitration agreement will be construed as effective despite the existence of some defective intent, thus encouraging a pro-arbitration culture. Further, in case of two conflicting interpretations, the one that renders the contract effective will prevail. In addition, any unclear term in the contract will be interpreted against the party drafting it (*contra proferentem* rule). Moreover, good faith interpretation dictates that the contract must be read as a whole without focusing solely on its specific terms or phrases. Finally, a good faith interpretation underpinning the theory of confidence may be utilized to justify the extension of the effects of the arbitration agreement to non-signatories. It is ultimately stressed that contextual good faith interpretation, which is even endorsed by common law courts (see Section 6.3.5), may develop a synergetic effect upon formalistic interpretation, especially when the parties have failed to foresee a contingency *ex ante* the non-consideration of which may eventually frustrate their legitimate expectations.

Overall, in interpreting contractual rights and obligations or determining the proper law, two quintessential tests carve out the perimeter of what good faith entails for the arbitrator's interpretive mission. Satisfying reasonable and legitimate expectations is the first step. That test does not canvass what the parties hoped or wished for.[6] Instead, it directs to the legitimizing foundation of the parties' intent. When language is obscure, the arbitrator will strive to read the contract in a commercially sensible way. It is decided that

> [t]he reasonable expectations and purpose of the ordinary business person when making an ordinary business contract may serve as a guidepost to determine the intent of the parties. Reasonableness is the test to be applied when there is doubt as to the intent expressed in writing.[7]

6 ICC Case No. 18051/CYK, Sept. 14, 2015, para. 438, *available at* https://jusmundi.com/en/document/decision/en-devas-multimedia-private-limited-v-antrix-corporation-limited-award-monday-14th-september-2015.

7 Rohm And Haas Company v. Arkema France (Final Award), ICDR Case No. 50 154 T00532 10, Oct. 9, 2012, para. 44 (Arbitrator Intelligence Materials, Kluwer Law International).

On another occasion, the reasonable expectations of the parties would prompt the arbitrator to intervene in case the parties intended to subject themselves to extremely unfair and unreasonable procedural deadlines. At any rate, the reasonable expectations of the parties should not be perceived as the back door to importing extra-contractual obligations and trumping party autonomy. Instead, they help arbitrators measure the parties' conduct by reference to the available pool of acceptable means and decisions that serve the purpose of the contract. However, nothing precludes the arbitrator from determining the standard of reasonableness by putting special weight on the surrounding circumstances.

Public policy is the second test. Good faith constitutes part of public policy and effectively plays an important role in the interpretation and performance of the contract, the choice of law and the enforcement of the award. There is no homogeneous understanding of how broadly or narrowly the notion of public policy should be construed, given its distinct scope in each legal system and multiple levels of public policy. For instance, it was reasoned in the recognition and enforcement of an award that "good faith should be understood and interpreted not broadly, as a person's general lack of sufficient attentiveness or carefulness, but narrowly, as a person's deliberate attempt to jeopardize fundamental values: fraud, corruption, or other evidently illegal activity."[8] As regards the enforcement of arbitral awards, the value of good faith lies in its filtering mechanism to uphold only such intentions that do not override international public policy.

9.4 Reasons for Legitimizing Interference with the Contract

Interference with the contract is a delicate issue. It has been extensively discussed that there is a grave risk that party autonomy is sabotaged. Interference with the contract may be justified *exceptionally* in terms of gap-filling or adaptation, with good faith being the main yardstick necessitating the social control of commercial conduct.[9] Whether the arbitrator is vested with the power to resolve the dispute or regulate the contractual relationship, essentially, they aim for the same result.[10] A wider conceptualization of arbitrator's competence (*unité de l'arbitrage*) has emerged out of transnationalism and the need to provide flexible yet pragmatic solutions instead of strictly applying the legal rules.[11] Indeed, a number of reasons support the paradigm shift from dogmatism to pragmatism.[12]

8 Lithuania No. 3, L. B. v. State Property Fund of the Republic of Lithuania, Supreme Court of Lithuania, Civil Case No. 3K3-363/2014, 27 June 2014, 39 Y.B. Comm. Arb. 437, at [66] (2014) (A.J. Van den Berg ed., Kluwer Law International 2014).

9 K.P. Berger, *Power of Arbitrators to Fill Gaps and Revise Contracts to Make Sense*, 17(1) Arb. Int'l 1, 16 (William W. Park ed., OUP 2001).

10 Berger, *supra* note 9, at 14–15.

11 Berger, *supra* note 9, at 14–16.

12 Berger, *supra* note 9, at 17.

Concrete examples include the adjustment of agreed penalty clauses that are quite disproportionate to the loss suffered or external unforeseen circumstances *i.e.*, war and ensuing increased energy prices. Gap-filling may also result from the arbitrator's interpretive mandate, the latter being rather a dynamic than just a static understanding of the contractual framework. In that sense, supplementation of the contract may be deemed critical by reference to a practice-orientated good faith hailed in customs or trade usages. On the other hand, good faith may have a drastic effect on the choice of law, especially when the invalidity of such law is attributed to fraud or some other illegality.[13] It shall be borne in mind that such interference with party autonomy could not have been justified had it not been for the reasonable and legitimate expectations of the parties and the utilitarian view that a contract should be rendered effective rather than ineffective. At any rate, certain safeguards must be in place. The power to adapt or correct the contract must not disturb the contractual equilibrium. Instead, it is used to restore the equilibrium in cases where the arbitrator determines that one of the parties has been treated in an unfair or unjustifiable manner *vis-à-vis* the other. Most importantly, the arbitrator is not allowed to protect parties from their own shady deals.

9.5 An Autonomous Standard

The theory of an autonomous obligation of good faith is underrated for no good reason. Good faith, as an open-ended rule, cannot introduce additional obligations into the contract. Its significance lies in its capacity to specify or supplement certain rules, discover certain obligations that the parties failed to explicitly insert into the contract or reduce their rights and question their responsibility.[14] However, the arbitrator's conscience, coupled with the permissiveness of the applicable law, may result in engineering certain self-standing good faith obligations that both business sense and fairness require. Concrete examples are the obligation of the aggrieved party to minimize the loss, setting off one claim to demand the whole payment against another, the standard of disclosure in the negotiations[15] and the standard of mutual cooperation in order to perform the contract smoothly and effectively (see Sections 2.2.2, 2.5.2, 3.2.1, 3.2.4.1 and 4.3.2). Further, an independent cause of action may be founded on an implied covenant of good faith (see Sections 3.2.3 and 4.1.1). Good faith may also be considered a source of attributing contractual liability as decided in the famous *Norsolor* award (see Section 5.2.2). Ultimately, arbitration rules and soft law instruments provide for a uniform conceptualization of good faith in the procedure (see Section 8.5).

13 See Yock Lin Tan, *Good Faith Choice of a Law to Govern a Contract*, SJLS 307 (2014).

14 Pierre Mayer, Le Principe de Bonne Foi devant les Arbitres du Commerce International, Festschrift Pierre Lalive, Basel, Frankfurt a. M. 1993, at 544, *available at* www.trans-lex.org/115700.

15 Mayer, *supra* note 14, at 544, 548.

9.6 The Enforcement Status

Good faith does not exist in a vacuum. Downplaying its enforceability would entail not recognizing that its normative content has a binding value: the capacity to impose certain consequences insofar as a failure to abide by good faith occurs. Not providing notice to the other party of the *force majeure* event, failing to renegotiate the contract upon the occurrence of an unforeseen impediment and abusing the right to terminate the contract may all form the cause of awarding damages. As much as a public policy notion of good faith can prohibit the enforcement of punitive damages or at least limit punitive damages to a proportional amount, the exceptional remedy of punitive damages, on the other hand, may also be the direct consequence of a breach of good faith. On the contrary, a breach of the procedural standard of good faith may result in cost sanctions for the parties, adverse inferences, the power of the tribunal to adjust the procedural timetable and the setting aside or non-enforcement of the award. Therefore, it must be concluded that it would have been a Pyrrhic victory for the integrity of the arbitration system had good faith been merely exhausted to an exercise of suasion.

9.7 In the Brink of a Uniform Transnational Standard

The idea of a uniform transnational good faith in arbitration penetrates the entire theory about the trichotomy of its functionality *i.e.*, substantive, interpretive and procedural good faith. It has been explained that the antipathy towards the elevation of good faith to a self-standing transnational standard is justified on its face. The critics point out that the scarcity of awards that resort to a transnational standard of good faith, as well as the lack of uniformity among legal cultures, render its application rather wishful thinking. In addition, the sophisticated nature of contemporaneous legal systems and the incapacity of a generic rule of good faith to replace all mechanical rules provide no support that transnational law is better suited than national law in situations[16] where sophisticated parties appoint an experienced arbitrator to just do her job: to resolve a technical dispute.

Nonetheless, the body of the *lex mercatoria,* as well as the UNIDROIT Principles and Trans-Lex Principles, the latter reflecting a creeping codification of the *lex mercatoria*, highlights the consistency in the way that different cultures treat an impermissible conduct. From the perspective of interpretation, an autonomous standard of good faith interpretation would produce a uniform effect in construing consent to arbitrate liberally without sticking to the constraints of national law. In addition, it would instill a deontological duty upon the business actors to comply with international public policy and further confirm that "transnational lawyers

16 Mayer, *supra* note 14, at 555.

intuitively assume that the business community unquestioningly accepts general principles of law as binding upon it."[17] A transnational interpretive standard of good faith reminds us that the reasonable expectations of international players are not always reflected in the strict application of national legal rules. Further, calibrating a transnational good faith standard in the wake of metaverse disputes would concretize specific rules of expected behavior and insulate the system from AI pitfalls or from parties' taking advantage of them. A uniform procedural standard of good faith, as enshrined in the IBA Rules on the Taking of Evidence, constitutes proof that the arbitration community is on the brink of witnessing less compromise and more harmonization across heterogeneous legal cultures. Although it is doubtful that a uniform procedural good faith adds an additional layer of protection or imposes further obligations on the parties, it facilitates the finding of a common understanding among different actors as to what a 'global' perception of propriety of conduct indicates.

9.8 Good Faith Fueling a Reform for the System

As much as in other areas of law, in international commercial arbitration, good faith resembles an elephant-in-the-room problem that is often misunderstood. Regardless, it would be myopic to perceive good faith as the silver bullet for every complex issue arising out of a dispute. The present monograph attempted to dispel the demonization of good faith by showing both at a theoretical and empirical level that good faith is not an empty shell. In this respect, the scope and content of good faith was determined. In particular, the flexibility of the doctrine to engineer solutions in the wake of unexpected challenges or inadequacy of the contract (or the law) was explained. Ultimately, the regulatory nature of good faith was portrayed in that the sanctity of contracts and parties' conduct should not be unrestrained. It is not advanced that contracts, laws and rules should be overwhelmed with detailed references to good faith or even liberal constructions of it at the expense of lengthy and pricy negotiations. Rather, the author critically revisits the skepticism toward the application of good faith due to several threats to the integrity of the system.

Rebuilding trust in business and the rule of law cannot be harnessed insofar as the currency of good faith, which also operates as a pillar of the system of international commercial arbitration, is consistently undervalued. A reform of the system for the purpose of increasing legitimacy cannot be effectively implemented absent a brave effort to spotlight the contribution of good faith to international commercial arbitration. That contribution is predicated on increasing parties' and arbitrators' *accountability*, instilling *transparency* in the procedure and enhancing the

17 Frédéric Gilles Sourgens, Good Faith in Transnational Law: A Pluralist Account 221 (Vol. 3, International and Comparative Business Law and Public Policy 2022).

soundness and *persuasiveness* of the arbitral reasoning.[18] Embarking on the new era of accelerated globalization and metaverse disputes embroiled with all kinds of distortions and forms of misconduct that parties, arbitrators and other stakeholders succumb to proves no less than the regulatory significance of decoding good faith and the need to illustrate its practicality.

18 *Cf.* Diego P. Fernández Arroyo & Alexander Senegacnik, *Global Governance's Inescapable Legitimacy Conundrum, in* 3 Cambridge Compendium of International Commercial and Investment Arbitration 1802–24 (Stefan Kroll et al. eds., 2023).

Index

FSC
www.fsc.org
MIX
Papier | Fördert
gute Waldnutzung
FSC® C083411

Kolibri 360 GmbH
Ferdinand-Jühlke-Straße 7
99095 Erfurt, Deutschland
produktsicherheit@kolibri360.de